THE YELLOWSTONE PRIMER

Land and Resource Management in the Greater Yellowstone Ecosystem

Edited by
John A. Baden and Donald Leal

PACIFIC RESEARCH INSTITUTE FOR PUBLIC POLICY
San Francisco, California

Cloth ISBN 0-936488-23-9
Paperback ISBN 0-936488-24-7

Library of Congress Catalog Card Number 88-64201

Printed in the United States of America.

Pacific Research Institute for Public Policy
177 Post Street
San Francisco, CA 94108
(415) 989-0833

Library of Congress Cataloging-in-Publication Data

Yellowstone primer : land and resource management in the
greater Yellowstone ecosystem / edited by John A. Baden
and Donald Leal.
      p.   cm.
   Bibliography : p.
   Includes index.
   ISBN 0-936488-23-9 : $29.95. — ISBN 0-936488-24-7
(pbk.) : $12.95
      1. Ecology—Yellowstone National Park.
2. Environmental policy—Yellowstone National Park.
I. Baden, John. II. Leal, Donald.
QH105.W8Y45 1990
333.78'3'0978752—dc19   88-64201
                                                   CIP

This book is dedicated to Sally Baden, devoted mother and conservationist, in recognition of her life-long commitment to conservation and education about people's stewardship obligations to the environment they share with God's other creatures.

CONTENTS

PART I   FOUNDATIONS FOR REFORM

1

The New Resource Economics

2

Saving an Ecosystem: From Buffer Zone to Private Initiatives

PART IV POSTSCRIPT

LIST OF FIGURES

LIST OF TABLES

Greater Yellowstone Ecosystem

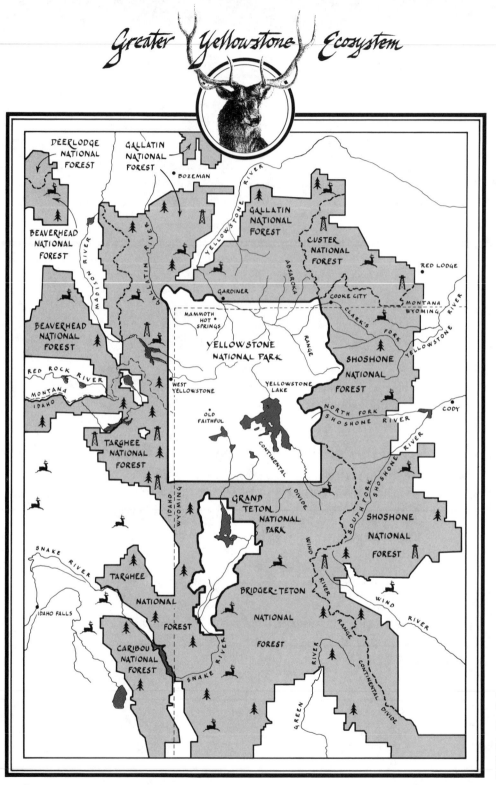

DEERLODGE NATIONAL FOREST

GALLATIN NATIONAL FOREST

BOZEMAN

GALLATIN NATIONAL FOREST

CUSTER NATIONAL FOREST

RED LODGE

BEAVERHEAD NATIONAL FOREST

MADISON RIVER

GALLATIN RIVER

YELLOWSTONE RIVER

ABSAROKA

GARDINER

COOKE CITY

CLARK'S FORK

MONTANA
WYOMING

YELLOWSTONE RIVER

BEAVERHEAD NATIONAL FOREST

RED ROCK RIVER

MONTANA
IDAHO

MAMMOTH HOT SPRINGS

YELLOWSTONE NATIONAL PARK

RANGE

SHOSHONE NATIONAL FOREST

WEST YELLOWSTONE

YELLOWSTONE LAKE

NORTH FORK SHOSHONE RIVER

CODY

OLD FAITHFUL

CONTINENTAL

SOUTH FORK SHOSHONE RIVER

TARGHEE NATIONAL FOREST

IDAHO
WYOMING

GRAND TETON NATIONAL PARK

DIVIDE

WIND RIVER

SHOSHONE NATIONAL FOREST

SNAKE RIVER

TARGHEE

WIND RIVER

IDAHO FALLS

NATIONAL

BRIDGER-TETON NATIONAL FOREST

CARIBOU NATIONAL FOREST

FOREST

SNAKE RIVER

GREEN RIVER

RANGE

CONTINENTAL DIVIDE

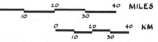

- OIL & GAS LEASE

- ELK HERD · WINTER RANGE

- TIMBER PRODUCTION

| 0 | | 20 | | 40 | MILES |
| 10 | | 30 | |

| 0 | | 20 | | 40 | KM |
| 10 | | 30 | |

PREFACE

The Greater Yellowstone ecosystem covers an area of approximately 31,000 square miles (19,900,000 acres). This is roughly equivalent to the state of Maine. The diversity in topography and wildlife is matched by the diversity in jurisdiction and ownership of the lands in the ecosystem. Private ownership covers 24% of the land while Indian reservations (4%) and state-owned property (3%) account for small but important areas. The remaining 69% of the ecosystem is owned by the United States government with specific areas managed by one of five separately funded agencies: the National Park Service, Forest Service, Bureau of Land Management, Fish and Wildlife Service, and Bureau of Reclamation.

As this book goes to press, the fires that swept Yellowstone National Park a year ago continue to generate debate and public concern. The debate tends to focus on issues such as whether the "let burn" policy of the Park Service should continue and how long it will take the 45% of the park that was burned to recover. Typical reform proposals call for controlled burns, more professional management, increased fire fighting capacity and similar adjustments to the status quo. Such proposals may lead to some site-specific, short term improvements, but ultimately they will be inadequate in protecting the park and surrounding lands because they fail to realize that the fires, though dramatic, were merely a reflection or symptom of a much larger problem. This is the problem of the institutions and incentives that govern all federal land management.

These institutions and incentives must be examined and fully understood if we are ever to achieve environmentally sound resource use and management. Using the Greater Yellowstone Ecosystem as a model, this volume provides the analytical framework and insights that are applicable to federal lands throughout the United States. With such insights comes the potential for dramatic reform.

The Pacific Research Institute has published eight books on resource, environment, and energy policy. These books all challenge conventional wisdom and attempt to prompt fresh discussion on issues of vital concern. *The Yellowstone Primer* is a worthy and welcome addition to our catalog.

A significant portion of this book came from papers and a conference organized and funded by the Political Economy Research Center, Bozeman, Montana. These papers were received by the Pacific Research Institute, supplemented and edited for publication. The final product is thus a group effort and I would like to thank the individuals and organizations involved for their work in making this book a reality. In the production of any book, there are those behind the scenes who play a key role in the process. In this instance, Martin Morse Wooster was such an individual and I thank him for his fine work in reviewing and commenting on the final draft of the manuscript.

William H. Mellor III
President
Pacific Research Institute
for Public Policy

INTRODUCTION

John A. Baden

"Yellowstone National Park is not an island," writes Rick Reese, author, environmentalist, and a principal founder of the Greater Yellowstone Coalition. "Geographically, biologically and ecologically it is part of and highly dependent upon millions of acres of adjacent lands, which together with the park itself comprise the "Greater Yellowstone" area. The environmental integrity of Yellowstone Park is dependent upon the careful management of these lands."[1]

More than 3.5 million people visit the Greater Yellowstone ecosystem each year. With over 19 million acres the area is massive. It is also politically and administratively complex, encompassing two national parks, six national forests, three federal wildlife refuges, five "gateway" towns, thirteen counties, and portions of three states.[2]

One major problem is that the boundaries enclosing Yellowstone and Grand Teton national parks do not protect all of the resources vital to the environmental integrity of the two parks. These resources are susceptible to potentially harmful activities that occur outside the two parks' boundaries on private, state, and national forest lands. Reese illustrates this interdependence in his discussion of the land

1. Rick Reese, *Greater Yellowstone: The National Park and Adjacent Wildlands*, Montana Geographic Series, No. 6 (Helena: Montana Magazine, 1984), p. 8.
2. National Park Service and U.S. Forest Service, "The Greater Yellowstone Area," September 1987.

requirements of elk and grizzly bear.[3] To sustain healthy populations, these animals require areas for winter grazing, breeding, solitude, and protection. Some of these areas extend over 20 miles beyond park boundaries. Whatever the management philosophy exercised within national park boundaries, the elk and grizzly are vulnerable to management decisions made in neighboring jurisdictions.

The surrounding region, as a critical habitat for threatened and endangered species, receives special recognition in the Endangered Species Act of 1973, which calls for the protection and management of wildlife species that the secretary of the interior determines to be threatened and endangered. Statutory mandates require federal agencies to "conserve such species, carry out specific programs in this conservation effort, and ensure that other agency actions do not result in the destruction of wildlife habitat." However, not all critical habitat is under the control of the federal agencies directed to conserve the threatened and endangered species.

The geothermal resources located in and adjacent to Yellowstone National Park are another environmental consideration. The Island Park geothermal region just outside the southwest border of the park is a focus of concern, as is the thermal well at the Church Universal and Triumphant near Gardiner, Montana, nearly 100 miles away. Environmentalists fear that the development of thermal resources outside park boundaries may adversely affect geysers inside the park.

Another concern is watershed protection in Gallatin National Forest, which may provide water sources that feed the park's northwest geyser system, including Old Faithful. Yet every year decisions having a major impact on the Gallatin watershed are made by the U.S. Forest Service without regard to the water needs of the geyser systems.

Under the Wilderness Act of 1964, nearly 4.5 million acres of the national forests encircling the park have been set aside to preserve their solitude and beauty. Additional roadless areas are currently under study for inclusion in the Wilderness Preservation System. Although these areas also form a vital part of the Greater Yellowstone system, they are managed by a different bureaucracy than is the park.

---

3. Rick Reese, *Greater Yellowstone: The National Park and Adjacent Wildlands,* Montana Geographic Series, No. 6 (Helena: Montana Magazine, 1984), p. 8.

AGENCY MANAGEMENT OF GREATER YELLOWSTONE

Of the roughly 19 million acres of land in Greater Yellowstone, more than 14 million acres fall under the jurisdiction of federal agencies. Most conspicuously, the National Park Service in the Department of the Interior is charged with managing Yellowstone and Teton national parks, which together comprise over 2.5 million acres. National forests managed by the U.S. Forest Service (USFS) surround the parks: the Gallatin, the Targhee, the Bridger-Teton, the Shoshone, and the Beaverhead are the most prominent. The Bureau of Land Management (BLM) in the Department of the Interior has management responsibility for subsurface resources on Forest Service lands. The U.S. Fish and Wildlife Service, also in the Department of the Interior, has three federal wildlife refuges in Greater Yellowstone: Red Rocks Lake National Wildlife Refuge, the National Elk Refuge, and Gray's Lake Refuge. Wyoming, Idaho, and Montana all have state lands within the system.

Many of the problems facing Greater Yellowstone that are discussed in this book can be tied directly to public management. How did a nation supposedly dedicated to private management of its resources end up with nearly 75 percent of its land in this key area managed by inefficient government bureaucracies? Understanding the origins of public management may help us to extract ourselves from this policy conundrum. We must go back one hundred years to the Progressive era of the late 1800s and early 1900s. This period in our history produced several important reforms and generated the American "counter-revolution," a series of events that had lasting effects on land and natural resource management. This counter-revolution was a profound shift from private to governmental management of natural resources.

PROGRESSIVE ERA REFORMS

Yellowstone National Park, created in 1872, stands as one of the finest monuments to the good intentions that led to the Progressive era reforms. The seven national forests surrounding Yellowstone and Teton national parks also originated in the Progressive era—specifically, in the Withdrawal Act of 1891. The Progressives had faith in "scientific management"; they also believed that federal bureaucrats could be insulated from political pressures. These sincere beliefs underly the creation of the agencies that manage most of Greater Yellowstone.

The Progressives assumed that scientific managers would act on the basis of some higher values. They apparently believed that an environmentally sensitive Platonic despot would emerge as the bureaucratic norm. This creature would combine the knowledge of Aldo Leopold, America's revered pioneer wildlife ecologist, with the spirit of St. Francis, the patron saint of the environmental movement. But the results of one hundred years' management of Greater Yellowstone reveal this idealized bureaucrat to be an impossible dream.

Unfortunately, the Progressives' faith in scientific management created a vast array of environmental costs, inequities, and economic inefficiencies. When the Progressives substituted governmental control for private management, they dramatically altered the calculus of the individual decision maker. As an unintended consequence, they also introduced perverse incentives into the decision-making system.

In both political economy and ecology, unintended consequences can be exceedingly important. Just as pesticides in the natural environment adversely affect the hatching of eagles, perverse incentives in the political environment adversely affect land management.

Although the Progressives' model was well intended, the founding fathers a hundred years earlier had a more accurate sense of human behavior when they designed our Constitution. In the *Federalist* No. 10, James Madison warned the people of New York State of the hazards factions posed to the fledgling union.

> Among the numerous advantages promised by a well-constructed Union, none deserves to be more accurately developed than its tendency to break and control the violence of faction. . . . Complaints are everywhere heard from our most considerate and virtuous citizens, equally the friends of public and private faith, and of public and personal liberty, that our governments are too unstable; that the public good is disregarded in the conflicts of rival parties; and that measures are too often decided, not according to the rules of justice and the rights of the minor party, but by the superior force of an interested and overbearing majority.[4]

4. Roy P. Fairfield, ed., *The Federalist Papers: A Collection of Essays Written in Support of the Constitution of the United States* (Baltimore: Johns Hopkins University Press, 1981), p. 16.

Madison's discussion has striking relevance to us today as we examine special interests operating in Greater Yellowstone.

AN OVERVIEW OF THIS BOOK

All contributors to this book want to preserve the environmental values of Greater Yellowstone. Like the environmental groups focused on Yellowstone, the authors are advocates for an area they cherish.

The Greater Yellowstone ecosystem is, to use the wildlife biologist's term, home range to most of the authors. We live—or have lived—in Greater Yellowstone or near its border, and we believe our home range deserves protection. Each author recognizes that Greater Yellowstone will be affected by both natural ecological processes and conscious human decisions. Each accepts the reality of continued federal ownership and assumes that decisions will continue to be made in a political environment.

This book's fundamental subjects are human decision making, the reality checks imposed by nature, and the evolution of administrative systems in a changing political culture.

We begin with Michael D. Copeland's introduction to the new and important field of New Resource Economics, through which we view the problems and possibilities of Greater Yellowstone.

In Chapter 2, a survey of Greater Yellowstone's environment is provided by Donald Leal, a research associate in the Political Economy Research Center in Bozeman, Montana, just outside Greater Yellowstone. Because the ecological boundaries do not coincide with those delineated by ownership classification, activities in one area can redound to other, even distant, areas. These interactions can threaten the ecosystem's integrity; hence, there are increasing demands for federally managed buffer zones in the private lands that are part of Greater Yellowstone.

Leal argues that the greatest threats come from the activities of federal agencies. With the U.S. Forest Service, the Bureau of Reclamation, and the National Park Service driven primarily to maintain and increase their budgets, environmentally destructive and economically wasteful activities are promoted by bureaucrats and by their special interest clientele. Leal suggests several reforms that would improve this situation by addressing decision makers' incentives.

Part II deals with the issue of balancing use and preservation in

Greater Yellowstone, with the four chapters devoted to water, land, wildlife, and energy. Each necessarily relates to the others—interdependence is a defining characteristic of all systems.

Water management is critical to the ecological integrity of Greater Yellowstone. In Chapter 3 Andrew Dana, a geographer and a graduate of Stanford University Law School, explores water quality and allocation and the conflicts between consumptive uses of water (for example, irrigation and municipal supplies) and nonconsumptive uses (for example, fishing and floating).

Unfortunately, many of the alternative uses of water are incompatible. The management decisions that govern water use are highly complex and emotionally charged. Threats to the ecosystem are omnipresent and solutions are difficult to obtain. Dana concludes that many of these problems result from poorly defined and defended property rights, jurisdictional confusion, and external threats. Modest reforms, however, offer significant promise of relief to this critically important resource. Eliminating subsidies for development and improving clarity of property rights with concurrent transferability are central to reform.

Although private lands represent only a small percentage of Greater Yellowstone, they are of disproportionate importance. They provide critical winter range for thousands of animals and are the site of businesses that accommodate millions of tourists. The ecological network of the ecosystem does not recognize political and legal boundaries. Once again, interdependence dominates. Jo Kwong, a political economist specializing in natural resources, addresses this issue in Chapter 4. Applying property rights theory to land management conflicts, she emphasizes the protective/preservation function of property rights when the decision maker faces the consequences of decisions.

Dr. Kwong analyzes case studies of land use conflicts involving private lands in Greater Yellowstone. Specifically, she seeks alternatives to federal occupation and control of these lands by examining mechanisms that increase the contributions of private ownership and ensure ecological integrity. Conservation easements and transfers to nonprofit conservation groups are among the alternatives she explores.

Wildlife and geological formations are Greater Yellowstone's best-known attractions. Tom Blood, an avid outdoorsman, addresses the man-wildlife relationships in Chapter 5. Blood focuses on the interdependence of predator and prey in any ecosystem and identifies the wolf as a missing link in the system. Although the absence of this predator has degraded the ecosystem's integrity, politically powerful livestock interests have vehemently opposed the wolf's reintroduction. The government that exterminated this creature has lately come to appreciate its key role in the system but seems prevented by politics from reintroducing it. Blood proposes private-sector alternatives for wolf recovery and critical habitat management. His discussion of private land trusts outlines a way to bridge the political chasms that currently prevent reforms.

Oil and gas developments receive little public attention in Greater Yellowstone, yet this region is a part of the important "overthrust belt" portion of the oil patch. Donald Leal, Geoffrey Black, and I discuss this issue in Chapter 6. There is a common assumption that oil and ecology do not mix, but a great deal of experience, in Yellowstone and elsewhere, indicates that this perception is erroneous. Environmentally sensitive technologies for exploration and production of oil and gas are well known. The primary problem of sensitive development is political rather than physical, institutional rather than ecological.

Under current institutional arrangements neither agency personnel nor environmentalists have anything to gain from environmentally benign and economically productive oil and gas production. Yet environmentally destructive and economically wasteful timbering activities are strongly promoted by the USFS and the forest products industry. This perverse situation can be rectified by changing the incentives under which both activities occur.

Part III, Politics and Ecological Reform, features three papers. Each recognizes that political systems as well as ecological systems have feedback loops. Those who challenge the existing authority over resource allocation and management cannot anticipate a passive reception. The spirit of these environmentally sensitive times is fundamentally bureaucratic and collectivist. When challenged, the bureaucracy acts as predictably as a sow grizzly who believes her cubs are threatened. When actions are evaluated in political terms, ecological integrity and economic productivity become secondary to political considerations. This fundamental reality must be understood if reform is to occur.

Alston Chase, author and naturalist, writes about the ecology of information in Chapter 7. He is concerned with the gap between research results and management decisions. Chase develops an ecological model of agency behavior, stating that "human organizations are also ecosystems." In the organization of the Park Service, we find, "an explicit mechanism for preventing embarrassing information from escaping the parks." In an analysis consistent with public choice theory, Chase argues that the work of science has been subverted by the forces of bureaucratic politics. At least in the short run, scientific information unconstrained by political pressures is seen as destabilizing to the organization.

Chase is not an adherent of the New Resource Economics, but his proposed reforms are consistent with that approach. He notes that within a large bureaucracy, truth—in the form of scientific knowledge—and power are inversely related. Thus, he advocates the establishment of a quasi-independent agency and other organizational reforms that would better insulate science from politics.

Gene Lyons, a lifelong and ardent practicing sportsman, presents a compelling story from the literary trenches of *Newsweek.* Armed with a Ph.D. in English from the University of Virginia and a title of Books Editor, he approached the Yellowstone story with skepticism regarding tales of mismanagement. In directing this project for *Newsweek,* Dr. Lyons learned firsthand of the problems of the university/agency complex. Specifically, he learned that speaking truth to power is not a survival characteristic. Further, he discovered that if you challenge the collectivist ethos of conventional environmentalism, the zeitgeist will bite back.

In Chapter 9, economist Richard Stroup, a Montana resident, develops an idea he and I originally published in the *Cato Journal* in 1982 as "Endowment Boards: A Clearing in the Policy Wilderness?"[5] Recognizing that decisions are constrained contracts, heavily influenced by the information and incentives confronted by those in decision-making positions, Stroup suggests the creation of park endowment boards with responsibility for management. These organizations would be bound by the common-law doctrine of trust and fiduciary responsibility and would be accountable to Congress. Endowment boards would be charged with preserving the values of the

---

5. The most recent statement developing this idea appeared in the *Wall Street Journal's* editorial page of November 23, 1988, in the article "Take Politics Out of the National Parks: Let Nature Groups Bid for Control," an article by John Baden.

parks and fostering appreciation of them. In function, they would closely resemble the boards of the nation's great private museums of art and natural history. The challenge of balancing competing demands and making delicate trade-offs is clearly beyond the scope of politically driven organizations. The independence and judgment of a trust organization could be a formula for environmental policy success.

Dr. Vernon Smith was trained in engineering and economics at California Institute of Technology and Harvard. He is best known among economists for his pathbreaking and highly original work in developing the field of experimental economics. He is, in addition, a highly respected resource economist who has published in the areas of land, water, and wildlife economics. He is an active outdoorsman and sportsman with many years experience in the wildlands and waters of the West. The conjunction of qualities he brings to the task makes him the ideal author for the concluding chapter of this volume.

CONCLUSION

When we seek the cause of almost any problem in Greater Yellowstone, we find destructive ecological practices coupled with economic inefficiencies. There are striking opportunities for reform. Changes in the system to link good environmental management with economic growth would generate substantial environmental and economic benefits. These are precisely the kinds of reforms that we propose in this book. And, although most of these papers were written before Yellowstone burst into flames in the summer of 1988, the controversy of those months has underscored the urgency of examining the problems of policy and institutions addressed in these papers. By the same token, Alston Chase's conclusions in his criticisms of the Park Service in *Playing God in Yellowstone,* published in 1986, are more valid than ever. If the park had been managed as Chase says it should have been, the disastrous conflagrations of 1988 would never have occurred.

PART I

FOUNDATIONS FOR REFORM

1

THE NEW RESOURCE ECONOMICS

Michael D. Copeland

Yellowstone National Park, the "jewel in the crown" of the U.S. park system, and its environs, the Greater Yellowstone ecosystem, are a national treasure. It is hard to imagine a more concerned, dedicated, and professional group of stewards than the elite corps of scientific managers assigned to Yellowstone Park. If qualified managers with good intentions were sufficient to ensure sound decision making, Yellowstone would be the Eden of national parks. But as Alston Chase points out in *Playing God in Yellowstone,* National Park Service policy in Yellowstone is rife with mistakes, inefficiencies, poor judgment, and politically motivated decisions.[1]

Many of the problems are related to the Park Service's attempts to follow a preservationist policy, stopping further change and ensuring that all that happens is natural. Natural regulation and the "let-burn" policy have led to widespread criticism following the fires of the summer of 1988. Mismanagement of the northern elk and bison herds has led to overpopulation, causing overgrazing in areas where these animals thrive. This has caused erosion and stream sedimentation and has adversely affected a number of plant and animal species in the park. Chase blames natural regulation policies for the decline of de-

---

1. Alston Chase, *Playing God in Yellowstone: The Destruction of America's First National Park* (New York: Atlantic Monthly Press, 1986).

ciduous trees such as cottonwood, mountain alder, red birch, aspen, and willow. He also notes a decrease in forbs, a drying of soil, the development of short and sparse grasses, and the spread of sagebrush. The inherent conflict between preservation of the resources and use of the resources by people has been an ongoing problem.

If governmental ownership, management, and control lead to poor decision making in an intensively used and highly visible area such as Yellowstone Park, it would not be surprising if the situation were even worse in areas managed by the U.S. Forest Service (USFS), the Bureau of Land Management (BLM), and the Bureau of Reclamation. This is, in fact, the case. In these agencies, unlike the National Park Service, management decisions are not subject in the same sense to public scrutiny.

Yet, despite decades of land use management, most Americans still believe that only government can effectively manage natural resources. Private market-based options are automatically ruled out.

The New Resource Economics (NRE), developed by scholars at the Political Economy Research Center, based in Bozeman, Montana, critically examines the prevailing environmental orthodoxy. The perplexing problem of government-endorsed environmental destruction is explained in terms of public choice theory. The NRE offers a prescription for reform based on individual property rights and incentives.

NRE developed from a concern for the environment, the integrity of which was being compromised—not only by seemingly irresponsible individuals, but by the very government agencies assigned to protect the environment! The U.S. Forest Service's penchant for consistently undertaking logging activities that *cost* taxpayers hundreds of millions of dollars annually is well covered in Chapter 2 by Donald Leal. The adverse effects on fish, wildlife, and streams caused by these "deficit timber sales" cast doubt on the ability of the Forest Service to effectively manage its lands.

Yellowstone National Park is not immune to the same types of criticism. Political scientists Jeanne Nienaber Clarke of the University of Arizona and Daniel McCool of Texas A & M University include Yellowstone among the agencies that "muddle through."

In 1949 [National Park Service] Director Newton B. Drury issued a report called "The Dilemma of Our Parks," which described the deterioration and destruction of park land and park property caused by so many visitors and so few staff. A similar report was issued twenty-six years later, and it reached essentially the same conclusions. This one was titled "The Degradation of Our National Parks." The solution to this problem, as envisioned by the Park Service in 1949, was to initiate a massive development program in the national parks to accommodate increased visitation. . . . To keep up with public demand, in 1956 the agency launched its Mission '66 program. This was an ambitious ten-year development program that increased visitor capacity enormously but that "has done comparatively little for the plants and animals" and "nothing at all for the ecological maintenance of a park." Another author observed that "some of the Park Service's problems . . . will be traced to its own effort to attract the public."[2]

Typically, the solution offered for bureaucratic mismanagement is to replace agency managers with people who are competent, well intentioned, and well educated. It is clear, however, that the problems with government command-and-control management are not caused by bad people, but rather by flawed institutions and inappropriate incentives.

NRE AND PUBLIC CHOICE

Public choice economics provides some answers for those trying to explain the apparently perverse behavior of the institutions that manage our valuable resources.

Bureaucrats, like private business people, act to further their self-interest. Instead of financial gain, their reward is the perquisites resulting from advancement. Because they do not "profit" from their decisions, they do not necessarily manage their bureau in a manner designed to generate the most satisfaction or benefits for the users of the bureau's services. Decisions by the bureaucrat do not result in more or less profit as the customers or users react by purchasing more or fewer goods or services. People in private business, seeking profit, consider their customers. If their business decisions produce more satisfaction, they gain more income. A successful bureaucrat, in contrast, would gain salary, rank, and prestige. The bureaucrat's most advantageous policy, therefore, is one that increases the size of the

2. Jeanne Nienaber Clarke and Daniel McCool, *Staking Out the Terrain* (Albany: State University of New York Press, 1985), p. 51.

bureau, the size of its budget, and the number of people the bureaucrat supervises.

Not only do bureaucrats have little incentive to carefully monitor the cost of each program, but in some cases they are even motivated to generate more costs. For example, by spending a bureau's entire budget in one fiscal year, the bureaucrat can increase the likelihood of raising its funding in the next fiscal year. Private business people undertake only those activities that they expect to be valuable enough (as evidenced by customers' willingness to pay) to warrant the cost.

Because the products or services of a government agency are usually available free or at a nominal cost, there is no basis for ascertaining the true value of these services or the worth of the project or activity. However competent professional managers may be, they have no edge in determining the value that users or "customers" derive from government agencies' services. The information needed to assess the true value and cost of goods and services can be revealed only in the marketplace.

The information-generating function of prices cannot be overestimated. Prices provide information on the value and cost of proposals—information that is necessary to determine the "economic efficiency" of a project. For example, the U.S. Forest Service has to make decisions regarding competing uses (such as logging, recreation, agriculture, or mining) for forest land. Assuming (and this is a big assumption) that USFS managers want to generate as much satisfaction or enjoyment as possible among the users of their services, how do they determine how to allocate the resources they control? The price of logs in the lumber market may be known, but for activities which are not leased or sold such as hunting, biking, and fishing, no system exists for establishing accurate value.

Of course, many government agencies charge for their services or products, and when the prices reflect the true values and costs, they generate strong incentives to make sound or efficient decisions. However, government agencies' prices are typically below those of the market. Fees charged to ranchers for grazing their cattle on BLM lands are typically lower than grazing fees on comparable private land. This discrepancy generates inappropriate signals about the value of resources and the environmental costs of activities.

If the Forest Service must manage its resources for competing uses (such as grazing, hiking, camping, hunting, fishing, and logging), price distortion or lack of price information leads to perverse decisions. Timber sales generate a major share of the Forest Service's revenue. Congressional appropriations and funds retained by the Forest Service from timber sales through the Knudson–Vandenberg Act are strong incentives to utilize Forest Service land for logging, even if the other uses of the land are adversely affected.

In addition to the inherent lack of knowledge and information, scientific managers in government agencies are limited by a perverse set of incentives that channel their activities into unproductive activities.

Agency managers often believe that their bureau has a mission mandated by Congress that frees them from the responsibility of considering the costs of their acts. U.S. Fish and Wildlife Service personnel and state fish and game officials, therefore, might support land restrictions (such as zoning to prohibit subdivision of land) that would enhance game habitat, regardless of the effect such an action would have on other recreational activities, the value of the surrounding private property, or the rights of the landowner.

If an owner of resources or an employee of the owner makes decisions that lead to losses or to diminished profits, he or she is responsible for those actions. But for government bureaucrats, having the authority to make decisions does not mean taking the responsibility for those decisions. Agency managers are not accountable for their decisions in the sense as private owners. Wasting a resource does not result in a loss or a reduced profit, because prices are typically not charged. Whereas a private manager might be fired because of losses resulting from poor decisions, a governmental manager is largely immune from firing because of civil service laws and has much greater latitude to make bad decisions without being held responsible.

Park Service managers' decisions regarding the Yellowstone forest fires generated enormous costs. The urgency and national visibility of the situation meant that the Park Service could get substantial funds from Congress to fight the fire. But if the Park Service had to fight the fires *without* additional aid from Congress, different decisions might have been made. Prescribed burning, earlier and more vigorous fire-fighting efforts, and the use of prohibited vehicles (such as bulldozers to clear fire lanes and off-road motorized vehicles) were all possibilities. The additional costs of the current Park Service policy included air pollution extending for hundreds of miles, destruction of private property, interruption of vacation plans, and loss of income to businesses on the perimeter of the park. Private owners, when faced with paying for these costs, might have reacted very differently to the fire than did the Park Service bureaucrats.

Public choice literature offers many explanations for seemingly perverse behavior by government managers and politicians. Several of these warrant discussion. The generally recognized tendency of government agencies to cater to the interests of narrow special interest groups is not surprising when the incentives of the decision makers are considered. Voters tend to be ignorant about many issues. Their individual share of the cost of most programs is very small, and obtaining accurate information on the cost and the effect of a program on their lives is difficult. Thus they remain "rationally ignorant." On any given issue, however, not all voters are ignorant. Members of groups whose well-being is strongly affected will become informed and will go to great lengths—campaign contributions, lobbying, mobilizing members, advertising—to influence a government decision. Politicians and bureaucrats do respond to such efforts.

When strong constituencies are involved, political decisions are easy to predict. Politically feasible rather than economically efficient actions are taken. A program that generates much greater costs than benefits might very well be carried out if the benefits are concentrated in the hands of a strong, well-organized group and while the cost is diffused among a large number of taxpayers, each of whom pays a small price. Bureaucrats also tend to favor programs with visible benefits and invisible costs. Protecting animals by forbidding logging and mineral development on specific tracts of land often has considerable popular support. The resulting rise in the price of housing might not be given appropriate consideration.

Not only will bureaucrats respond to special interests, they will also seek out special interests and tailor decisions and legislation to win support and votes. The Greater Yellowstone Coalition (GYC), an umbrella group of organizations interested in the Yellowstone region, represents a strong constituency for preservation policy in Yellowstone. That policies of Yellowstone managers tend to be consistent with GYC proposals is probably no accident. And because the bureaucrats, the agency, and the special interest will all gain from an increase in the bureau's budget, strong pressure in that direction can be expected.

When an individual's self-interest conflicts with the interests of society, the public tends to lose. The New Resource Economics suggests that, instead of seeking "better managers" to operate with public interest in mind, we should recognize that people are motivated by self-interest. We should design institutions that link a manager's interest with the interests of people affected by that manager's decisions.

IMPROVING YELLOWSTONE WITH THE NEW RESOURCE ECONOMICS

Unlike the standard assumption that there is a "public interest" that managers can ascertain, New Resource Economics begins with the individual entrepreneur. If entrepreneurs pay the full cost of their actions and if the revenue they receive represents all of the value generated by those actions, they will undertake only actions that will lead to net gains for themselves and society. If the owner of water rights, for example, finds a higher valued use of that water than irrigating crops (such as leaving water in the stream for the benefit of fish and wildlife), the owner stands to gain personally if the value of the water in its new use is greater than the water's cost. Here, the owner's profitability is consistent with sound decision making for society if the owner's decision takes into consideration all costs and benefits.

Problems arise when the costs of the project are paid by others. The entrepreneur, in deciding whether the project is profitable, will consider only his or her own costs. The project might be carried out even when the costs are greater than the benefits, because only part of the costs have been considered. The project is profitable for the owner but not reasonable or efficient for society. For example, one of the costs of developing oil in Alaska is oil spills. This cost will be incurred by local residents, fishermen, and anyone who feels harmed by the effects on the environment. Whether or not oil production or development should occur is not clear. What is clear, however, is that the cost of the oil spills may not be taken into account by the oil companies—in which case the decision will be biased in the direction of development.

The private sector entrepreneur must be "responsible" for all costs, either by bearing the costs, or, at a minimum, by reimbursing those who have incurred costs because of the entrepreneur's actions. If the owner of the water rights decides to leave water in the stream during low flows to sustain fish, he must bear the cost of his reduced agricultural production. He feels that the value of the water in the stream is greater than the cost he incurs. If increased flows cause problems for people downstream, he must be responsible or legally liable for those costs and must consider them in determining his actions.

The assignment of property rights will determine ultimate responsibility for the costs. If hunters have a clearly defined property right to hunt on Forest Service land, decisions by the Forest Service to allow grazing or logging must take into consideration the effects of their actions on game herds, access, and game habitat. If a decision to allow logging interferes with hunting, hunters would have to be compensated for their loss. A legal system that recognizes the property rights of *all* parties forces decision makers to consider these interests.

An entrepreneur must also be able to capture all benefits of an action if the costs and benefits he faces are to represent net benefits to society. If his benefits are enjoyed by people who do not pay for his services, he is less likely to perform those actions. When the owner of a resource excludes nonpayers from using the resource, nonpayers become motivated to pay. The value they receive is considered by the owner in deciding the use of the resource.

For example, a landowner considering expensive stream improvement activities, such as fencing cattle away from the stream bank, would enhance the fishing value of the stream for his private use or for the use of fee-paying fishermen who would eventually help pay for the improvements. If the public had the legal right to fish this stream, which is the case in some areas in Montana, fishermen would have no motivation to pay and the landowner would be less likely to make the improvements.

As long as the wealth and income of the decision maker are affected by his decisions, he is forced to consider costs and benefits. The private owner is strongly motivated to protect against resource waste if he is the residual claimant and can claim as his own any increased value of his resources that result from conservation. Thus, well-defined, enforced, and transferable property rights will create incentives for practical decisions, efficient actions, promotion of environmental quality, and sound resource stewardship.

To ensure incentives so that resources are moved to other uses, the rights to the resources must be transferable to other uses and other owners. If water is more valuable left in the stream to sustain fish populations than used to irrigate fields, the owner must have the right to choose the use. Of course, the owner must also be able to charge fishermen and capture a share of the benefits resulting from conserving his property.

Many cases of environmental degradation are blamed on greedy individuals, the market system, and the lack of governmental ownership, control, and regulation. The demise of the Great Plains bison in the nineteenth century, for example, is blamed on greedy market hunters and the absence of government control. In fact, the problem developed because no one had property rights to the bison; no one owned them. They were what economists call an open-access resource. Had bison been privately owned and valuable, the owner would have protected his asset, managed the herd efficiently, and sold rights to harvest bison. Domestic cattle are valuable and privately owned (government, through its subsidy programs, is involved) yet appear to be in no danger of extinction. Game species are thriving on huge tracts of land owned by the International Paper Company in the southeastern United States. A significant portion of the company's profits on these tracts comes from marketing the rights to hunt deer, turkey, and quail. As long as they own the rights to hunt on this land, they will ensure the value of their resource by preserving the game.

Unfortunately, some situations do not lend themselves to the assignment of property rights. Provision of wildlife habitat for far-ranging animals is a case in point. Following the fires of the summer of 1988, which destroyed a significant portion of wintering area for Yellowstone's northern elk herd, a brutal winter caused thousands of elk to die. Local newspapers chronicled a public outcry for the private purchase of additional elk wintering areas. Elk are far-ranging animals that cover considerable territory. Many of the hunters who would gain from new wintering areas would refuse to pay for their maintenance. Therefore, because the value of elk habitat is understated, there would tend to be underinvestment in this purpose.

These uncaptured benefits are the domain of the entrepreneur, however, and innovative market solutions have sprung up in recent years. Groups such as the Nature Conservancy, the Montana Land Reliance, and Ducks Unlimited, acting in the interest of a widely dispersed constituency, purchase land critical to their goals.

Even in cases where uncaptured benefits or costs imposed on third parties are widespread enough to warrant government involvement, there is often considerable opportunity to alter the incentive structure to effect efficient changes in bureaucratic behavior. Randal O'Toole in "Reforming the Forest Service" suggests eliminating the Forest Service's government funding and allowing the agency to earn what it can by *marketing* its considerable resources for competing uses—logging, recreation, grazing, and mining.[3]

In many cases all that natural-resource markets need to flourish is the removal of the obstacles imposed by government. Prohibiting water marketing except diversion, leasing of large blocks of Forest Service land for hunting, and allowing private, for-profit provision of hunting, fishing, and camping are examples.

New Resource Economics does not propose market solutions for all situations. There is a role for government, albeit a much smaller one than currently exists. In certain cases private decision making will fail to take significant considerations into account, resulting in what economists call market failure. Public goods are those consumed by everyone, whether they pay or not. If the result of certain activities is cleaner air, the people benefiting would often not be willing to pay their share since they benefit whether they pay or not. Market failure also occurs when costs are incurred by people not involved in the decision-making process. If logging causes stream siltation, the costs imposed on downstream users may not be considered by decision makers. These cases of market failure mean that market decisions may be imperfect.

In the same sense that private decisions will not be efficient (the case of market failure), NRE shows that government failure is a pervasive and serious problem. Revealing market failure is not sufficient reason to substitute government involvement. Market solutions, even with the problems discussed above, will often lead to better resource decision making than will government management. Imperfect government may be worse than imperfect private decisions.

A constituency that is concerned only with preservation of a resource will view NRE as a threat. Although preservation is an important goal—and the NRE paradigm suggests that the private sector will often preserve resources much better than government—private ownership and decisions will sometimes make preservation a secondary concern. If other activities are valuable enough, they will take

---

3. Randal O'Toole, *Reforming the Forest Service* (Washington, D.C.: Island Press, 1988).

place at the expense of preservation, with reasonable environmental safeguards. If the proposed activity (mining, for instance) poses too great a threat to the long-term value of the resource, the owner will forgo it. Preservationists who feel a resource is so valuable that it must be preserved at all costs are free to purchase the resource. Giving such groups the opportunity to purchase such "priceless" resources would provide a reality check on the "preserve at all costs" mentality.

The private ownership of resources is often criticized as leading to "rape and pillage" behavior; this attitude assumes that capitalists will exhaust a resource as quickly as possible. But if a resource is expected to be more valuable in the future than it is now, owners interested in increasing their wealth will preserve the resource for the future, even if the resource owner does not expect to live to see the resource finally utilized. A classic example is that of a landowner considering planting trees as a cash crop. Even though many years may pass before trees are harvested, the value of the property increases as harvest time approaches, thus enabling the resource owner to profit from his actions while saving the resource for future generations. Of course, sometimes owners make mistakes and misuse resources, but the government alternative is fraught with the same danger.

New Resource Economics provides some alternatives to the present comand-and-control management techniques. There is still room for governmental ownership, management, and control, but on a much smaller scale. While private solutions to resource problems are not a panacea, they offer an opportunity for constructive reform.

New Resource Economics would create private incentives and institutions whenever possible. It would utilize the market system to generate the price information needed to make good decisions. It would create property rights that motivate decision makers to consider true costs and benefits before making their decisions. Private ownership could, in many cases, replace government ownership. The following chapters present numerous examples of New Resource Economics analysis.

2

SAVING AN ECOSYSTEM
From Buffer Zone to Private Initiatives

Donald Leal

Signs of abuse are multiplying in the Greater Yellowstone ecosystem. In the national forests, road construction and timber cuts deplete precious wildlife habitat and increase sediment in the region's streams and rivers. At the same time, growing recreational use is putting added strain on the region's crown jewels, Yellowstone and Grand Teton national parks.

Resolving these problems is a formidable task in such a large and administratively complex system. The region, which encompasses more than 19 million acres, includes areas administered by the federal government, such as the national parks, national forests, wilderness, wildlife refuges, and Bureau of Land Management lands. In addition, there are private lands and lands administered by the states of Wyoming, Idaho, and Montana. The region also contains tourist towns such as Jackson Hole, Wyoming, and Big Sky and West Yellowstone, Montana.

Many environmentalists think that the solution lies in the creation of a "legal buffer zone" around Yellowstone and Grand Teton national parks.[1] Such a zone, they contend, would legally protect the whole ecosystem from activities considered threatening to the envi-

---

1. T. R. Reid, "The Land Set Aside for Yellowstone Was a Great Mistake," *Washington Post,* July 15, 1985, p. 23; Timothy Egan, "Land Sought as Buffer Around Parks," *New York Times,* March 3, 1989, p. 8.

ronment, such as oil and gas development, logging, and new housing construction. The idea won support from Yellowstone National Park superintendent Robert Barbee and the Reagan administration's National Park Service director, William Penn Mott, Jr.

Defined in a broad sense, the buffer zone includes a region that varies from 40 to 60 miles beyond the boundaries of Yellowstone and Grand Teton national parks. Under the zone concept, proposed developments such as commercial logging, road construction, oil and gas development, hardrock mining, geothermal development, livestock grazing, and ski resort development in the surrounding national forests (these forests constitute 89 percent of the buffer zone) would be "sharply limited."[2] Environmentalists insist that these developments can cause irreparable harm to wildlife, habitat, and geothermal features in the region. But exactly how decisions to limit development would be carried out remains a mystery. For instance, what specific criteria would be used to determine rejection of a proposed activity? Would potential benefits of an activity be weighed against environmental costs? In addition, how would a buffer zone affect uses occurring on private land in the buffer zone? Protest by environmentalists of use of a well on land owned by the Church Universal and Triumphant near the northeast boundary of Yellowstone Park and a push for government acquisition of other private land in the region indicate environmentalists' desire for more government control in the region.

People living in Greater Yellowstone's rural communities worry that a buffer zone could be carried to extremes and ban the activities that sustain their fragile economies. Energy developers see the current buffer zone proposal as arbitrary and fear that they could be denied access to some very promising energy reserves. They contend that the buffer zone concept blocks their ability to conduct development in an environmentally safe manner. They point to the Audubon Society's Rainey Preserve in Louisiana and the Kenai National Wildlife Refuge in Alaska to demonstrate that oil and gas development can be conducted safely.

To those of us who want to prevent further environmental deterioration in the region, a buffer zone sounds—at first hearing—like an excellent idea. But there remain questions about implementing this

---

2. T. R. Reid, "The Land Set Aside for Yellowstone Was a Great Mistake," *Washington Post*, July 15, 1985, p. 23.

approach. For example, determining which activities are harmful is not a cut-and-dried issue. There is substantial evidence that oil and gas development can occur in Greater Yellowstone to a degree without harming the environment.[3] Thus, while there is agreement that certain kinds of development (such as logging and road building along hillsides with slopes of 60 percent or more) are creating environmental problems, there is not a consensus that all development is damaging.

The buffer zone concept needs to be precisely defined to avoid needless prohibition of activities that do not endanger the environment. The economic well-being of the communities in the region must always be kept in mind.

To ensure that only sensitive and beneficial activities take place, we should first examine how the dominant landowner in the region— the federal government—is protecting Greater Yellowstone. We should find out to what extent environmentally harmful and economically unsound activities are occurring. What policies are promoting such activities? Which activities lack economic incentives to protect the environment?

Since much of Greater Yellowstone falls under the jurisdiction of the U.S. Forest Service, the management policies for our national forests provide a logical starting point.

THE FOREST SERVICE AND YELLOWSTONE'S NATIONAL FORESTS

Environmentalists hailed the passage of the National Forest Management Act in 1976 as a major breakthrough. Support for the act grew out of criticism that the agency tended to emphasize timber harvesting at the expense of the environment. At long last, the Forest Service would be forced to value wildlife and wilderness—not just board feet.

One of the results of the act was the implementation of an extensive forest planning process. Since the passage of the act, the Forest Service has laboriously planned for the national forests, specifying the areas where logging, road construction, mining, oil and gas development, and livestock grazing are allowed, and areas where they are not. The agency had expected to finish these plans by the end of 1984 at a cost of $100 million, but many were not completed by then because of changes prompted by environmental appeals. As a result, the

---

3. See Chapter 6.

costs of forest planning soared to triple the original estimate.[4] Meanwhile, the Forest Service still emphasizes timber harvesting in regions where timber is of marginal quality and the costs of production far outweigh the returns. The Forest Service's decision to harvest timber in those regions resulted in a net operating loss of $1 billion in 1985 and again in 1986.[5] Private forestry consultant Randal O'Toole voices concern about the Forest Service's penchant for spending more than it collects: "Although [the Forest Service] produces annual revenues of about $1 billion, in order to do so it spends $2 billion per year, producing net earnings of minus $1 billion. Few companies in the Fortune 500 can produce losses this large."[6]

The Forest Service runs deficit timber programs in the forests of Greater Yellowstone. A recent Wilderness Society study states that "this is the least defensible activity in the Greater Yellowstone Ecosystem."[7] For the period 1979–1984, annual timber-cutting costs exceeded timber receipts in all seven of the region's national forests. "Regionwide losses over the six-year period averaged nearly $7 million per year, or 55 cents for every dollar invested in timber production. Six-year average losses ranged from $241,000 per year in the Caribou National Forest to $2.2 million per year in the Beaverhead National Forest."[8] The study's statistics for each national forest are presented in Figure 2–1.

Consider the Gallatin National Forest timber program in fiscal year 1986. Administration and preparation of timber sales and salvage sales of dead timber cost about $443,000, reforestation of timber-depleted areas cost $266,000, planting new trees and thinning cost $158,000, road building and maintenance of existing roads cost $747,000, and trail building and maintenance cost $238,000. All told, the timber

4. Randal O'Toole, "Below-Cost Sales, Budget Maximization, and the Conservation Ethic: A Process of Natural Selection" (Paper for 1986 Policy Seminar on Privatization, Political Economy Research Center, Bozeman, Montana, September 26, 1985), p. 9.

5. In 1988 the agency showed a profit of $690 million, mostly due to profitable timber cuts in the Pacific Northwest and in the Southeast. However, of 122 national forests, 65, including those surrounding Yellowstone Park, collected significantly less than they spent on their timber programs.

6. Randal O'Toole, "Reforming the Forest Service." Working Paper 87-7. Political Economy Research Center, Bozeman, Montana, January 1987, p. 1.

7. Wilderness Society, "Management Directions for the National Forests of the Greater Yellowstone Ecosystem." Wilderness Society, January 1987, p. 21.

8. Ibid., pp. 22–23.

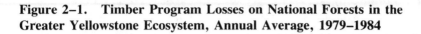

**Figure 2–1.   Timber Program Losses on National Forests in the
Greater Yellowstone Ecosystem, Annual Average, 1979–1984**

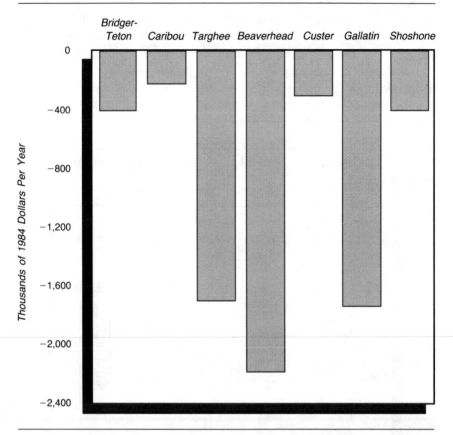

program cost the taxpayer $1,852,000 and brought the government
$669,800 in revenue.[9] The Forest Service released figures in 1989
indicating that it lost another $1 million on Gallatin National Forest
from the timber harvested there in 1988.[10]

National forest plans over the next ten years indicate that the timber
program is still the dominant activity. O'Toole estimates that the tim-

9. Craig Johnson, "Forester Calls Macroserve Unrealistic," *Bozeman Daily Chronicle,*
January 25, 1987, p. 1.

10. Robert Ekey, "Timber Program Lost $1 Million," *Billings Gazette,* March 17, 1989,
p. 2C.

ber programs for these forests will lose between $200,000 and $5 million per year in the 1990s.[11] Losses for six of the Yellowstone national forests are presented in Figure 2–2.

The Forest Service's explanation for continuing with these activities even though they are operating at a loss is that they are helping stabilize the economies of the small communities in the region. Yet the timber program can inhibit the opportunities for recreation by jeopardizing fish and wildlife and degrading visual amenities. The comparison of timber- and recreation-related jobs illustrated in Figure

Figure 2–2.   Projected Annual Losses Due to Timber (in thousands of 1978 dollars)

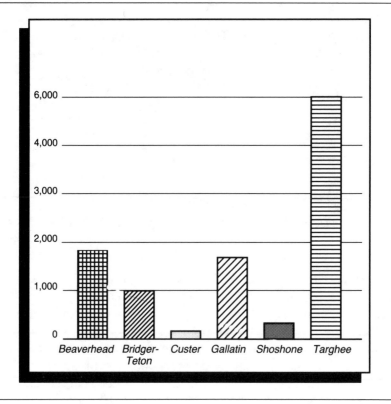

11. O'Toole, "Below-Cost Sales, Budget Maximization," p. 10.

Figure 2–3.   Recreation and Timber Employment from Six Rocky Mountain Forests (direct full-time equivalent job generated by each forest)

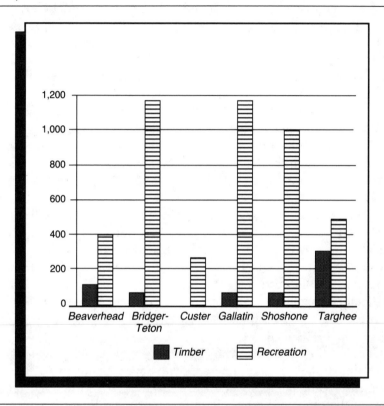

2–3 reveals the shaky ground on which this economic stabilization argument is erected.[12]

The Forest Service also claims that its road-building and logging activities provide additional recreational access and enhance wildlife habitat. If these nonmarket benefits were factored in, according to the Forest Service, the total benefits would outweigh the costs of the overall timber program. But there are serious omissions in this argument.

12. O'Toole, "Reforming the Forest Service," p. 31.

While new roads give more access for motorized recreation, the agency provides less of what backcountry hikers, hunters, and fishermen want. The Forest Service's argument also ignores the sedimentation problems created in many of the streams and rivers by road building and logging. This sedimentation adversely affects the region's natural trout fisheries, one of the main attractions for tourism in the region. And while a logged area will regenerate itself with new grasses and shrubs and thus produce more food for elk and deer, logging reduces other necessities for the animals, including thermal protection and security from mature stands of trees (see the discussion of the survivability of bull elk in the Gallatin National Forest later in this chapter).

What constitutes a proper mix of roaded and roadless, logged and unlogged lands in the Greater Yellowstone ecosystem? The fact that certain goods such as hiking, hunting, and fishing are not marketed creates a dilemma for forest officials. In the absence of prices they must rely on their best judgments of the mix of uses the public wants. But without prices there is no way to determine the amount of good roads or hiking trails, for instance, desired by the public, and even worse, the officials and the public must rely on the political process to search for the correct mix. This approach hardly ever reaches a satisfactory conclusion for all interests involved: somebody wins and somebody loses—as the rash of protests and lawsuits on these issues in the late 1980s have attested.

Contrast this situation with that of resource management on the large timber holdings of International Paper Company (IP) in the Southeast. Unlike the situation in the Greater Yellowstone region, most of the timber land base is in private hands. Prices exist for services such as hunting, fishing, and hiking, as well as for timber. As a result, resource managers can make informed choices on the joint production of logging and recreation. Their choices will be guided by their attempt to maximize profits.

The returns from recreational activities on IP lands have increased steadily in the late 1980s. As a result, wildlife's share of the resource pie has become an increasingly critical factor in timber operations on IP lands. Evidence of this can be seen by the new approaches taken by IP to protect wildlife habitat. For example, buffer zones where no logging is permitted are established for all riparian areas. Road building is minimized whenever possible; where roads for logging already exist, closures to protect wildlife security during hunting are strictly enforced.[13]

Such approaches are noticeably absent in Forest Service management. Lands in increments of hundreds of thousands of acres are either classified suitable for logging or they are not. Road closures on logging roads are rare. Buffer zones to protect riparian areas are non-existent. The political process may be the only element that the Forest Service uses that the IP arrangement does not.

How do timber programs hurt the environment? The Wilderness Society expresses the concerns of many conservationists about the Forest Service's timber-cutting practices:

> Each of the long-term management plans issued by the Forest Service in the ecosystem calls for a continuation of timber harvesting in areas that are unsuitable for timber production. These sites are often characterized by steep slopes, less stable land types, and harsh climatic factors that can prevent successful reforestation within the five year requirement of the NFMA.[14]

By law, the Forest Service must manage its lands on a sustained yield basis by not harvesting trees faster than their rate of growth. The National Forest Management Act directs the Forest Service to cut timber only on lands that can be restocked within five years and to use clear-cutting only where it is consistent with forest regeneration.

Clear-cutting, which is used extensively in Greater Yellowstone's national forests, removes all trees in a stand during a timber harvest. Such practices are quite damaging to the environment. Forestry consultant O'Toole explains that "clear-cutting often requires herbicides . . . [and] creates the harshest possible conditions for seedlings: hot, dry soils in summer, frost pockets in winter."[15] Nevertheless, the Forest Service maintains that such conditions do not limit the suitability of lands for timber production. The Wilderness Society notes that Forest Service plans for "Gallatin, Shoshone, and Bridger-Teton National Forests do not remove any land from their suitable timber bases because of possible reforestation difficulties. These decisions ignore

13. International Paper Company, "A Forester's Guide to Wildlife Management in Southern Industrial Pine Forests." Technical Bulletin 10, January 1980.

14. Wilderness Society, "Management Directions," p. 26.

15. O'Toole, "Reforming the Forest Service," p. 23.

the fact that each of these forests contains land types of shallow and rocky soils, steep slopes, and high elevations."[16]

Along with logging has come extensive road building. For example, in the Gallatin National Forest 807 miles of inventoried forest roads have been constructed. Another 1,000 miles of uninventoried roads (roads not maintained) is estimated to exist, and the projected amount of additional roads to be built over the next ten years is more than 2,200 miles.[17] There are environmental problems when roads are built in critical wildlife habitat and watersheds. The disturbance to wildlife can be serious when road building results in more motorized access into previously unroaded areas that are relied on by elk and grizzly as places they can breed and escape hunters. It is critical for their survival that certain areas not be accessible by motorized traffic.

In addition, both road building and clear-cutting can cause watersheds to be flooded by excess sediment, as the Wilderness Society found.

> Sediment generated by land-disturbing activities poses one of the greatest threats to water quality and fisheries within the ecosystem. Many of the ecosystem's watersheds are steep and consist of unstable soils ill-suited for road building and other land-disturbing activities. When disturbed these lands can dump tons of sediment into streams, smothering important fish habitat.[18]

The Gallatin River is easily damaged by sedimentation. Beginning in Yellowstone National Park and flowing through a beautiful canyon north of the park, the Gallatin provides excellent trout fishing, rafting, and sightseeing. The Forest Service reckons that Gallatin River fishing and recreation "account for about $815,000 a year in direct income forest-wide."[19] This figure, of course, does not reflect people's willingness to pay for use of the river, but it does illustrate the river's economic importance to the region.

This river is located in a geologically fragile area. Smaller drain-

16. Wilderness Society, "Management Directions," p. 26.

17. U.S. Department of Agriculture, U.S. Forest Service, *Final Environmental Impact Statement to the Gallatin National Forest Plan* (Bozeman, Mont.: U.S. Forest Service, 1988).

18. Wilderness Society, "Management Directions," p. 27. For a study of sedimentation problems, see Brad Shepard, "Sedimentation Impacts from Clearcutting on the Flathead National Forest," *Trout,* Spring 1985, p. 85.

19. Craig Johnson, "Beautiful, Bountiful Gallatin River," *Bozeman Chronicle,* September 21, 1986, p. 17.

ages, such as Taylors Fork, Porcupine Creek, Bush Creek, and West Fork—each of which has sparse vegetation and soil highly susceptible to erosion—empty tons of sediment into the Gallatin during spring run-off or heavy rains. Even with these sediment-laden tributaries, there is still enough forest cover and other vegetation in the rest of the Gallatin drainage system to keep the river stabilized. This is fortunate because trout need clean water to reproduce. If sediment increased, it would not be long before the Gallatin River would cease to be the exceptional trout fishery it is today.[20]

Under the Forest Service's current plans, this will eventually happen. While calling for increased logging in the Gallatin Forest, the Forest Service says that additional water run-off will occur, resulting in larger water supplies for downstream users. They don't point out the effect the increased water supply will have on the Gallatin's blue-ribbon fishery.[21]

State fish and wildlife officials are also concerned that road building and clear-cuts have seriously reduced protective cover for elk, especially mature and trophy elk. These animals seek areas that have maximum cover and protection during the long hunting season. A detailed study of the effects of timber harvesting, road construction, and recreational traffic reveals a reduction in usable habitat for elk and an increase in stress among elk.[22] In recent years there have been fewer mature elk because they lack sufficient protective habitat. In the Gallatin National Forest, Montana wildlife biologist Terry N. Lonner has seen a disturbing trend in the quality of elk hunting. In the mid-1980s, the elk harvest was approximately 65 percent "spikes," or male elk approximately one to two years old; ten years earlier, 50 percent of the harvest were spikes; in the mid-1950s only 35 percent of the harvest were spikes.[23]

In addition to timber cutting and road building, other federal government-subsidized activities threaten habitat. Both the Forest Service and the Bureau of Land Management, for example, run livestock grazing

20. Ibid., p. 23.
21. U.S. Department of Agriculture, U.S. Forest Service, *Gallatin National Forest Plan* (Bozeman, Mont.: U.S. Forest Service, 1985), pp. 11–68.
22. L. Jack Lyon, Terry N. Lonner, et al., *Coordinating Elk and Timber Management: Final Report of the Montana Cooperative Elk-Logging Study 1970–1985* (Bozeman, Mont.: Montana Department of Fish, Wildlife, and Parks, 1985), pp. 37–48.
23. Mark Henkel, *The Hunter's Guide to Montana* (Helena, Mont.: Falcon Publishing Co., 1985), p. 17.

programs on their Greater Yellowstone holdings. Like timber cutting, grazing is heavily subsidized. The current grazing fee is $1.54 per animal unit month (basically a cow and a calf grazing for one month). Grazing fees on comparable private lands in the region are nearly three times as high.[24] If grazing were turned over to the private sector, the level of activity would probably be greatly reduced. In the Shoshone National Forest, for example, the cost to maintain and administer grazing and mitigate damage to riparian habitat is over $6.73 per acre in 1985 dollars. Yet the fair market value of the grazing land is only $6.57.[25]

With artificially low fees, users have an incentive to overstock the range. Range damage has already occurred in Greater Yellowstone. For example, the Targhee National Forest has categorized 125,000 acres of the range in "poor or very poor" condition due to overgrazing by livestock.[26] In addition to being charged below-market prices for use of range, livestock owners are not assessed the full costs for damage their cattle cause to riparian habitat (the banks of streams). As the Forest Service's plan for Targhee National Forest reports,

> Livestock, (especially cattle), and road construction have had the greatest impact on riparian areas of any resource activities. Damage in the form of stream bank trampling and overgrazing of willows and other riparian vegetation, loss of cover for shade and food production for fish and increased erosion are the adverse impacts.[27]

It should also be noted that many recreational activities including fishing and hunting are provided to users free of charge. Indications are that the Forest Service's subsidies for recreation may be as high (if not higher) than its timber program. This in turn can lead to overuse of fragile resources in the region by recreationists.

Since fish and wildlife are two of the major reasons people visit these national forests, one has to ask what logic leads the Forest Service to subsidize logging, road building, recreational traffic, and grazing. Millions of dollars are spent every year by the private sector on travel, motel accomodations, and sporting equipment in Greater Yel-

24. Randal O'Toole, "Inefficiency in the National Forests—A Review of the Sales-Below-Cost Issue," *Forest Watch*, September 24, 1985, p. 16.

25. Ibid., p. 17.

26. U.S. Department of Agriculture, U.S. Forest Service, *Targhee National Forest Plan* (St. Anthony, Idaho: U.S. Forest Service, 1985), p. 10.

27. Ibid., p. 86.

lowstone, while the Forest Service spends millions to subsidize activities that stress wildlife and habitat. Clearly something is wrong.

Other federal government subsidies pose threats to the region. Small Business Administration loans, federal insurance programs, and federal grants for rural development (for example, for municipal water-treatment plants) frequently promote unwise development. More than fifteen years ago, a road was proposed from U.S. Highway 191 in Gallatin Canyon to Big Sky Ski Resort. Environmentalists protested, charging that the road would harm an ecologically fragile area. Despite an appeal by the Montana Wilderness Association and subsequent delays, federal highway funding eventually paid most of the costs of road construction.[28]

Current government policy creates problems in the region beyond the national parks. The federal government uses tax dollars to subsidize activities that endanger fish and wildlife habitat. In the absence of subsidies, these activities would be substantially reduced and the environment would be greatly improved.

THE PARK SERVICE AND YELLOWSTONE NATIONAL PARK

One might assume that the problems described above are inherent in managing multiple-use national forests, but surely the federal government does a better job of managing the national parks! Yet National Park Service policy produces just as many problems.

Under the 1916 Organic Act, Congress directed the National Park Service

> to conserve the scenery and the natural and historic objects and the wildlife therein and to provide for the enjoyment of the same in such manner and by such means as will leave them unimpaired for the enjoyment of future generations.

The agency is not authorized to determine the proper balance between timber cutting, mining, and conservation in its jurisdiction. Despite Congress's clear mandate, controversy continues.

One conspicuous controversy has been the steady rise in humans

28. Gallatin Canyon Study Team, "Impacts of Large Recreational Developments Upon Semi-Primitive Environments: The Gallatin Canyon Synthesis Report Executive Summary," Institute of Applied Research and Montana State University, Bozeman, Montana, 1976.

killed by grizzly bears.[29] Explanations for this increase have included the decision to close the garbage dumps, the bears' primary food source, and the Park Service's handling of bears—for instance, tranquilizing the bears and moving them to other areas of the park. John and Frank Craighead, naturalists who carried out a ten-year study of the grizzly, claim that when the dumps were closed, the bears were forced to look for food at campsites and nearby towns, inevitably increasing their contact with humans. Bears that posed persistent problems were eventually killed by park rangers.

The number of bears killed by park rangers over the last eighteen years is at the minimum greater than the total number of bears remaining in the Greater Yellowstone ecosystem today—around 200. The Park Service claims that 261 grizzly bears have been killed; the Craigheads think the number is closer to 320.

Others believe that elk and bison populations have grown out of control because of the Park Service's natural regulation policy. The Park Service chooses not to intervene in controlling the size of elk or bison populations because the park's flora and fauna are assumed capable of regulating themselves. Coinciding with this hands-off approach has been a growth in the elk population; elk in Yellowstone's northern range reached a thirty-year peak at the end of 1988. Wildlife biologist and researcher Charles E. Kay, who has studied aspen growth in the park's northern range, argues that too many elk grazing in the region has significantly reduced the aspen. This in turn has led to the disappearance of the beaver that depend on aspen for food and shelter. Loss of the beaver is alarming because this species has played a critical role in stabilizing water flows, according to research by biologists in the 1920s and 1950s.[30]

Finding that the aspen regeneration rate just outside the park where there is much less pressure from elk grazing was 60 percent compared to 4 percent inside the park, Kay makes a strong case that the elk population has grown beyond control of the range. Even the casual observer senses something is wrong in this region. A July 1986 *News-*

29. Congressional Research Service, *Greater Yellowstone Ecosystem: An Analysis of Data Submitted by Federal and State Agencies* (Washington, D.C.: U.S. Government Printing Office, 1987), p. 145.

30. Charles E. Kay, "Aspen Reproduction in the Yellowstone Park–Jackson Hole Area and Its Relationship to the Natural Regulation of Ungulates" (Paper for Western Elk Management Symposium, Utah State University, Salt Lake City, Utah, December 1985).

week article reported, "A day's hike in Yellowstone's northern range showed plants cropped down to the dirt and the foliage on most trees 'high-lined.' "[31]

The park's bison are also becoming a serious problem. The beasts who can walk through livestock fences roam across the park boundary and onto ranchland in search of better pastures in winter. Ranchers are concerned because a lot of the bison carry brucellosis. This disease poses a serious risk to livestock; if contracted by cows it causes them to abort their calves. To date the Park Service has done little to control the bison population nor has it successfully addressed the problem of bison roaming onto ranchland. In fact, the responsibility has been shouldered by the Montana Fish, Wildlife, and Parks, which has initiated special public hunts on the bison once they cross the park boundary. Animal rights groups are protesting the hunting of bison just outside the park.

There are other controversies in the park. For instance, the Park Service has been embroiled in debate over the closing of the Fishing Bridge tourist facilities on the northern end of Yellowstone Lake, near trout-spawning areas where grizzly bears feed. Between 1976 and 1984, there were forty-five incidents involving grizzly bears and humans, mostly in the campground. Environmentalists want all tourist facilities in the Fishing Bridge area removed because the area is prime grizzly bear habitat. Merchants just outside the park fear that closing these facilities would cost them tourist dollars.[32]

The Park Service's current plan is gradually to phase out the Fishing Bridge campground but to allow the RV park and some concessions to remain. Environmentalists have filed suit against the Park Service, demanding that it close the Fishing Bridge facilities. A Park Service newsletter notes that the agency has to consider economic and political factors in deciding not to close all services.[33] One can understand the Park Service's dilemma. As a public agency, the Park Service is trying to satisfy both environmentalists and those whose incomes depend on tourism. Unfortunately, neither side is satisfied by compromise.

31. Jerry Adler with Mary Hagler and Jeff Copeland, "The Fall of the Wild," *Newsweek*, July 28, 1986, p. 54.

32. Robert Ekey, "Park Service Stands Pat on Fishing Bridge," *Billings Gazette*, February 27, 1987, p. 1C.

33. Ibid.

Tourism is threatened by other factors besides environmental activism. In early 1986, to meet proposed budget cuts, park officials announced the closing of the popular campground at Madison Junction, near the northwest entrance to the park. After a public uproar over the proposed closing of the campground, the Park Service eventually reversed its position. It was puzzling at the time, however, that the Park Service's reason for closing the campground was to reduce operation costs. Proceeds from the Madison camping fees outweighed the costs of operating and maintaining it. So it was not a matter of closing a money-losing operation.

Why did the Park Service choose to close a popular campground? Some have suggested that park bureaucrats were cutting highly visible tourist services to ensure that the agency budget would remain large. After all, what member of Congress wants to be accused of denying the public a valued service by cutting the Park Service budget?

There is cause for concern about not only what occurs beyond Yellowstone National Park—in the proposed buffer zone—but also what occurs inside park borders. To design necessary reform in Greater Yellowstone, it is important to understand the problems of the Forest Service and the Park Service.

REFORMING PUBLIC LAND POLICY

The biggest step that can be taken toward protecting Greater Yellowstone will save taxpayers money and reduce the size of government. Elimination of federal subsidies would halt the deficit timber sales and end such programs as Small Business Administration loans, federally backed insurance, rural development grants, and Environmental Protection Agency-funded municipal waste-treatment programs. Although their effects have not been as extensive as deficit timber sales in Greater Yellowstone, the smaller programs also encourage environmentally damaging activities that the private sector would never encourage. Activities that do not stand on their own economically would be eliminated.

A model that can be applied to Greater Yellowstone already exists. The Coastal Barriers Resources Act was passed in 1982 to stop the subsidized destruction of coastal barriers along the Atlantic and Gulf coasts of the United States. This act eliminated federally subsidized insurance for new developments on these ecologically fragile areas.[34]

Another key step toward reforming the system is the fair market pricing of noncommodity goods taken from public lands. Granted, goods produced from the forests and Yellowstone National Park already entail user fees, ranging from livestock grazing rights to campground and park entrance charges. But these fees are very low compared to similar activities in the private domain. People are willing to spend $15.00 to $27.50 for a daily ski lift ticket, yet the entrance fee to Yellowstone is now $10.00 for one vehicle for a seven-day stay at the park, raised in 1988 from $5.00. The fee charged for livestock grazing on federal land was recently raised from $1.35 to just $1.54 for an animal unit month, still only about one-third of that charged on comparable private land.

Arbitrarily low user fees force people to compete for goods through means other than prices. In public campgrounds, this means waiting in long lines or making reservations months in advance. Furthermore, underpricing goods on our public lands encourages overconsumption of resources. Hunting pressure on public lands during the deer and elk seasons grows steadily, as more hunters pursue dwindling numbers of animals. And more hunters are turning to private sources, leasing hunting rights on private lands.

Reform could begin with higher entrance fees in Yellowstone and Grand Teton national parks and fees for fishing and hunting in national forests. But first and foremost would be the requirement that each unit operate within a budget based solely on proceeds from user fees. Because it would no longer receive congressional appropriations, management would have to adjust its operations and establish a new fee schedule. If such a system were implemented, we would no doubt see a raise in the user fees, perhaps to $7.00 per vehicle per day instead of per week.

Such an action would have important benefits. Charging realistic fees and retaining them in the budget would force managers to be aware of what services the paying public desires most. Under the current system, managers devote too much attention to trying to please the most well-organized special interest groups, rather than the public

---

34. Douglas Wrenn, "Barrier Islands," *Environmental Comment*, February 1981, pp. 3–11. Also see Coastal Barrier Resources Act, Public Law 97-348, 97th Congress.

at large. These special interest groups currently provide political support for higher appropriations from Congress. In return they want the Park Service and the Forest Service to follow the policies that benefit them. This change in funding source would also give managers more freedom to manage the region's natural resources according to sound research and current conditions. For instance, without the political pressures from environmental groups advocating natural regulation, the Park Service would be more inclined to actively control wildlife populations when overpopulation problems appear.

This new approach is likely to face stiff opposition in the political arena. Until modest fee hikes in 1986 and 1987, the weekly fee per vehicle for Yellowstone Park had been stuck at $2.00 since 1916. When the intention to raise fees in 1986 was announced, there was protest from local merchants and several local recreation groups. Charging realistic fees for services in the political arena is difficult and controversial, and forcing public managers to operate within a budget based on user fees is less attractive to bureaucrats. So a move for significant reform must come from outside the Park Service—from environmentalists disenchanted with the park's resource policy, recreationists disenchanted with the customer service, and millions of Americans disenchanted with the growing problems in national parks and national forests.

Charging recreational fees for activities such as fishing, hunting, and wilderness hiking in the surrounding national forests would be one way to sensitize Forest Service officials to the great recreational value these forests provide. Each forest would retain all fees from recreation as well as proceeds from all development activities and would use all of these returns to offset the cost of operating the forest. Without funding from Congress, each forest would be required to not operate at a loss. This plan would be an important first step toward reforming management of the national forests in the ecosystem.

Another approach would go even further in taking resource-use decisions out of the political arena. Allocating rights to differing land uses can best be accomplished through market competition and private property rights. Well-defined, transferable, and enforceable property rights foster accountability, and efficient markets send clear signals on what goods people prefer. When market prices and property rights reign, owners have to account for the preferences of others as well as their own. Whatever restrictions they place on their property or whatever goods they decide to produce, they must consider the opportunities they forego. For example, even if owners of land with wilderness and mineral potential are concerned solely with preserving the site's pristine character, they must still consider the potential income from oil and gas reserves they would forego if they left the land undeveloped.

Solutions to land use problems in Greater Yellowstone range from long-term leasing to transferring public lands to private ownership. Leasing allows the private sector to manage resources directly. Grazing and mineral rights are already leased in the national forests; expanding this practice to include other uses could accommodate other interests. An environmental group holding the surface rights to critical grizzly habitat, for example, would directly control the area. The group would be able to reallocate their organization's resources, preserving critical habitat instead of publicizing injustices or carrying out political battles. Leasing is best accomplished through competitive bidding, which overcomes the problem of undervaluation that is typical in the Bureau of Land Management's current leasing of grazing rights.

In some cases, complete sale of land may be the best choice. The government has little reason to hold lands that lack wilderness value, and it is logical to auction off such land to the private sector. Those concerned with the environment may object to this approach, claiming that if lands are leased or sold to the highest bidder, only the rich will be able to afford the wilderness. But many environmental groups, such as the Nature Conservancy, the National Audubon Society, and the National Wildlife Federation have multimillion-dollar endowments. Environmental organizations could devote their resources to preserving the land through acquisition rather than to lobbying and bringing lawsuits. Buying or leasing land is much more productive than waging political warfare.

It may be argued that under a market-oriented approach some environmental goods will suffer from the free-rider problem. A sporting club should be able to lease hunting or fishing rights for its members in the national forest, but what about preserved habitat or wilderness? The free-rider problem is obvious in this case. People can enjoy the existence of grizzly bear habitat without having to visit the area themselves, so employing a user fee would be impossible. But organizations concerned with such goods are becoming increasingly successful in obtaining contributions. They employ many creative methods—

magazine subscriptions, field trips, special travel rates—to attract people and money to their cause.

Where environmental amenities are the chief concern, there is another alternative for divesting public lands. Richard L. Stroup has suggested that wilderness endowment boards be established to manage unique environmental assets.[35] The boards, composed of leaders of environmental groups and other highly committed citizens, would be charged with preserving wilderness. Board members would be bound by a fiduciary responsibility to preserve the public's interest in the wilderness. Under this structure, members would be at liberty to weigh alternative uses for the land as long as the environment was protected. Areas with large oil and gas reserves might be slated for environmentally sensitive development of these resources. Royalties from oil and gas development could be used to further environmental goals, such as acquiring more critical habitat. There would be strong incentives to achieve compatible arrangements between environmentalists and industry where commercial activities could be conducted in ways that would not hurt the environment.

Private, nonprofit organizations whose objective is to preserve the environment are also a logical choice to manage the parks. Private management would be an attractive experiment for some of the smaller national parks. In larger parks like Yellowstone, private organizations could assume authority for particular areas of the park, such as the upper Lamar valley. Nonprofit groups could also manage a particular species and habitat. A step in this direction has already begun in Yellowstone with the Yellowstone Fishery Fund, a private fund for the research and protection of cutthroat trout that was recently established to offset federal budget cuts.[36]

SUMMARY

The Greater Yellowstone area can be reformed without increasing governmental intervention. The Forest Service's timber program is running a deficit in all of the national forests surrounding Yellowstone. This damages the environment and wastes money. Rather than demanding buffer zones to protect the parks, environmentalists should

---

35. Richard L. Stroup, John Baden, and Jane Shaw, "Wilderness Endowment Boards: Alternative to Wilderness Disputes," *Forest Planning,* June 1985, p. 9.

36. Thomas R. Pero, "Yellowstone Fisher Fund," *Trout,* Autumn 1986, p. 46.

work to reform existing institutions. If government is prevented from distorting signals from the market, our worst ecological fears would be laid to rest.

An end to deficit timber sales as well as other forms of government subsidies in the region would stop overstressing the environment and save taxpayers money. In addition, imposing realistic user fees and allowing national parks and forests to keep these fees for their own use would be an effective means of checking recreational overuse of the national parks. Greater efficiency is ultimately obtained when we rely on private stewardship. Only through private ownership is authority aligned with responsibility. Innovative proposals such as the wilderness endowment board support the environment yet force stewards to recognize that other uses of the region are equally valid.

PART II

BALANCING USE AND PRESERVATION: Land, Water, Wildlife, and Energy

3

WATER RESOURCE MANAGEMENT

Andrew Dana

Yellowstone Park and the mountainous country surrounding it legitimately may be called the pinnacle of the United States. Three of the nation's greatest rivers—the Missouri, the Columbia, and the Colorado—begin in the Yellowstone ecosystem. Water has shaped and continues to mold the ecosystem's landscape—the mountains, the valleys, and the dramatic canyons. In the arid west, this water is inextricably tied to local settlement and economic development. Water is crucial to the Yellowstone region's world-renowned wildlife populations, and, of course, to its fisheries. Beyond the immediate vicinity of Yellowstone, these waters support navigation and commerce downstream along the Mississippi and Columbia Rivers; they provide flows crucial to salmon and steelhead fisheries in the Pacific Northwest; and they even provide southern California with drinking water and electricity from the Colorado River.

Despite their importance, however, Yellowstone's waters face various threats, ranging in scope from site-specific pesticide contamination, to sedimentation from overgrazing by wildlife, to general acidification from acidic rain and snow. The structure of the water resources management system greatly complicates efforts to control these threats. Jurisdiction over control of water resources is divided between states and the federal government. The states delegate control over water resources to various state agencies, private landown-

49

ers, and conservation and irrigation districts. The federal government likewise fractures responsibility for water resources management and divides this responsibility among such agencies as the National Park Service, the U.S. Forest Service, and the Bureau of Reclamation.

Central to the problems of water resources management in the Yellowstone ecosystem are the incentives generated by these institutions and organizations that control water. Incentives in an unregulated market system are generally unambiguous: resources must be used efficiently and responsibly. The owner who does not use his resources efficiently will not realize their full value, and he (and society) will be poorer as a result. The market system tends to eliminate inefficiency, because entrepreneurs buy out inefficient resource owners in order to take advantage of the gains to be derived from more efficient resource management.

In the public sector, however, bureaucrats often have few incentives to manage resources efficiently. Agency officials are often more concerned with protecting their budgets—hence, their own careers—than with managing resources. The key to maintaining and increasing agency budgets is political support. Thus, governmental agencies and the well-intended bureaucrats who staff them tend to become captive to the special interests that control political purse strings.[1] This is particularly true for the water resources of the Yellowstone ecosystem, where there has never been a true market for water and where federal and state agencies control the use of millions of acre-feet of water.

The many public and private factors that shape water resource management make it extremely difficult both to encourage economic development and to protect the environment. This chapter introduces the reader to the complexities of water resource management in the Yellowstone ecosystem and suggests some reforms to improve opportunities for economic growth and to safeguard environmental assets.

THE WATER RESOURCES OF THE YELLOWSTONE ECOSYSTEM

The mountains of Yellowstone commonly receive over 40 inches of precipitation annually—more moisture than New York City receives

---

1. John Baden and Richard Stroup, *Bureaucracy vs. Environment* (Ann Arbor, Mich.: University of Michigan Press, 1981).

in a typical year.[2] Within the Yellowstone area, twelve rivers of major regional importance drain the ecosystem. Stream flows in these rivers are highly variable (see Table 3–1). The flows in several of the rivers are regulated by dam releases. When the dams need repair, river flows sometimes must be completely blocked. This explains, for example, the extremely low flows recorded on the Red Rock and Shoshone Rivers. Such low flows have devastating impacts on fish and wildlife habitat. Other low flows may result from irrigation diversions.[3]

The average annual discharge figures for rivers originating in the ecosystem as set forth in Table 3–1 may be misleading. Snow begins to fall in the high country in September and often does not start to melt until May. Much of this precipitation runs off during seasonal high water. For example, almost 50 percent of the Yellowstone River's annual run-off occurs in May, June, and July (see Figure 3–1). In drought years, the Yellowstone's annual discharge may be less than half the river's average annual flow.[4] On paper, the Yellowstone ecosystem is "water rich," supplying the West with over 12.5 million acre-feet in an average year and much more in wet years. Due to frequent drought, however, only half that amount of water is dependable. Even in wet years, most of the water leaves the ecosystem in spring and early summer. This has led to concerted and largely successful efforts to dam the ecosystem's rivers for water storage.

When discussing water resources management, it is necessary to distinguish between two broad types of management issues: water quality and water allocation. Sedimentation, acid rain, and herbicide and pesticide pollution are issues of water quality. Questions of entitlement to use water involve water allocation. Water allocation and water quality are related. Extensive reuse of water for irrigation, for example, can destroy water quality, as rivers pick up sediment and pesticide and herbicide residues from irrigation return flows.

An important aspect of water allocation issues is the distinction between consumptive and nonconsumptive uses of water. Consump-

2. Missouri River Basin Commission, *Report and Environmental Assessment, Yellowstone River Basin and Adjacent Coal Area Level B Study, Vol. 1–2* (Omaha, Neb.: Missouri River Basin Commission, 1978).

3. The highest flow in the Madison River occurred in 1959 when a wave created by an earthquake measuring 7.1 on the Richter scale crested Hebgen Dam, and the lowest flow was measured the following spring when dam repairs were made.

4. U.S. Water Resources Council, *Section 13(a) Water Assessment Report: Synthetic Fuel Development for the Upper Missouri River Basin* (Washington, D.C.: U.S. Water Resources Council, 1981).

Table 3–1.   Average Annual Discharge of Rivers Originating in the Yellowstone Ecosystem.

	Historical Peak Flow (cubic feet/ second)	Historical Low Flow (cubic feet/ second)	Discharge (acre feet/year)
Missouri basin			
Red Rock River	2,500	0	103,600
Madison River	10,200	5	722,300
Gallatin River	9,690	117	592,200
Yellowstone River	36,300	590	2,770,520
Boulder River	9,840	10	451,400
Stillwater River	12,000	58	704,200
Clark's Fork,			
Yellowstone River	12,700	32	691,200
Shoshone River	17,300	14	819,400
Wind River	13,000	130	898,400
Colorado basin			
Green River	4,840	31	370,000
Columbia basin			
S. Fork, Snake River	28,600	740	3,336,000
Henry's Fork,			
Snake River	6,220	53	1,054,000
Total average discharge (af/yr)			12,513,220

Note. Discharges were measured at points near the boundaries of the Yellowstone ecosystem (e.g., Livingston, Montana, for the Yellowstone River and Ashton, Idaho, for the Henry's Fork of the Snake River). Period of record varies by river basin (minimum period is 29 years for the Boulder River; maximum period is 69 years for the Madison River).

SOURCE: U.S. Geological Survey data, 1984, 1980, 1979.

tive uses deplete the available water supply; these uses include irrigation and industrial and municipal uses. Nonconsumptive water uses include preservation of instream water flows for fish and wildlife maintenance, recreation, navigation, and hydroelectricity generation. Nonconsumptive uses do not reduce water flows, but they do preclude using water to support industries such as agriculture and mining. Some nonconsumptive uses also affect water quality. Water released from hydroelectric facilities, for example, is sometimes supersaturated with nitrogen, causing a disease fatal to trout.

Both consumptive and nonconsumptive uses are crucial to Greater Yellowstone's economy. Although Wyoming, Montana, and Idaho

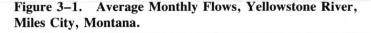

Figure 3–1. Average Monthly Flows, Yellowstone River, Miles City, Montana.

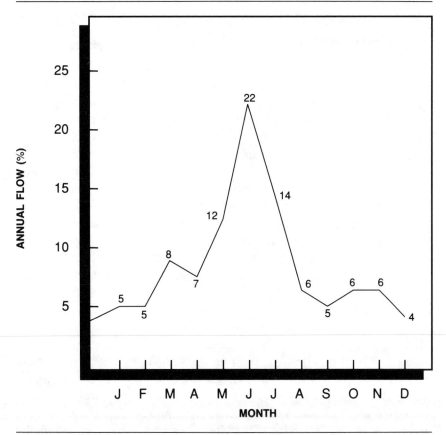

were settled first by miners, ranchers and farmers brought economic stability to the region. Agriculture remains an important activity, and today irrigation constitutes the largest consumptive use of water in the ecosystem. In the Yellowstone River basin, for example, irrigation accounts for about 85 percent of consumptive use.[5] As the population surrounding Yellowstone Park has grown in recent years,

5. Congressional Research Service, Environment and Natural Resources Policy Division, *Water Resources of the Missouri River Basin* (Washington, D.C.: Government Printing Office, 1976).

however, municipal and domestic demands for water are on the increase.[6]

Energy development—especially the expansion of coal mining—has also placed high demand on the region's waters. Montana and Wyoming contain almost half of the nation's strippable coal reserves. Unlike eastern coal, western coal is low in sulphur and when combusted produces fewer of the noxious emissions that are associated with acid rain. Burning more western coal is therefore an attractive way to minimize air pollution. The Montana and Wyoming coal beds are found in the eastern parts of those states, where water is especially scarce. Water is required for both mining and converting coal to electricity.[7] Other potential consumptive water uses associated with the coal industry include coal liquification and gasification and the transport of coal to eastern and southern markets by slurry pipeline. Although the industry has fallen on hard times recently and consequently no liquification or gasification plants or slurry pipelines have been built, many predict that the western coal industry will expand because of the richness of the deposits and the attractiveness of low-sulphur coals. If there is another coal boom, demand for water to support the industry will rise, and the coal industry will turn, as it has in the past, to the waters of the Yellowstone ecosystem.

Nonconsumptive demands for the ecosystem's water are also increasing. Outdoor recreation enthusiasts stress the value of Yellowstone's fish and wildlife, pointing to the dozens of superb trout fisheries within 200 miles of the center of the national park. Almost all of the major rivers in this ecosystem are trophy trout streams, including the Yellowstone, the Madison, the Gallatin, Henry's Fork and South Fork of the Snake, the Green, and the Wind rivers. Smaller rivers, such as the Boulder, Stillwater, and Gros Ventre, also offer outstanding recreation. The thousands of alpine lakes in the Absaroka, Beartooth, Gros Ventre, Teton, Wind, Centennial, Madison, and Gallatin mountains nurture five species of trout and a remnant population of grayling—a legacy of the last ice age.

The fisheries of the Yellowstone ecosystem have become an im-

6. Missouri River Basin Commission, *Missouri River Basin Management Plan* (Omaha, Neb.: Missouri River Basin Commission, 1980).

7. Connie Boris and John Krutilla, *Water Rights and Energy Development in the Yellowstone River Basin: An Integrated Analysis* (Baltimore: Resources for the Future and Johns Hopkins University Press, 1980).

portant factor in the local economy. In Montana alone, the state Department of Fish, Wildlife, and Parks estimates that "the annual value of Montana's lake and stream fisheries totals $215 million."[8] The Madison River, flowing out of Yellowstone Park, registered the highest value of any stream in the state, and the Gallatin and Yellowstone rivers also rank highly.[9] Demand for wild river protection is rising because trout fisheries depend directly on high water quality and sustained instream flows. Environmentalists have pushed for inclusion of many of the ecosystem's rivers in the Wild and Scenic River System. To date, portions of the Yellowstone, Henry's Fork of the Snake, the Snake itself, the Clark's Fork of the Yellowstone, and the Wind Rivers have been considered for Wild and Scenic River designation.

More generally, tourism demands protection of adequate instream flows; Yellowstone Falls, for instance, would lose its grandeur if no water flowed over them. Generation of hydroelectricity also demands protected instream flows; water must flow through turbines to generate power.

That conflicts over water quality and allocation are on the rise is not surprising. To understand these conflicts, we must examine the water resource management infrastructure that has been established in the Greater Yellowstone ecosystem.

THE WATER RESOURCE MANAGEMENT SYSTEM

From ecological, political, and geographical points of view, river basins represent attractive management units. An individual river basin is a natural land subdivision, unified by its watershed, and management units can easily be determined by simple, hierarchical stream classification. *First-order streams* have no tributaries; they tend to be small brooks or creeks. *Second-order streams* are formed when two first-order streams flow together. As a second-order stream travels down its course, it may be joined by numerous first-order streams, but it still retains its second-order classification. When two second-order streams meet, however, the resulting stream—or river—is classified as a *third-order stream*. Again, first- and second-order streams

8. John Duffield, "The Worth of Fishing," *Montana Outdoors,* 19 (1988): 34.

9. John Duffield, John Loomis, and Rob Brooks, *The Net Economic Value of Fishing in Montana* (Helena, Mont.: Montana Department of Fish, Wildlife, and Parks, 1987).

may join third-order streams, but the third-order stream does not move to a higher classification until it is joined by another third-order stream.[10]

This classification system illustrates the natural order of river systems. If river management units are broken down into basins and sub-basins and if a single agency is given responsibility for managing a tenth- or eleventh-order river basin, coordination of water allocation and water quality decisions would be achieved relatively easily and efficiently. The downstream impacts of water diversion from a fourth-order stream, for example, would be readily apparent to managers charged with maintaining navigation on a tenth-order river.

Unfortunately, river basin management is not so simple. Today's resource management units have been determined by political considerations, not by ecological or hydrological criteria. The great natural river basins of the Yellowstone ecosystem—the Missouri, Green, Snake, and Yellowstone basins—have been pared into distinct and uncoordinated political jurisdictions. As a result, Yellowstone's rivers cross numerous political boundaries as they flow from the ecosystem.

The political fragmentation of the Yellowstone area has disastrous implications for water resource management. Consider the difficult task of coordinating management decisions among the following federal, state, and local agencies and the private sector:

The U.S. Forest Service, National Park Service, Bureau of Reclamation, Army Corps of Engineers, Bureau of Land Management, U.S. Soil Conservation Service, U.S. Fish and Wildlife Service, U.S. Geological Survey, Bureau of Indian Affairs, Environmental Protection Agency, and Federal Energy Regulatory Commission;

> The States of Wyoming, Montana, and Idaho, each with its own water resource, fish and wildlife, agriculture, state lands, pollution control, and energy regulatory agencies;
>
> Other states downstream that have formal and informal vested interests in water leaving the ecosystem;
>
> County irrigation and soil conservation districts, public utilities, and municipalities;
>
> A host of private-sector water users, including private utilities, individual landowners with private water rights, industry, and special interest conservation and water development groups.

10. Robert Muller and Theodore Oberlander, *Physical Geography Today* (New York: Random House, 1978).

Each of these public and private groups has a voice in determining water use in the Yellowstone ecosystem, and each often has goals and management objectives that differ from the others.

This diffusion of responsibility often presents serious problems for downstream water users. Near Cooke City, Montana, for example, there is mine tailing adjacent to Soda Butte Creek. Years ago, when the mine was operated, no water quality statutes existed and instream flows were not appreciated. The miners dumped their waste material without regard to the effects on the stream. Now, whenever a summer thunderstorm passes over the area, sediment washes into Soda Butte Creek from these mine tailings.[11] The sediment is then carried downstream, upsetting recreational fishing opportunities for a week at a time on a 100-mile stretch of the Yellowstone River. The cumulative impact of such sedimentation on fish and aquatic insect populations is not yet known. This situation and others like it throughout the ecosystem result from ill-defined public and private rights and from the fragmented resource management system.

Given the host of agencies and private-sector groups that influence water management decisions, the factor ensuring both that any water at all flows in some rivers and that most areas continue to maintain high water quality is the existing system of water rights.

WATER RIGHTS IN THE YELLOWSTONE ECOSYSTEM

From the earliest days of western settlement, water has been an extremely valuable—though often underpriced—resource. Historically, property rights evolved so that individuals could capture the benefits of valuable resources, including water.[12] Property rights to water evolved very early in the arid West, and they differ considerably from water rights in the wetter, eastern portions of the United States.

In general, individual states determine how and to whom to allocate their waters. The fledgling federal government granted these rights to each of the thirteen original states, and the other thirty-seven states entered the Union with the same powers.[13] Each state is free to choose how to allocate its water resources to its citizens.

11. Jana Mohrman, telephone interview, Yellowstone National Park, Mammoth, Wyoming, May 12, 1986.

12. Terry Anderson and P. J. Hill, "The Evolution of Property Rights: A Study of the American West," *Journal of Law and Economics* 18 (1975): 163–179.

13. *Martin v. Waddel,* 1842, 41 U.S. (16 Pet.) 367; *Pollard v. Hagen,* 1845, 44 U.S. (3. How.) 212.

Western water law is dominated by the *prior appropriation* system of water rights, which has its roots in the mid-nineteenth-century mining camps of California. In its most basic form, the prior appropriation system holds that rights to use water depend on the date on which an individual claimed the water and devoted it to a beneficial use. Beneficial use of water normally means that water must be diverted or withdrawn from a stream or impounded in a lake and must be used to foster traditional economic activities, such as mining and irrigation. Early water claims are "senior" to later claims; that is, in times of shortage, appropriators with the most recent claims may not use any water until all claims filed prior to their own are satisfied.[14]

Montana, Idaho, Wyoming, and other western states adopted the prior appropriation system of water rights to allocate their limited resources. For over a century, this system allowed the western economy—especially agriculture—to flourish; it permitted ranchers and farmers to secure crucial water resources. By granting private water use rights, states essentially transferred the control of water to private parties.[15] The private sector had to put the water to beneficial use, or rights to use the water were lost.

In recent years the demand from environmentalists and sportsmen for instream flows has placed a *de facto* restriction on the amount of water that is available for private diversion.[16] Individuals and corporations can no longer simply go to their county courthouses, file notices of appropriation, and construct headgates to divert water without addressing the instream flow question. As Ralph Johnson writes:

> Courts everywhere now recognize that in-place water uses must be legally protected, and that the prior appropriation doctrine itself fails to provide adequate protection. The question is not *whether* but *how* this protection is to be provided.[17]

14. Frank Trelease and George Gould, *Cases and Materials on Water Law*, 4th ed. (St. Paul, Minn.: West Publishing Co., 1986).

15. Appropriation rights are not full ownership rights. Rather, they are usufructory rights that state governments grant to private parties.

16. Terry Anderson, "The Public Trust vs. Traditional Property Rights: What Are the Alternatives? In Proceedings from Western Resources in Transition: The Public Trust Doctrine and Property Rights, sponsored by the Political Economy Research Center, Bozeman, Montana, 1986.

17. Ralph Johnson, "Public Trust Protection for Stream Flows and Lake Levels," *U.C. Davis Law Review*, 14 (1980): 265–267.

The instream flow question has altered the entire debate over water resource management in the Yellowstone ecosystem. Every state in the ecosystem now has a statute that protects instream flows from excessive private appropriation. The Montana Department of Fish, Wildlife, and Parks, for example, holds instream flow rights to about two-thirds of the Yellowstone River's average annual discharge.[18]

Although states have general discretion over their water resources, state jurisdiction over water is limited by powerful federal doctrines. Under the Commerce Clause of the U.S. Constitution, federal rights extend over all of the nation's waterways in order to protect interstate commerce. These "navigation servitude" rights apply regardless of whether stream or lake beds are held privately or by the states. Commerce Clause rights also allow the federal government to regulate water use on the nonnavigable tributaries of navigable rivers when the purposes of commerce are served by regulatory action.[19] Thus, the federal government can intervene to prohibit Montana, Wyoming, or Idaho from granting water development rights in the Yellowstone ecosystem that might interfere with interstate commerce.

The federal government also holds "reserved" water rights in the Yellowstone ecosystem. The seminal U.S. Supreme Court case that established these rights was *Winters v. United States* (1908).[20] In *Winters,* the Supreme Court ruled that when the federal government set aside the Fort Belknap Indian Reservation, enough water to meet the needs of the reservation was implicitly reserved for use on tribal lands. The Court reasoned that without water the Indian lands were practically valueless.

The scope of the *Winters* decision is not limited to Indian reservations. In 1976, the Supreme Court held in *Cappaert v. United States* that water was reserved on *all* federal reservations, including national parks, national forests, national monuments, wildlife refuges, and military reservations. The Court summarized the scope of the reserved rights doctrine:

> When the Federal Government withdraws its lands from the public domain and reserves it for a federal purpose, the Government, by impli-

18. William Clark, "A Free-Flowing Yellowstone: The Reservations Challenge," *Montana Outdoors*, 10 (1979): 22–23.

19. *United States v. Rands*, 1967, 389 U.S. 121, 88 S.Ct. 265; *United States v. Appalachian Electric Power Co.*, 1940, 311 U.S. 377, 61 S.Ct. 291.

20. *Winters v. United States*, 1908, 207 U.S. 564, 28 S.Ct. 207.

cation, reserves appurtenant water then unappropriated to the extent needed to accomplish the purpose of the reservation. In doing so the United States acquires a reserved right in the unappropriated water which vests on the date of the reservation and is superior to the rights of future appropriators.[21]

The Court clarified *Cappaert* two years later in *United States v. New Mexico*[22] by specifying that the quantity of water that is reserved is the amount necessary to serve the specific purposes for which the reservation was originally created (for example, timber growth and watershed protection in the national forests).[23]

Two aspects of the reserved rights doctrine have had enormous effects on western water law: first, the quantity of water reserved under the doctrine need not have been specified at the time the reservations were created, and second, the priority date of reserved waters under the appropriation doctrine stems from the date the reservations were established. As a result, potentially huge, but unquantified, amounts of water are reserved to the federal government and Indian tribes, often with very early priority dates.

For example, the Wind River Indian Reservation in the southern portion of the ecosystem was established in 1868. When these reservation water rights are finally determined, privately held water rights granted by Wyoming and in use for over 100 years may be junior to Indian reserved rights, which have remained latent over the past 120 years. Similarly, Yellowstone Park's water rights carry an 1872 priority date, the year the Park was established. Enough water is reserved to the federal government in all of the waters flowing into and through Yellowstone Park to fulfill the purposes for which the Park was created, and the scope of these purposes ultimately depends on judicial interpretation of Congress's intent when it formed the national park. Quantification of these reserved rights is crucial to Montana's ongoing statewide adjudication of water rights. Without Park Service quantification of the amount of water reserved to it, Montana cannot be sure of the amount of water it may allocate to its own citizens.

The rivers and streams of Greater Yellowstone retain healthy instream flows and high water quality largely because there has not yet

21. *Cappaert v. United States,* 1976, 426 U.S. 128, 96 S.Ct. 2062.

22. *United States v. New Mexico,* 1978, 238 U.S. 696, 98 S.Ct. 3012.

23. Lands administered by the Bureau of Land Management have never been withdrawn from the public domain and, thus, have no appurtenant reserved rights.

been much demand from agriculture and industry for the waters. Even if such demand grows in the future, however, environmental values may be protected if federal land managers aggressively assert the reserved rights doctrine. The doctrine may be invoked to prevent economic development that may be detrimental to the purposes for which the national parks and forests were created.

A final level of water resource management exists in the Yellowstone ecosystem—interstate water allocation compacts. These compacts are negotiated agreements between states that must be approved by the President and Congress before they become effective. Interstate compacts serve to regionalize water resource management, creating another level of government between the state and the federal systems. Interstate compacts reflect state attempts to overcome management difficulties resulting from the political subdivision of natural river basins. The compacts attempt to create administrative systems in harmony with hydrological constraints (for example, flow regimes and water quality standards) on water use. In theory, states are more likely to solve their conflicts over water through negotiation, rather than through litigation, by working within a mutually acceptable interstate compact framework. Three drainage basins in the Yellowstone ecosystem are affected by interstate compacts: the Yellowstone, the Snake, and the Green (Colorado).

THREATS TO THE YELLOWSTONE ECOSYSTEM'S WATER RESOURCES

The complex institutional structure for managing water resources in the Greater Yellowstone ecosystem creates many threats to environmental integrity and erects numerous barriers to efficient and sensitive economic use and development of the resources. Each private and public water user and each state and federal agency with jurisdiction over the region's water has separate interests and promotes certain types of water use. Such narrowly focused goals and "enclave thinking" within government bureaucracies leads to a lack of coordination in regional water resource management. Poor coordination, in turn, leads to cumulative environmental damage.[24]

24. Joseph Sax (Greater Yellowstone Coalition Annual Meeting, Yellowstone National Park, Lake, Wyoming, 1986). Sax has written about the tendency of federal bureaucracies to pursue shortsighted goals in the context of management of Glacier National Park. Joseph Sax

For example, the Forest Service actively promotes the harvest of timber on marginally productive timber lands in the ecosystem (see Chapter 2, which discusses the problem of deficit timber sales). With each new road it builds, the Forest Service pumps more sediment into the region's rivers. At the same time, ranchers who neglect to rotate their cattle in a timely manner allow their stock to overgraze riparian zones, thereby increasing soil erosion. Zealous national park wildlife managers, eager to see ungulate herds thrive, ignore the disastrous effects that elk and buffalo can have on willow trees. Without the willows, beaver populations decline in Yellowstone National Park, and without beaver dams a natural sediment filtration system is eliminated from the ecosystem's rivers.[25] The sedimentation of the ecosystem's rivers is not caused by a single villain or nefarious agency; it is a cumulative problem, stemming from many narrowly focused resource management decisions.

No formal mechanism allows water managers to deal with incremental problems like sedimentation. Because jurisdiction is split, solutions to synergistic environmental problems must be creative and cooperative. In the Yellowstone River basin, for example, a local chapter of Trout Unlimited pressed several federal agencies, especially the National Park Service, to study the sediment problems that plague the Yellowstone River. As a result, the National Park Service; the U.S. Geological Survey; the U.S. Soil Conservation Service; the U.S. Fish and Wildlife Service; the Montana Department of Fish, Wildlife, and Parks; the Montana Department of Water Quality and Health and Environmental Sciences; and Trout Unlimited are cooperating to determine whether the sediment levels in the river have increased because of diverse government management policies or natural processes. This sedimentation data will be particularly useful for gauging the impact of the fires of 1988 on soil erosion in Yellowstone Park, highlighting the importance of scientific study to ecosystem management.[26]

---

24. (*Continued*)
and Robert Keiter, "Glacier National Park and Its Neighbors: A Study of Federal Interagency Relations," *Ecology Law Quarterly*, 14 (1987): 207.

25. Alston Chase, *Playing God in Yellowstone: The Destruction of America's First National Park* (New York: Atlantic Monthly Press, 1986).

26. John Bailey, former president, Joe Brooks Chapter of Trout Unlimited, Livingston, Montana. Interviews May 8, 1986 and March 27, 1989.

Unfortunately, the sediment study on the Yellowstone River is the exception rather than the rule. Most often, scientific study of water problems takes a back seat to political agendas.[27] There is an acute need to know more about many environmental problems, including acid rain, *Giardia* infestations, overgrazing, and instream flow requirements. Even without this knowledge, the ecosystem's political institutions are ripe for reform. Flaws in the prior appropriation system, intra- and intergovernmental conflicts, special interest agency goals, conflicting attitudes in the private sector, and even air pollution emissions from thousands of miles away pose threats to the integrity of Yellowstone's water resources.

PROBLEMS WITH THE PRIOR APPROPRIATION SYSTEM

Although the prior appropriation system in its pure form is a relatively efficient means to allocate water resources, it has some flaws that require modification in light of current demands for water. One of the most serious problems is that private individuals and groups cannot obtain instream water rights, even though all three states in the Greater Yellowstone ecosystem currently recognize instream water uses as beneficial. When the appropriation system was first adopted, the most valuable water uses—irrigation and hydraulic mining—required diversion, withdrawal, or impoundment of water. Water diversion and impoundment made possible the settlement of the West and the transformation of territories into states. Unfortunately, the appropriation doctrine's diversion requirements are legacies of an outdated value system that forbade private individuals and groups from obtaining instream water rights—rights that are rapidly increasing in value.[28]

Another problem with the prior appropriation system is its "use it or lose it" credo; that is, a water right holder must *use* his water or *lose* the right altogether. The original intent of this provision was to prevent appropriators from hoarding water they did not need. Unfor-

27. Luna Leopold, Address (Greater Yellowstone Coalition Annual Meeting, Yellowstone National Park, Lake, Wyoming, 1986).

28. There is one exception. Individuals can appropriate instream flows for stock water. Albert Stone explains the irony of this situation: "No 'dam, ditch, reservoir, or other artificial means'" is used for watering cattle. "Should instream use by people . . . have less recognition and dignity than instream use by cattle?" Albert Stone, *Montana Water Law for the 1980s* (Missoula, Mont.: University of Montana School of Law, pp. 51–53, 1981).

tunately, the provision has the reverse effect today. Individuals who have rights to large quantities of water—often senior rights—have incentives to use every drop of the water to which they are entitled, partly because lost water rights depress land values. Instead of promoting water conservation, the use it or lose it doctrine encourages appropriators to be profligate in their water use. If appropriators do conserve water, by installing a sprinkler irrigation system, for example, they may lose their right to the water they conserve after five years, when the water becomes available to other appropriators.

One remedy to the problems created by diversion statutes and the use it or lose it credo would be to amend state water laws to allow private instream appropriation of water rights and easy transferability from one use to another.[29] Under this arrangement, an appropriator need not lose his water right and priority date if he adopts more efficient means of using water; he could transfer his right from one beneficial use to another (for example, from irrigation to ecological preservation).

Both individual appropriators and those who value instream flows would benefit from easily transferable water rights. This system would allow the Sierra Club, the Nature Conservancy, and other environmental groups to have equal standing with other private appropriators to preserve instream flows. In the past, such conservation organizations have had to purchase entire ranches and transfer the water rights to the states to protect riparian resources. If private instream appropriation were possible, conservation groups could purchase water rights apart from the land and retain private ownership of the water. Such reform would foster efficiency and enhance the environment.

Montana, Wyoming, and Idaho have not adopted these reforms; all three states have established cumbersome and controversial mechanisms to allow government appropriation of instream flows.[30] These public-sector appropriations of instream flows are highly political, and because each state has acted independently, the instream flow statutes are not coordinated. For example, Montana has implemented an instream flow "reservation" system. These reservations are awarded to

29. Terry Anderson, *Water Crisis: Ending the Policy Drought* (Baltimore: Johns Hopkins University Press and the Cato Institute, 1983).

30. James Huffman, "Instream Water Use: Public and Private Alternatives," in Terry L. Anderson, ed., *Water Rights: Scarce Resource Allocation, Bureaucracy, and the Environment* (Cambridge, Mass.: Pacific Research Institute for Public Policy, Ballinger Publishing, 1983).

public agencies with specific priority dates, but they do not carry the full weight of private water appropriations. As a result, there is speculation that neighboring states may not recognize them as valid water rights.[31] Montana's instream flow protection system focuses primarily on the need to preserve fish and wildlife habitat and water quality for health, and the statute was passed largely to prevent the construction of reservoirs on free-flowing rivers.[32] The statute was instrumental in the defeat of a major dam proposed for the Yellowstone River.

On the other hand, Wyoming's instream flow statute permits only the state to hold rights to instream flows and requires the approval of various state agencies before a valid instream flow right may be issued.[33] In some cases, the state water Development Commission must study the feasibility of constructing stream impoundments to provide for instream flows, and only if an impoundment is not feasible will the state consider appropriation of natural instream flows.[34] The statute may authorize construction of dams on the ecosystem's free-flowing rivers in the name of instream flow preservation.[35] This approach to instream flow protection varies considerably from Montana's approach.

Another strategy for instream flow protection recently adopted by sportsmen and state bureaucrats is to invoke the "public trust doctrine," which may potentially override many private rights in the name of the "public good."[36] In essence, the public trust doctrine is the state's counterpart to the federal navigation servitude powers; it asserts that an unspecified amount of water is reserved to the public to preserve public values, most commonly instream flows. The doctrine may be asserted retroactively to strip individuals of their vested water rights without compensation in the name of the public good. The public trust doctrine therefore undermines the traditional water rights system, creating uncertainty for established users of water and hampering

31. Wright Water Engineers and Frank Trelease, *A Water Protection Strategy for Montana: Missouri River Basin* (Helena, Mont.: Montana Department of Natural Resources and Conservation, Water Resources Division, 1982).

32. Mike Aderhold, "Yellowstone Water: There's Only So Much," *Montana Outdoors,* 8 (1977): 13–18; Jim Posewitz, "A Free-Flowing Yellowstone: No Longer Just a Dream," *Montana Outdoors,* 10 (1979): 35–37.

33. *Wyo. Stat. Ann.* §§41-3-1001-1014 (Michie Supp. 1988).

34. *Wyo. Stat. Ann.* §41-3-1006(b) (Michie Supp. 1988).

35. *Wyo. Stat. Ann.* §41-3-1005 (Michie Supp. 1988).

36. *Montana Coalition for Stream Access v. Curran,* 1984, 683 P.2d 163; *Montana Coalition for Stream Access v. Hildreth,* 1984, 684 P.2d 1089.

economic growth. Determination of "public" values presents an obvious difficulty. Ranchers, for example, have significantly different views of public rights than do environmentalists. The effect of the public trust doctrine has been to antagonize private property owners, rather than to create inducements for them to recognize environmental values.[37]

CONFLICTING DEMAND IN THE PRIVATE SECTOR

The classic conflict over instream flow preservation is between agriculturalists, who desire maximum amounts of water for irrigation, and recreationists, who want water to remain in the rivers for fish and waterfowl. But other, equally serious conflicts between potential water users exist in the Yellowstone ecosystem. Conflict over water between agriculture and industry, for example, has been highly charged in the past. When the coal industry eyed the ecosystem's water during the early 1970s, a coalition of family farmers and environmentalists formed the Northern Plains Resources Council and helped thwart large-scale industrial water appropriation and the 380-foot Allenspur dam, proposed for the Yellowstone River.[38]

More recently, a conflict has erupted between entrepreneurs, who have applied to the Federal Energy Regulatory Commission (FERC) to build federally subsidized hydroelectric facilities throughout the region, and preservationists, who want no further development of the ecosystem's watercourses. The roots of this problem are in federal legislation that authorizes FERC to subsidize low-head hydroelectrical development.[39] This has prompted scores of entrepreneurs to propose small dams and generators throughout the ecosystem.[40] In response, environmentalists have mobilized substantial opposition. The Federation of Fly Fishermen, based in West Yellowstone, Montana, spon-

37. Political Economy Research Center, Proceedings from Western Resources in Transition: The Public Trust Doctrine and Property Rights, Bozeman, Montana, 1986.

38. Alvin Josephy, "The Agony of the Northern Plains," in Lon C. Ruedisili and Morris W. Firebaugh, eds., *Perspectives on Energy: Issues, Ideas, and Environmental Dilemmas,* 2d ed. (New York: Oxford University Press, 1978), pp. 205–225.

39. 16 U.S.C.S. §824a-3 (Lawyers Ed. Supp. 1988).

40. Congressional Research Service, *Greater Yellowstone Ecosystem,* Committee on Interior and Insular Affairs, Committee print #6, 99th Cong., 2d sess., 1987, 82.

sored publication of a handbook that outlines methods of interference with FERC's licensing of hydropower units.[41]

Even environmentalists and sportsmen—long the closest of allies—are coming to loggerheads over water resource management. This growing conflict pits preservationists against recreational users of the ecosystem's waters. The membership of Trout Unlimited, for example, finds itself caught on the horns of this dilemma. Trout Unlimited's philosophy is: "We believe . . . that what's good for trout and salmon is good for the fishermen and that managing trout and salmon for themselves *rather than for the fishermen* is fundamental to the solution of our trout and salmon problems" (emphasis added). Yet the majority of the organization's membership *are* fishermen, and they are members because Trout Unlimited works to improve fishing opportunities. Marshall Bloom succinctly summarized this dilemma in a recent issue of *Montana Troutline:*

> There is no such thing as a nonconsumptive, totally benign use of a [fishery] resource. Everybody who uses a river takes from it. . . . Just because we love the rivers, don't think we can't love them to death. Toilet paper, beer cans, jet boats, and stereo music systems degrade the [fishing] experience to be sure, but so does a flotilla of sleek Avons [rafts for fishing] regardless of who is at the oars.
>
> What should Trout Unlimited members, dedicated to cold water fisheries and quality fishing experiences, do? I wish I knew. . . . [T]here is not an easy solution. Should the [Montana] Department of Fish, Wildlife, and Parks limit the number of outfitters? Should private users be required to pay a fee every time they float? Aren't the problems of hydroelectric dams, pesticides, industrial wastes, clear-cutting, in-stream flows, and lousy agricultural practices more urgent? Few would deny that they are, but floating is also a problem . . . and what makes it particularly difficult is that we [Trout Unlimited members] are part of this problem. As Pogo said, "We have met the enemy and he is us."[42]

Those who subscribe to environmental preservation principles would limit recreational use of the ecosystems' waters, but organizations like

41. R. Roos-Collins and the Friends of the River Foundation, "Intervention in the Federal Energy Regulatory Commission's Review of Hydro-Power," pamphlet sponsored by the Federation of Fly Fishers, West Yellowstone, Montana, 1982.

42. Marshall Bloom, "The Montana Jungle Boat Ride," *Montana Troutline,* 6 (1986): 1, 3.

Trout Unlimited find it difficult to endorse such limitations because some of their members would be excluded from use of the resource. In addition, many members are philosophically opposed to restrictions on access to trout streams.

All of these conflicts—over instream flows, industrial water development, small-scale hydroelectrical development, and recreational use of the region's rivers—illustrate the profound differences within the private sector over how to manage the ecosystem's water resources. What is good for one segment of the public is often disastrous for another. A rancher who returns muddy irrigation water to a river may be assured of good crop growth, but he may also devastate a fisherman's recreational opportunities as silt settles over trout spawning beds and smothers the incubating eggs. Conversely, the fisherman's demand for instream flows deprives ranchers of the water they need for their livelihoods. In short, there is no way that either private or public water resource managers can ever unilaterally manage the region's waters to "serve the public good." There are, in fact, many publics to be served.

In theory, a private water market with well-defined, enforced, and transferable property rights would ensure that the demands of all parties would be served. Under such a system, water resource uses would gravitate to their highest and best applications. The best trout streams would be preserved and the private sector could allocate recreational use by price; ranchers and farmers would irrigate efficiently; and hydroelectricity developers would have to bid for development rights in a nonsubsidized market against environmentalists and other water users. A smoothly operating market could solve many of the continuing conflicts among water users.[43]

Establishing such a system in the foreseeable future may be impossible, however. Given its present structure, the appropriation doctrine cannot accommodate a market for water; it would have to undergo fundamental reform. If instituted too quickly, such reform would be socially disruptive, as water appropriation rules change. Another problem stems from the difficulty of determining the economic and social value of nonconsumptive water uses, such as the provision of fish and game habitat and the existence value of free-flowing rivers.

43. Terry Anderson, *Water Crisis.*

These values are poorly reflected in any market and are normally not transferable.

There has been one positive development: western governors recently endorsed a report that recommended adoption of market-oriented water policies to help reduce economic inefficiency and to enhance environmental preservation.[44] While the governors' action is an important first step toward widespread adoption of market principles, reform has to overcome a century of history and social inertia. Like it or not, water allocation decisions are largely in the hands of public agency administrators, where they will stay for the foreseeable future. This condition is alarming because conflicts between public agencies are, if anything, more acute than conflicts within the private sector.

PUBLIC-SECTOR WATER RESOURCE MANAGEMENT

As in the private sector, government agencies—and the bureaucrats who run them—have well-defined goals for the use of water resources, and these goals are often diametrically opposed to one another. Unfortunately, the potential for making disastrous water management decisions is greater in the public sector. Generally, private water users control only limited amounts of water in small geographical areas. The U.S. Forest Service and the National Park Service, however, have control of enormous amounts of water over huge areas. Other agencies—the Bureau of Reclamation and the Army Corps of Engineers—see their mission as building massive government-subsidized dams.

The two basic types of governmental conflict are intragovernmental disputes, which include conflicts between agencies at the same level of government (for example, the U.S. Forest Service and the National Park Service); and intergovernmental disagreements, which involve conflicts between different political administrations (for example, Montana and Wyoming, Wyoming and the U.S. Forest Service, the Yellowstone Compact Commission and the Bureau of Indian Affairs).

44. Bruce Driver, *Western Water: Tuning the System* (Denver: Western Governors Association, 1986).

Both types of conflicts pose serious management problems and impede economic development and environmental preservation.

Intergovernmental Disputes

On a broad scale, intergovernmental disputes have enormous potential to shape water use in the Yellowstone ecosystem. Disputes between states and the federal government over water development are numerous and widespread, usually over the issue of states' rights. None of the western states appreciate federal meddling in what they perceive to be state water rights. With the widespread assertion of federal reserved rights, states have found themselves in a disquieting situation: much of the water that they long thought was available for allocation to their citizens may well be owned by the federal government or by Indian tribes. This has created uncertainty in western water law, and uncertain property rights slow—or halt—economic development. On the other hand, environmental preservation goals may be advanced by this uncertainty, at least for the immediate future. Without clear property rights to water, developers are less eager to pursue water resource development plans, and this allows water to continue to flow downstream.

As a consequence of newly asserted federal rights, the states are negotiating with Indian tribes and with various branches of the federal government to quantify reserved rights. For nearly a decade Wyoming has tried to reach a settlement with the Arapahoe and Shoshone Indians living on the Wind River Reservation, and since 1979 Montana's Reserved Rights Compact Commission has been attempting to codify federal, Indian, and state rights. In both cases, the negotiations have been extremely difficult and politically sensitive. No progress in defining federal rights in the Yellowstone region has been made in Montana, and several potential settlements for Wind River allocations have fallen through. Most recently, the Wyoming Supreme Court determined that the Wind River Reservation tribes are entitled to 477,000 acre-feet of water with an 1868 priority date.[46] This represents approximately half of the water on the reservation. Although the decision is being appealed to the United States Supreme

---

46. *In re the General Adjudication of All Rights to Use Water in the Big Horn River System*, 753 P.2d 76 (Wyo. 1988), *cert. granted, Wyoming v. United States*, 109 S.Ct. 863 (1989).

Court, the implications of this decision are that Wyoming users will have to share their water with the tribes. Wyoming recognized this fact in 1989 and entered a one-year water-sharing agreement with the Arapahoe and Shoshone tribes.[47]

Another manifestation of the conflict between federal and state governments has been played out over Wild and Scenic River designation. In at least two cases, the main branch of the Yellowstone in Montana and the Clark's Fork of the Yellowstone in Wyoming, state governments have removed rivers from congressional consideration or have delayed their designation by asking their federal representatives to withdraw bills. Both Montana and Wyoming have been unwilling to surrender any jurisdiction over their waters to the federal government, despite federal recommendation that the two rivers be included in the national system.[48]

Conflict between states is also a problem in the Yellowstone ecosystem, particularly when two or more states share water rights in the same drainage basin. Montana and Wyoming often disagree over how to administer interstate streams in the Yellowstone basin, and Wyoming must work with Colorado, Utah, New Mexico, Arizona, Nevada, California, and Mexico when setting policy for the Green River. The Yellowstone, Green, and Snake Rivers are governed by interstate water allocation compacts, which were designed to reduce interstate conflict. Nevertheless, disagreements are common.

The Yellowstone Compact, for example, divided the flows in the four major tributaries to the Yellowstone River between Montana and Wyoming, with allocations based on percentage of average annual flows. Since the compact was ratified in 1951, the two states have been unable to agree on how to translate the negotiated percentages into precise acre-feet shares of the flows. After a series of proposals and counterproposals,[49] the states are still haggling over how to quantify their water rights. Currently, Montana is reviewing a proposal by Wyoming to govern application of the compact, and Wyoming is reviewing a plan for compact administration submitted by Montana.[50]

47. *The High Country News,* March 13, 1989, p. 5.

48. Jim Posewitz and Larry Peterman, Montana Department of Fish, Wildlife, and Parks, Helena, Montana, telephone interview, April 5, 1983; Tom Mitchell, Shoshone National Forest, Cody, Wyoming, telephone interview, May 16, 1986.

49. Boris and Krutilla, *Water Rights and Energy Development.*

50. .Yellowstone Compact Commission, *Thirty-Seventh Annual Report,* 1988, p. iv.

Meanwhile, Wyoming has embarked on an aggressive, subsidized water development plan in the Yellowstone basin (and elsewhere in the ecosystem and the state) in an attempt to establish rights to the water before it flows into Montana and other states. When a severe drought strikes, Wyoming will have in-place water users deriving economic benefit from the subsidized water projects. Even though downstream states may hold legal rights to flows from Wyoming, they may not have the economic infrastructure to support such claims during a crisis year. Wyoming's philosophy seems to be that it is easier to protect water uses that are already in place than it is to protect bare legal title to water without any established beneficial uses.[51]

Single-Purpose Agency Goals

Like private-sector special interest groups, individual government agencies tend to favor one resource management goal over others: the Army Corps of Engineers stresses flood control, the Bureau of Reclamation promotes agricultural development, the U.S. Fish and Wildlife Service focuses on habitat preservation and enhancement, and the Environmental Protection Agency monitors water quality. Pluralistic political theory holds that these competing governmental missions will tend to balance each other and ensure that socially unpopular and inefficient policies will never be approved. As Robert Dahl writes:

> Because constant negotiations among different centers of power are necessary in order to make decisions, citizens and leaders will perfect the precious art of dealing peacefully with their conflicts, and not merely to the benefit of one partisan but to the mutual benefit of all the parties to a conflict.[52]

In the arena of water rights, governmental power is not continually shifting through constant negotiation. Rather, agency powers are carefully split, and bureaucrats are fiercely territorial.

A classic example of this territoriality is found in the history of the 1944 Flood Control Act, which planned a system of water storage reservoirs in the Missouri River basin. Both the Bureau of Recla-

51. Andrew Dana, *An Evaluation of the Yellowstone River Compact: A Solution to Interstate Water Conflict* (M.A. thesis, Department of Geography, University of Washington, Seattle, Washington, 1984).

52. Robert Dahl, *Pluralist Democracy in the United States: Conflict and Consent,* Chicago: Rand McNally, 1967.

mation and the Army Corps of Engineers submitted proposals for the dam system. The Corps' proposal included plans for a dam on the Yellowstone River at Allenspur—50 miles north of Yellowstone Park. The Bureau of Reclamation developed its own plan for Missouri basin development and proposed a dam at the inferior Mission site, 16 miles downstream from Allenspur. Eventually the Bureau of Reclamation was awarded jurisdiction over development in the Yellowstone basin, and throughout the 1950s the bureau promoted its Mission dam. In 1960, however, the Bureau suddenly shifted its emphasis to the Allenspur site. Apparently, enough time had elapsed for the bureau to propose building a dam at a site originally suggested by the Army Corps of Engineers.[53]

The impacts of the Allenspur dam on the Yellowstone ecosystem would be immeasurable. It would impound 4.0 million acre-feet of water, destroy 30 miles of "blue-ribbon" trout water (including prime habitat for the rare Yellowstone cutthroat trout), flood 32,000 acres of the upper Yellowstone River valley, and inundate prime agricultural land and wildlife habitat, all at a cost of hundreds of millions of dollars. Fortunately, due to great public outcry and a concerted battle waged by environmentalists, the Allenspur dam has not been built, despite strong pressure for it from the coal industry and the Bureau of Reclamation during the coal boom of the early 1970s. The Yellowstone remains the longest free-flowing river in the forty-eight contiguous states.[54]

Other rivers in the ecosystem have suffered a different fate. The Wind, Shoshone, Red Rock, and Henry's Fork and South Fork of the Snake rivers all have sizable dams. The Madison River has been impounded by two Montana Power Company dams. If funds were available, Wyoming would like to construct a dam on the Clark's Fork of the Yellowstone. The lesson is simply stated: if public funds are available, public agencies will build dams in the absence of massive public opposition.

The pluralistic vision of interagency competition is inadequate. Agency activities are *not* determined by constant negotiations; they are largely determined by their budgets. Therefore, activities that reap

53. Robert Anderson, "A Report on Allenspur Dam," insert in the *Livingston Enterprise,* October 1974, Allenspur Committee to Save the Yellowstone, Livingston, Montana.

54. William Clark, "A Free-Flowing Yellowstone."

the most dollars from federal and state coffers will receive the most favor from bureaucrats.[55] For the Forest Service, these activities are forestry and road building; for the Federal Energy Regulatory Commission, hydroelectrical development; for the Bureau of Reclamation, dam building. Most state agencies are motivated by the same factor— dollars from public treasuries.[56] The result is that governmental agencies prefer to concentrate on one or two management objectives to the detriment of other resources. This tendency to specialize poses the single greatest threat to waters in the Yellowstone ecosystem because it precludes cooperative and comprehensive management over an entire river basin. The environmental threats resulting from this "enclave" mentality include stream siltation from road building and overgrazing on Forest Service and Bureau of Land Management lands, subsidized hydroelectricity and irrigation development, ineffective controls on herbicide and pesticide use, and recreational overuse (see Table 3–2).

State and federal agencies, funded to pursue their uncoordinated goals, pose at least as much threat—if not more—to the environmental integrity of Yellowstone's waters as does private development. Federal agencies often strongly support the most environmentally destructive and economically inefficient water development projects. Although coal industry demand led to renewed interest in constructing the Allenspur dam in the 1970s, the Bureau of Reclamation took up the cause and lobbied hard for the project alongside potential industrial users. With some justification the private sector is frequently blamed for creating environmental problems for water users downstream. Governmental agencies, however, often create problems that are equally troublesome. Governmental control of Yellowstone's waters is part of the water resources management problem, not necessarily the solution.

THREATS FROM OUTSIDE THE ECOSYSTEM

Two significant threats to the Yellowstone ecosystem's waters come from outside the region: acid rain, which threatens water quality, and

55. Baden and Stroup, *Bureaucracy vs. Environment.*

56. Wildlife agencies are largely supported by sportsmen's license fees and by taxes on recreational equipment. Thus, their activities are more often biased toward providing opportunities for the maximum number of recreationists.

Table 3–2. Threats to the Yellowstone Ecosystem's Waters: Causes and Consequences.

Threat	Causes	Consequences
Sedimentation	1. Forest Service road building 2. Overgrazing of BLM, Forest Service, and Park Service lands 3. Poor timber harvest practices 4. Careless state and federal road maintenance	a. Decline in water quality b. Smothering of aquatic insects c. Degradation of fish spawning beds d. Heightened water temperatures e. Lost recreational opportunities
Stream impoundment	1. FERC-subsidized hydrodevelopment 2. Bureau of Reclamation, Soil Conservation Service, and state subsidies for agriculture 3. Army Corps of Engineers flood control	a. Loss of free-flowing rivers b. Flooded fish and wildlife habitat c. Lost recreational opportunities d. Increased erosion downstream from dams
Overappropriation	1. Biases within state government for agricultural and industrial water uses	a. Loss of instream flows b. Lost fish and wildlife habitat
Pollution	1. Careless monitoring of herbicides and pesticides use by agencies concerned with timber and crop production 2. Careless mining practices	a. Diminished water quality b. Loss of fish and wildlife habitat c. Loss of aquatic insects and plants
Recreational overuse	1. No regulation of wilderness use 2. No state regulation of floating and fishing traffic 3. Inability of sportsmen to regulate themselves	a. *Giardia* contamination b. Decline in quality of recreational experience c. Litter d. Displacement of fish and wildlife

water demand from states downstream, which threatens water allocation. Neither poses imminent disaster, but each could considerably alter the structure of water resource management in the Greater Yellowstone ecosystem.

Acid rain is formed when sulphur dioxide and nitrogen oxides, emitted primarily by industry and automobiles, react with water vapor in the atmosphere to produce sulfuric and nitric acids. These acids then fall to the ground as rain and snow. There is some debate about whether acid rain occurs naturally, or whether industrialization in the past century, especially escalation in the rate of fossil-fuel combustion, has created a new environmental problem. The general consensus is that industrial and automobile emissions have aggravated a naturally occurring phenomenon.[57]

The control of acid rain (or the lack of control) represents a classic economic/environmental trade-off. To control the problem, industry must pay enormous costs to retrofit emission stacks with air pollution control devices. If industry does not pay these costs and if acid rain is permitted to continue, there is mounting evidence that environmental damages will be massive. In sensitive areas, the phenomenon increases the acidity of lakes and streams and kills aquatic flora and fauna, including fish. Acid rain also retards the growth of certain tree species.

The situation is complicated further because the sources of sulphur and nitrogen emissions are often hundreds of miles away from affected areas. Potential sources of acid rain in the Yellowstone ecosystem include smelters in the Salt Lake City area and in Arizona and Mexico.[58] Sulphur dioxide and nitrogen oxides are emitted from tall stacks and are transported by the strong winds in the upper atmosphere. They are precipitated several days later, hundreds of miles away. Acid rain is an externality problem: the polluters in one area do not pay the costs of their pollution in other areas.

The dangers of acid rain vary substantially within the ecosystem, depending primarily on geologic factors. Because granitic rocks have poor acid-buffering capacities, granitic mountain ranges, including the Beartooth, Teton, and Wind River ranges are highly susceptible to acid contamination. Other ranges that are primarily composed of sedimentary rocks, such as the Gallatin range, are better able to withstand acid precipitation.

In 1985 the Environmental Protection Agency studied the high

---

57. Phillip Shabecoff, "Science Group Ties Acid Rain to Earth Harm," *New York Times*, March 14, 1986, p. 8.

58. Robert Fox, Environmental Protection Agency, Helena, Montana, telephone interview, May 16, 1986.

mountain lakes of the Yellowstone ecosystem to evaluate whether acid precipitation was a problem in the region. No significant acidification of the ecosystem's waters was detected.[59] Nevertheless, the potential for damage remains high.

When this chapter focused on geographical scale and water resources management, we argued that one means of reducing conflict might be to manage entire river basins as single entities, rather than dividing basins among many political jurisdictions as is done today. One conflict that might be avoided with basinwide management is the tendency of upstream states in a river basin to fight over water with downstream states.

One reason these conflicts are increasing is found in the history of water subsidization in the American West. To a large degree, western water resources were developed by the public sector, and water development costs were spread to state and national taxpayers. Western water resources are therefore relatively inexpensive for users; the cost of water is priced below its true value. As a result, demand has begun to outstrip supply, creating what economist Terry Anderson has labeled a "water crisis." Anderson writes:

> Water prices have been kept below market-clearing levels, and the inevitable shortages have followed. The government has responded by attempting to constrain demand, ration water, and increase the available supply. . . . Increased water supplies have only been possible through construction of massive water projects, which have dammed many of our free-flowing rivers and built thousands of miles of aqueducts. . . . Without a price mechanism operating on water supply and demand, crisis situations will continue to arise.[60]

Anderson argues persuasively that market mechanisms must be structured into water allocation systems in the West to reflect true demand and supply. Otherwise, "water-hungry" states will continue to seek to develop resources in "water-rich" areas at enormous economic and environmental costs.

One of these water-rich areas is the Yellowstone ecosystem. Mon-

---

59. Landers, D.H., J.M. Eilers, D.F. Brakke, W.S. Overton, P.E. Kellar, M.E. Silverstein, R.D. Schonbrod, R.E. Crowe, R.A. Linthurst, J.M. Omernik, S.A. Teague, E.P. Meier. 1987. Characteristics of Lakes in the Western United States. Volume I. Population, Descriptions and Physico-Chemical Relationships. EPA/600/3-86/054A. U.S. Environmental Protection Agency. Washington, D.C.

60. Terry Anderson, *Water Crisis*, p. 5.

tana, Wyoming, and Idaho are surrounded by thirsty states. Under the Colorado River Compact, perpetually dry southern California has some say over Wyoming's use of the Green River. The Ogallala Aquifier, which has for many years supplied water for agriculture in west Texas, Oklahoma, eastern Colorado, and Nebraska, is being depleted through extensive pumping. States downstream on the Missouri River are beginning to object to water development plans in Montana and Wyoming, afraid that they will lose adequate instream flows to support navigation. Private industry has pressed for rights to pipe water out of the Yellowstone basin to transport coal. While there is no immediate prospect of major water development projects downstream, attention will eventually turn to the undeveloped headwaters of the Yellowstone, Missouri, Columbia, and Colorado rivers. The simplest and best way to avoid development of these rivers is to force downstream states to pay the full costs of the development, including the loss of environmental amenities.

CONCLUSIONS

The confused condition of water resources management in the Yellowstone ecosystem is the result of muddled property rights, confused jurisdictions, and sensitive riparian systems. Chances for quickly improving this state of affairs are remote, but some modest reforms will provide better than marginal improvements.

First, there must be a concerted effort to improve knowledge about the ecosystem's water resources. As Luna Leopold suggested at the 1986 annual meeting of the Greater Yellowstone Coalition, both government agencies and private groups must understand the hydrology of Yellowstone's rivers and streams before meaningful policy reform can be achieved. The initiative shown by the Joe Brooks Chapter of Trout Unlimited in Livingston, Montana, is a step in the right direction. This private, nonprofit group spurred a half-dozen federal and state agencies into collecting baseline data on Yellowstone River sediment levels with the goal of eventually reforming policy. The private sector is crucial to this process. Without efforts like those of Trout Unlimited, government agencies tend to ignore science, and bureaucrats find it easy to ignore the problems they create in pursuit of narrow goals. Private-sector groups must act as watchdogs, keeping bureaucrats from concentrating on their favorite single goal at the expense of environmental quality and economic efficiency.

Second, government agencies should be reformed to increase sensitivity to the effects of their resource management decisions. Economic efficiency and environmental values must become overriding goals. Incentives must be changed so that pork barrel water projects become as abhorrent to Bureau of Reclamation officials as they are to the nation's taxpayers. The Federal Energy Regulatory Commission's subsidization of small-scale hydroelectricity development should be dismantled.

Third, Montana, Wyoming, and Idaho should eliminate restrictions on private appropriation of instream flows for protection of fish and wildlife habitat and recreational opportunities. These restrictions are outdated and do not reflect heightened public demand for environmental preservation. Restrictions on water transfers should be eased to allow appropriators to transfer water rights from one use to another without jeopardizing their vested water rights. Such reforms would create incentives for private conservation and would more closely approximate the true market value of water resource uses, promoting economic efficiency.

Finally, federal reserved water rights must be quantified. Without quantification, economic development of the region's water resources will be hampered by uncertainty. In addition, the use of the public trust doctrine to limit private water use rights must be curtailed. Otherwise, no water rights will be dependable. Traditional private appropriators, especially the agricultural community, must recognize the growing value many individuals place on instream flows and environmental preservation. Environmentalists and recreationists must be sensitive to the water needs of ranchers and farmers. Antagonistic action can only mean reduced economic efficiency and environmental preservation.

Additional References

U.S. Geological Survey. *Water Resources Data for Idaho, Volume 1: Great Basin and Snake River Basin Above King Hill,* Water Data Report ID-80-1. (Washington, D.C.: Government Printing Office, 1980).

————. *Water Resources Data for Montana,* Water Data Report MT-79-1 (Washington, D.C.: Government Printing Office, 1979).

————. *Water Resources Data for Wyoming, Water Year 1984,* Water Data Report WY-84-1 (Washington, D.C.: Government Printing Office, 1984).

4

A PRIVATE PROPERTY RIGHTS APPROACH TO LAND USE CONFLICTS

Jo Kwong

Yellowstone National Park is a symbol of pride in America. Together, Yellowstone and Grand Teton national parks are world renowned for their wildlife, their thermal and geological marvels, and their millions of acres of natural wildlands. It is not surprising that preservationists have focused on the lands encircling the national parks that together with the parks make up the Greater Yellowstone ecosystem.

Environmentalists often argue that maintaining the integrity of the ecosystem is critical to preserving the splendor of the parks themselves. Approximately 9 million acres of land in the Greater Yellowstone belong to the federal government and are under the jurisdiction of several federal agencies, including the U.S. Forest Service (USFS), the Bureau of Land Management (BLM), the National Park Service (NPS), and the U.S. Fish and Wildlife Service.[1] The existence of approximately 1 million acres of private landholdings and state-owned lands within Greater Yellowstone, however, poses a major constraint on government agencies' "control" of activities in the ecosystem. Often the interests and goals of private landowners do not coincide with the

1. Defining the land contained in Greater Yellowstone depends on which of its characteristics (for example, geologic or hydrologic) are used as criteria for delineating boundaries. For this study, the Greater Yellowstone ecosystem consists of approximately 1 million acres of state and private lands, 2.5 million acres in national parks, and 6.5 million acres of U.S. Forest Service land.

broader "public interest," leading to potential land use conflicts. This chapter examines some of the problems that have occurred between private and public land uses in the Greater Yellowstone ecosystem, and proposes a property rights and public choice perspective to conflict management.

THE LAND USE CASE STUDIES

Concern over land use conflicts in Greater Yellowstone has led to the formation of a number of local conservation organizations, including the Greater Yellowstone Coalition (GYC), headquartered in Bozeman, Montana. The GYC was founded in 1983 to coordinate management of the parks, forests, and private and state lands and to support the protection and preservation of Greater Yellowstone. As part of its mission, the GYC has developed an inventory of development projects and management issues affecting the ecosystem. The inventory educates agency personnel, elected officials, and the public about the effects of these activities in Greater Yellowstone.

The 1984 inventory[2] identified a number of threats relating to land uses on private inholdings in various areas of the ecosystem. Three of those problem areas are examined here from the property rights and public choice perspective: the Grand Teton National Park protection plan, West Gardiner access, and inholdings at Squirrel Meadows.

Grand Teton National Park Protection Plan

Grand Teton National Park lies south of Yellowstone National Park, separated from Yellowstone by the John D. Rockefeller, Jr., Memorial Parkway. There are approximately 3,500 acres of inholdings within Grand Teton, of which 2,100 acres are privately owned and 1,400 acres are owned by the state of Wyoming.

These lands are the target of the National Park Service's 1983 Land Protection Acquisition Plan, which was developed to gain greater public control over the inholdings through land purchase, easement acquisition, eminent-domain acquisition, and other means.[3] Although pri-

2. "Inventory of Management Issues and Proposed Projects in the Greater Yellowstone Ecosystem," Greater Yellowstone Coalition, December 1, 1984.
3. Under eminent domain the government can confiscate private property by paying "fair market value" to the landowner. Final determination of fair market value is made by the government.

vate ownership of these lands predated the establishment of the park, the NPS is eager to seize these properties because activities there potentially conflict with the NPS goal of maintaining open space within the park. Road development and subdivision development, for example, can interrupt elk migrations and other wildlife patterns. As a result, the use of these lands is continually under scrutiny by the NPS, environmental organizations, and other special interest groups.

The plan identified the private, state, and county inholdings in the park, established the priority for acquiring each parcel, and determined the potential methods for acquiring the lands. A 160-acre land parcel at the north end of Black Tail Butte was one of the first areas targeted for acquisition because it comprises a large, undeveloped block of private land. The acquisition proceeding illustrates some of the issues that can lead to conflicts between public and private land owners.

Private inholders often enjoy their location among the public lands and are reluctant to sell their property to developers, government agencies, or other interested parties. In the Black Tail Butte case, however, the landowners were willing to sell their land to the National Park Service. The conflict arose in determining an exchange price. Appraisals by the National Park Service and independent appraisers hired by the landowners caused divergent expectations about the value of the land. The Park Service refused to pay the owners' asking price, halting negotiations for almost ten years.

The Park Service changed its acquisition strategy, however, when the frustrated landowners applied for subdivision approval for the property. Under the existing zoning, the landowners could subdivide the land and sell the parcels to purchasers who were willing to pay the market value of the land. In effect, the landowners were willing to sell the land to the Park Service for conservation purposes, but the reluctance of the Park Service to pay the landowners' selling price forced the owners to consider development options.

Faced with these development threats, the Park Service initiated a declaration of taking to acquire the land, using the justification that the property is "critical to the traveling public," a prime piece of real estate with significant scenic value and an important area for elk migration. Once the land was condemned, the NPS made a down payment on the land without determining an actual purchase price. The price was to be later determined by the courts.

Although the conflict will eventually be ended by the combination of condemnation proceedings, eminent-domain acquisition, and court ruling, this has been a lengthy process. How might the conflict have been better resolved?

Less costly measures than eminent-domain seizures could be used by preservationists to preserve both the ecosystem and individual rights to ownership. For example, preservation through conservation easements can lead to cooperative public and private management of an ecosystem. This approach is not restricted, of course, to private-sector activity, but if private groups are able to secure more funding for acquisition, they can offer a higher bid to the landowner.

A conservation easement is a property deeded to a conservation organization or governmental entity that prohibits, as part of the deed of trust, uses of that property that are incompatible with conservation or preservation objectives.[4] Typically, a conservation easement will

> Prohibit subdivision of the property, construction of commercial buildings or operation of a commercial enterprise, the dumping of trash or waste materials and the conduct of activities which would result in a significant soil erosion, water pollution, loss of aesthetic value, or degradation of habitat for fish and wildlife or plant species. Conservation easements ordinarily do not provide public access to the property, nor do they prohibit construction of buildings, fences, or other improvements necessary to carry on activities compatible with conservation objectives.[5]

A conservation easement is an attractive approach to land conservation for several reasons, the most powerful being that the land remains in private ownership. As private property, the land stays on the tax rolls—an increasingly important consideration in the face of budget cuts. The maintenance and upkeep of the land remain in the landowner's hands, which represents savings to the public sector. Furthermore, the landowner often faces greater incentives to manage the land efficiently and in a manner consistent with conservation goals. Because conservation easement contracts are developed both by the landowner and the trustee, the landowner formally commits the land to conservation uses and agrees to abide by the terms of the contract. The conservation easement is a legal document enforceable through the courts.

Conservation easements have been used for a variety of purposes

---

4. Montana Land Reliance, "Conservation Easements," pamphlet, 1983.
5. Ibid.

in the public sector since the early 1900s. Easements have protected big-game habitat, high-quality fisheries, waterfowl habitat, natural and undisturbed ecosystems, wild and scenic river resources, productive agricultural land, educational resources, and historic sites and structures.[6] The increasing move toward ecosystem management, however, provides fertile ground for extending the use of easements.

The Nature Conservancy and the Montana Land Reliance are two private, nonprofit conservation organizations that preserve critical lands through conservation easements. The Nature Conservancy, a national organization, is committed to the preservation of natural diversity by protecting critical lands and waters. The Montana Land Reliance is a local organization that performs similar functions on a state level.

The Montana Land Reliance has recently expanded its efforts to preserve spring-fed creeks through conservation easements. A 1985 ruling by the Montana Supreme Court opened all streams to public access for recreation. The change in property rights has provided a potential incentive for conserving spring creeks. The Land Reliance maintains that landowners perceive the stream access law as a major threat to their property rights and proposes a program in which landowners would maintain control of stream access by granting conservation easement over certain areas of their property. Sportsmen would give up access to easement-protected spring creeks, and landowners would give up development rights in order to conserve spring creeks.

The successful operation of organizations like the Nature Conservancy and the Montana Land Reliance, and of other private/public sector cooperative arrangements, demonstrates that economic efficiency and ecological preservation can be achieved through private ownership. The National Park Service and preservationists should continue to seek voluntary methods of land exchange, but they should also consider a "no action" approach where voluntary exchange fails, rather than resort to land taking through the power of eminent domain.

West Gardiner Access

North of Yellowstone National Park, approximately 40,000 acres of Gallatin National Forest land extend over parts of the Absaroka Mountains. The lower reaches of the area's eight drainages are ac-

---

6. Montana Land Reliance, *1978–1984 Annual Report,* Helena, Montana, 1984.

cessible by county roads. In three of the drainages—Divide Creek, Trail-Sunlight Creek, and Sphinx Creek—there is access to the national forest. In the other five drainages—Aldridge, Mol Heron, Upper Cinnabar basin, Horse Creek, and Skully Creek—a narrow band of private land lies between the county roads and the national forests, blocking convenient access to public lands.

For several years the USFS has wrestled with the issue of access in the five drainages, including both administrative access for protection and management of the forest and public access for recreation. According to the private landowners in the area, USFS policy has shifted markedly over the years, with increasing emphasis on public access.

Currently, the forest land can be reached through Yellowstone National Park. In addition, the USFS and cooperating agencies have been permitted to travel across some of the private lands for some administrative purposes. Individuals who ask landowners' permission are generally allowed to cross private land, but landowners tend to be less permissive during hunting season. One property owner recently reevaluated the situation, for example, when a couple asked permission to enter Forest Service lands to do nature photography and were caught hunting bighorn sheep in the park.

The Gallatin National Forest draft environmental assessment, which described the proposal to acquire access to the national forest lands, was released in 1984 for public review. Public response was incorporated into an environmental impact statement (EIS). The Forest Service has worked with affected landowners, interested organizations, and the public in preparing the EIS. It has also held several meetings with the Northern Yellowstone Rim Alliance (a local landowners' organization) and with representatives from the state of Montana, Yellowstone National Park, and recreational user groups to set up the process for deciding where and how to establish access to Forest Service lands.

Conflicts over access to the Gallatin National Forest have been resolved in a variety of ways. One ranch owner in Livingston, for example, donated a right-of-way easement giving the Forest Service rights to cross their inholdings under specified restrictions. In exchange, the USFS gave the landowner land that consolidated the ranch. In the Crazy Mountains, a landowner and the USFS established conditions for reciprocal rights. The landowner, who operated a timber company, and the USFS could then travel across both public and private land. Various other access acquisition procedures have been used in the Gallatin National Forest (see Table 4–1). Land swap proposals in the Crazy Mountains are also under consideration.

In the West Gardiner case, a year-long collaborative process has not led to any clear consensus on how access should be established. The landowners have questioned why access through their property is necessary, since the Forest Service land can be reached by more circuitous routes and through the park. The affected parties have different views on what *accessibility* should mean. If a hunter can reach Forest Service lands by hiking 6 miles around private property, is the public land inaccessible? The USFS believes the landowners, by not agreeing to land sales, easement sales, and land trades, are not meeting the agency halfway in the acquisition process.

The USFS asserts that proposed administrative and public access needs are consistent both with federal law and policy and with land management principles established by the March 1985 proposed forest plan. The agency argues that its specific needs include administration of grazing, permits for outfitters and guides, and special uses; law enforcement; wildlife and fish habitat management; administration of recreational uses and facilities; monitoring and protection of the grizzly bear; train maintenance; fire management; and other purposes as directed by national law and regulation. Cooperating agencies (the

Table 4–1. Negotiations for Parcels Involving Public Access Conflicts in Gallatin National Forest Lands in Montana (1975–1985).

	Secured Access to Parcels
1. Land exchange	11
2. Land purchase	6
3. Bypass around private land	8
4. Proving up on public roads (Documenting public rights to existing roads or trails)	4
5. Reciprocal rights (since 1980)	5
6. Easement acquired through cost sharing	31
7. Right-of-way acquisition	47
Negotiated or donated 42	
Condemned 5	

SOURCE: Gallatin National Forest district office, 1986.

Montana Department of Fish, Wildlife, and Parks; the interagency Grizzly Bear Team; and the U.S. Fish and Wildlife Service) also need access to private inholdings for wildlife management and law enforcement.[7] The USFS claims that the need for public access to national forest lands ranked third among the fifteen key issues identified by the public in the forest planning process.

Landowners, on the other hand, are guided by the basic need to protect their property. In choosing not to grant access, property owners are simply exercising their rights. Ownership in the United States is typically based on the right to exclude others. Landowners, therefore, can be expected to exercise this right. This fact should explain to the USFS why landowners are "denying that an access problem exists."

But since the landowners have agreed to participate in the collaborative process, let's examine why the USFS's proposals for voluntary, cooperative actions might be rejected. The landowners originally purchased the lands because they attach value to owning them. To persuade them to sell portions of their land, the USFS must offer compensation. The Grand Teton landowners probably rejected offers to buy their lands because the compensation offered was not sufficient. In the West Gardiner case, the USFS is supposedly constrained by procedural rules that restrict government purchases to "market value." Lands, therefore, must be appraised either by Forest Service or private appraisers. Once a market value is determined and accepted by the service, the agency generally will not exceed this amount when negotiating a purchase, even if the landowner receives a higher offer from private bidders.

The same reasoning applies to the purchase of right-of-way easements to inholdings. Easements can be developed, for example, to establish conditions permitting public or administrative access to a road or trail. In this case, however, property owners are also concerned that the resulting right of way might damage their property. If the easement permits public access, the landowner may doubt the Forest Service's ability to block recreationists from trespassing on other parts of the private property, littering on the grounds, leaving livestock gates open, and so forth. The landowners can avoid these problems by refusing to sign access agreements.

7. Ibid, p. 1.

These reasons may also explain landowners' reluctance to participate in land trades. When one portion of property is traded for another, areas adjacent to a landowner's property may be trespassed on. Or the proposed trades simply may not provide sufficient incentive. Other Forest Service voluntary proposals present similar difficulties. Thus, the Forest Service increasingly relies on compulsory access policies. Public choice theory sheds light on why the access problem may lead to conflict.

As the public increases its demands for access to private lands, the Forest Service can be expected to step up actions to obtain rights of way to these lands. The logic of rent seeking leads us to predict that the public will continue to seek access to inholdings in national forests because the recreational benefits of the land appear to be "free." No one pays for access to the lands; as part of the USFS's budget the costs are borne by all taxpayers. Thus, users will push for a modification of property rights to gain the benefits of access to the national forests.

Property owners can similarly be expected to fight to protect existing arrangements beneficial to them. Currently, adjoining landowners in the West Gardiner area have almost exclusive rights to public lands without paying the costs associated with ownership of those lands. They pay no property taxes nor do they maintain the property, yet they receive many of the benefits of ownership. For example, one of the current landowners is a hunting guide and outfitter; he advertises exclusive rights to hunting on public lands. It is obvious why this particular landowner is not interested in permitting access through his property.

The growing importance of this issue is demonstrated by a recent decision by the Montana Wildlife Federation. In May 1986, the group established public access to public lands for recreational use as their "top priority."[8] Another group, the Public Land Access Association, was created in 1985 specifically to secure access to public lands.

What are possible solutions to the problem? In June 1986, Montana senator Max Baucus recommended that hunting, fishing, and trapping fees be used to acquire public access easements. Since existing federal law does not allow such purchases, the Baucus amendment would allow states and federal agencies to levy new fees in addition to cur-

8. *Bozeman Daily Chronicle,* May 7, 1986, p. 12.

rent state licensing fees.[9] Although the issue continues to draw debate and controversy, the proposed amendment has not been implemented. Other, less conventional, market approaches can also be considered. For example, if the Forest Service cannot secure access through the cooperation of the landowners, it could consider turning the tables and selling either the forest lands or easements to the lands to surrounding private landowners.[10] This way, private landowners who currently benefit from the exclusive use of public lands would pay for the privilege. The agency could use the proceeds from the sales to purchase other lands or easements.

The USFS could also establish rights of way through the park. Shifting rights within the public lands system would be more equitable than confiscating them from private owners. If the costs of such access *within* the national forests are high (for example, in terms of ecological damage), private landowners should be given a proportionally higher price for their land.

The Black Tail Butte example suggests that certain governmental practices undermine the potential for an equitable and efficient outcome through voluntary exchange. We've seen how eminent domain provides a means to achieve public access with minimal regard for private landowner rights. Let's look at the problems surrounding eminent-domain takings.

The eminent-domain clause of the U.S. Constitution dictates, "nor shall private property be taken for public use, without just compensation." Under the clause, the government can use the power of condemnation to acquire land at "market value." The fact that land must often be condemned before eminent-domain proceedings occur, however, suggests that property is not acquired at the true market value.

Eminent domain gives the USFS the ability to circumvent the conditions for efficient and equitable exchange. But the agency does not particularly like to exercise these powers, because of the bad feelings that result. In the Gallatin Forest, a conflict over access has been going on since the early 1960s. The landowner has been reluctant to

9. New Mexico, for example, currently has a special fee. The state and the Forest Service agreed to levy a $10 fee on elk hunters and fishermen in the Valle Vidal area in the northeastern part of the state.

10. In instances where only surrounding private landowners of a public parcel can access the property, there is a limited market for the sale of such properties. Such limitations can lead to bargain sales of the Forest Service lands.

agree to any public access. The USFS could have acquired access through eminent domain over two decades ago, but the possibility of public outcry has blocked such action.

The USFS should consider forgoing public access across private lands if voluntary agreement with the property owner cannot be reached. This is likely to be the most efficient and equitable allocation of resources. A private landowner sometimes holds onto a house that can't be sold at a certain price, although the house could be sold if the price were lowered. Similarly, the USFS could probably purchase access rights easily if it offered a high enough price to the landowners. But the legal limitations requiring "market value" place certain spending constraints on the agency.

Squirrel Meadows

Squirrel Meadows is the only remaining private land between Yellowstone National Park and Grand Teton National Park. The 480-acre parcel has been subject to substantial scrutiny by those concerned with ecosystem management. Although the final destiny of the parcel has yet to be determined, there is cause for optimism in the innovative work of the American Parks Campaign, a private organization dedicated to acquiring threatened land adjacent to national parks. A compromise may be worked out between preserving specific land uses while respecting the rights of the current landowner.

In the early 1980s, Squirrel Meadows was put up for sale. Local U.S. Forest Service officials contacted the Nature Conservancy to discuss ways to ensure that the property would remain undeveloped. The officials suggested that the Conservancy purchase the land with the intention of later selling it to the USFS when sufficient funds became available. Although the Nature Conservancy was interested, they discovered several impediments to their acquiring the land. First, regional Forest Service headquarters in Ogden, Utah, declined to support the proposal, indicating that other financial commitments had higher priority. They could not guarantee that the Nature Conservancy would be immediately repaid. Then, on inspecting the property, the Nature Conservancy decided that the land did not meet the organization's criteria for preservation. Without a cooperative agreement for later transfer to the USFS, the organization could not justify the purchase.

Squirrel Meadows was sold to a partnership, which subsequently doubled the price and sold it to another individual who intended to maintain several acres for personal recreational use and to subdivide and sell the remainder. The Nature Conservancy discussed the potential consequences of subdivision development with the owner. The landowner has since become involved with exploring ways to minimize harm to the Greater Yellowstone ecosystem while preserving his investment. He proposed, for example, selling the land to the USFS for the price that he originally paid. Not surprisingly, the Forest Service turned down this offer just as they had rejected the earlier sale price that was 50 percent lower. Fortunately for conservation interests, the landowner sees the value of preservation and has been willing to explore ways to maintain the land's wilderness values.

The American Parks Campaign is working with Brigham Young University and Ricks College, both private institutions, to find ways to preserve the land without making the landowner pay the entire cost of preservation. One or both of the institutions hopes to take on Squirrel Meadows as a biological field station for use by their students. Purchase of the land will be arranged through direct contributions to the two colleges and through contributions made to the American Parks Campaign by various corporations that will dedicate part of their advertising budgets to the preservation project. Ricks College already holds title to some of the Squirrel Meadows property.

This effort will accomplish several objectives that are consistent with the property rights prescription for efficient and equitable allocation of resources. By operating within the marketplace rather than relying on the government's police powers to acquire property, the environmentalists in the American Parks Campaign ensure that the land is put to its highest valued use, enabling the resources to be used efficiently. It makes sense that those who pay for ownership rights will exercise those rights efficiently.

To achieve rights to ownership, special interests need to be more open to competing in the land market. Individual subdivision developers who invest in land operate on the expectation of a ready market for the subdivided land. Similarly, where environmental groups or the nation's citizens supply the purchase funds, they expect the payoffs from preservation to be sufficient to justify the purchase. Without this gauge, it is difficult, if not impossible, to determine an equitable resolution to land use conflicts.

The American Parks Campaign's success in its Squirrel Meadows project will provide a property rights solution to a current problem and a model for dealing with other conflicts between preservation and development.

SUMMARY

This property rights/public choice perspective on Greater Yellowstone shows how cooperative public- and private-sector activity can effectively and efficiently guide land use policies while highlighting the problems likely to be encountered in land use negotiations. Many of the preservation tools used in the past can be restructured to work as mechanisms to preserve property rights. Conservation easements and land purchase campaigns are alternatives that both protect traditional rights to land ownership and preserve wilderness areas.

5

MEN, ELK, AND WOLVES

Tom Blood

Sportsmen, environmentalists, and stockmen are becoming aware that the Greater Yellowstone ecosystem is experiencing ecological problems. These problems are significant because of the important wildlife species that depend on habitat in the ecosystem for survival.

Since the late nineteenth century, Yellowstone National Park has provided the last sanctuary for many species of wildlife. In 1885, naturalist George Grinnell wrote to the *New York Sun*: "There are, to my positive knowledge, not more than 700 bison . . . left [in the United States]. . . . About 180 are in Yellowstone." Although Grinnell's numbers are disputable, it is true that the park harbored the last herd of free-roaming bison.[1]

The threatened grizzly bear also roams the Greater Yellowstone ecosystem. Although grizzly bear numbers are declining in Yellowstone and some ecologists think that the species is headed for extinction, the Yellowstone population remains one of the two largest in the continental United States.

The Greater Yellowstone ecosystem also provides refuge for the once-endangered trumpeter swan. One of the swans' prime nesting sites is just west of Yellowstone National Park in Montana's Red Rock

1. Ruth Kirk, *Exploring Yellowstone* (Seattle: University of Washington Press, 1972), p. 49.

Lakes, which became a wildlife refuge in 1935. Since then, trumpeter swans have begun a remarkable comeback in the area. By the early 1970s, flocks of up to fifty swans could be seen on the Yellowstone River.[2]

The list of other species that depend on the Greater Yellowstone ecosystem for habitat is well known to most environmentalists. It includes the rare sandhill crane, which can be spotted in the lower Geyser basin; the protected peregrine falcon; the threatened bald eagle; the native Yellowstone cutthroat trout; and the cougar. Two wildlife species serve as key barometers of political management and ecological well-being in Greater Yellowstone: the Rocky Mountain elk and the timber gray wolf.

Growing populations of elk have been linked to a significant number of ecological disruptions in Greater Yellowstone, most conspicuously the deteriorating range within Yellowstone National Park. Wolves are a missing link in the Yellowstone ecosystem. They are the major predators of elk, and some have hailed the reintroduction of the wolf as a panacea to control elk numbers. Others—notably ranchers—have perceived the plan as a serious threat to their livelihoods, because wolves also occasionally prey on domestic livestock.

Wolves have been historically maligned in the West, to the point that the animal has become extinct in Greater Yellowstone. Strong emotions surround the idea of reintroducing wolves to this region. Ranchers in Montana, Idaho, and Wyoming view the wolf as threatening, controllable only by eradication. To many environmentalists, the wolf epitomizes wildness in a world dominated by man. To Yellowstone National Park wildlife managers, the wolf represents an answer to the rising elk population.

The wolf, however, will be neither a curse nor a cure-all for Greater Yellowstone. It is the political climate, more than the wolf's behavior, that is at the root of the standoff between environmentalists and ranchers over the issue of reintroduction.

This chapter offers alternatives from the private sector for each of the three proposed wolf management zones. Unless a political solution is created that is acceptable to ranchers, sportsmen, and environmental groups, establishing a viable population of Yellowstone wolves will not be feasible.

2. Ibid., p. 50.

ELK AND WOLVES IN YELLOWSTONE

Interpretations of the biological histories of the elk and wolf in Greater Yellowstone are shrouded in controversy. Incomplete and often conflicting historical records are one reason interpretations differ. Politics is another.

In the case of elk, the first question is whether the northern Yellowstone elk herd has historically used the Soda Butte Creek and Lamar River valleys for wintering grounds. Naturalists, wildlife managers, and historians dispute whether this herd traditionally wintered in the area or had been pushed and corralled into the 5,000 to 8,500 foot Lamar plateau by encroaching barbed wires and gunfire when the area was settled during the late 1800s and early 1900s.

Establishing the truth about elk settlement is important for justifying strategies to manage the animals. If the herd did not traditionally winter in this area, then the National Park Service's (NPS's) current "natural regulation" management practice becomes politically irrelevant. This strategy rests on the belief that elk are native to the region and should therefore be controlled only by natural factors, such as cold winters and limited browse, despite the apparent damage the growing elk herds are inflicting on the environment.

The elk herd in northern Yellowstone, conservatively estimated at 16,000 animals, is the largest herd in the Greater Yellowstone ecosystem.[3] The theory of natural regulation currently practiced in Yellowstone has profound consequences for these elk and their environment. Proponents of this theory believe that the Lamar drainage has wintered many thousands of elk over the centuries.[4] In addition, Park Service managers who support the natural regulation theory claim that food supply is the primary factor governing the size of this elk herd. In other words, when the herd size exceeds the carrying capacity of the range, a few harsh winters will bring the herd size back to "equilibrium."

> Over a series of years, naturally regulated ungulate populations were self-regulatory units. They regulated their own mortality and compensating

---

3. Rick Reese, *Greater Yellowstone: The National Park and Adjacent Wildlands* (Helena, Mont.: Montana Magazine, 1984), pp. 48–49.

4. Douglas B. Houston, "The Northern Yellowstone Elk, Parts I and II: History and Demography," Yellowstone National Park, Wyoming, April 1974, p. 5.

natality in relation to available winter feed and their population size. Predation on either wintering or newborn ungulates seemed a nonessential adjunct to the natural regulation process because it did not prevent populations from being self-regulatory by competition for food.[5]

This claim from a National Park Service official is loaded with assumptions, such as the notion that elk herds were never significantly controlled by predators, such as wolves. Current research to determine if this is true (and to establish the validity of natural regulation in today's Yellowstone ecosystem) is not possible since there are few wolves in or near Yellowstone.[6]

John Weaver, a wildlife biologist with the U.S. Forest Service (USFS), spent from 1975 to 1977 looking for wolves in Yellowstone National Park. He and his field assistants trekked more than 1,500 miles, "called" for wolves on more than 1,400 occasions, and planted animal carcasses with time-lapse cameras. Weaver saw only two sets of tracks that may have belonged to a wolf, and he once heard a series of howls that did not belong to either a dog or a coyote. But no wolves were spotted.[7]

The park has not been permanent home for a viable population of wolves since 1915, when the Park Service decided to eradicate the wolf from Yellowstone because the park's management had observed that the Yellowstone wolf was "a decided menace to the herds of *elk, deer, mountain sheep, and antelope*" (emphasis added).[8] Today's natural regulation advocates appear to have forgotten why wolves were eradicated from Yellowstone National Park earlier in the century.

Many biologists and range experts question the natural regulation theory.[9] Without the wolf in the Greater Yellowstone ecosystem, the

---

5. Alston Chase, *Playing God in Yellowstone: The Destruction of America's First National Park* (Boston: Atlantic Monthly Press, 1986), p. 59; from the report: Glen F. Cole, "An Ecological Rationale for the Natural or Artificial Regulation of Native Ungulates in Parks," *Transactions of the Thirty-sixth North American Wildlife and Natural Resources Conference* (Washington, D.C.: Wildlife Management Institute, 1971).

6. Tom McNamee, "Yellowstone's Missing Element," *Audubon*, 88 (January 1986): 12.

7. Ibid.

8. Ibid., p. 12.

9. Clay Marlow, a range scientist from Montana State University who specializes in vegetation-animal relationships, believes northern Yellowstone has been severely overgrazed and damaged by an unchecked elk population.

Bart O'Gara, an animal biologist at the University of Montana and head of the Northern Rocky Mountain Wolf Recovery Team established by the U.S. Fish and Wildlife Service, has food supply seems to be a poor means to check the northern elk herd. Elk herd growth continues unabated; many believe that the herd has exceeded the carrying capacity of the park's range.

In 1968, when the northern Yellowstone elk herd numbered 3,100, park wildlife managers estimated that the carrying capacity of the Lamar range would stabilize the elk population at between 4,000 and 6,000 animals. That estimate was soon raised.[10] By 1978, the elk population approached 12,000,[11] requiring that Park Service estimates of carrying capacity increase to match the rapid elk population growth in the Lamar and Soda Butte valleys. Outdated carrying capacity figures were rejected as "underestimates" of "environmental variability." The Park Service again revised the carrying capacity numbers and in 1974 matter of factly stated: "Records suggest that a total winter herd of around 12,000 (10,000–15,000) is most likely."[12]

Historical accounts contradict the park's theory. Records dating back to 1930 show that the elk population exceeded 11,000 animals only once (in 1933, the winter census counted 11,521). The theory of natural regulation was introduced for elk management in 1971. In 1975, the herd broke 11,000 and has consistently remained above 10,000 since.[13] During the 1980s, numbers have soared to between 16,000 and 20,000.

While natural regulation theorists wait for the elk population to stabilize, the range is showing signs of serious overuse. This may have negative consequences for wolves. Advocates of the plan to bring

---

9. (*Continued*)
worked in Yellowstone and says he has been impressed by the fact that there were no beaver, no snowshoe hare, very few field moles, and only an occasional blue grouse on the northern range. Tom Blood, "Wolf Reintroductions Producing Howls—Yellowstone Unsuitable for Wolves?" *Albuquerque Journal,* February 25, 1988.

10. Chase, *Playing God,* p. 73; Cole to Anderson, October 26, 1967 (obtained from Yellowstone Park Service by Alston Chase through the Freedom of Information Act); National Park Service, "Information Paper—Northern Yellowstone Elk Herd," September 17, 1968; Glen F. Cole, "Elk and the Yellowstone Ecosystem," Yellowstone Library, 1969; Douglas B. Houston, "The Status of Research on Ungulates in Northern Yellowstone National Park," (Paper for the American Association for the Advancement of Science Symposium on Research in National Parks, December 28, 1971).

11. Douglas B. Houston, *The Northern Yellowstone Elk: Ecology and Management* (New York: Macmillan, 1982), p. 17.

12. Houston, *History and Demography,* pp. 72–73.

13. Ibid., pp. 16–17.

wolves back to Greater Yellowstone assume that wolves translocated to the region will stay and flourish. There is some evidence, however, that the animals will not remain. According to Alston Chase's documented findings, the Park Service secretly returned wolves to Yellowstone in 1967. Marshal Gates, a summer seasonal ranger in the park, photographed a wolf near Soda Butte Creek in December of that year. Mr. Chase reports:

> In the following months [after the photograph] wolves were seen frequently, and in the four years after Gates's trip to the park, nearly four hundred sightings of wolves were reported, and although many were dismissed as erroneous, park authorities and independent experts agreed that many were solid evidence that wolves were indeed in Yellowstone.[14]

But the wolves did not stay. John Weaver's conclusive 1974 study found that no wolves inhabited Yellowstone. They had been spotted migrating northwest after 1967 toward Canada and were last seen in 1975. It has been hypothesized that elk alone were not enough to sustain the wolves, which must supplement a diet of big game with smaller prey, including beaver. Possibly because of overgrazing by elk, beaver no longer inhabit the park. Without the beaver, the wolf left.[15]

Will a second attempt at relocation be successful? Under the policy of natural regulation, the odds are against the wolf.[16]

Because the upset ecological balance in the park that has been created in the name of natural regulation, it is realistic to believe that the wolves might migrate elsewhere. Some "unnatural" management practices may have to be initiated, such as replanting willows and aspen to regenerate beaver habitat.

Private, state, and federal lands adjacent to the park also contain areas critical to the wolf's survival. Yet, private landowners' attitudes

---

14. Chase, *Playing God*, p. 120.
15. Ibid., pp. 135, 136. Tom Blood "Wolf Reintroductions."
16. Bart O'Gara, an animal biologist at the University of Montana and head of the Northern Rocky Mountain Wolf Recovery Team, is concerned that wolves may leave the park in search of a more diverse prey base. O'Gara, who has done extensive research on predators, sites his experience surveying wolves in Idaho with the Fish and Wildlife Service. O'Gara's team

> did these surveys in wilderness areas which were inhabited mostly by big game. But most of [their] wolf sitings were along the fringes of the wilderness areas where small game like beaver and rabbits were more plentiful.

and public land management policies would hurt the wolf's chances of survival if the species were reintroduced. Stockmen are unwilling to support the wolf's reintroduction because the predator presents a danger to their herds. However, political factors enter in as well.

Is the absence of wolves in the ecosystem haunting park wildlife policy makers? The reintroduction of wolves to Greater Yellowstone has been scrutinized by a group of agency personnel, professional biologists, livestock producers, and conservation group representatives appointed by the U.S. Fish and Wildlife Service. This group has released the Northern Rocky Mountain Wolf Recovery Plan, which describes the logistics, management, and possible implications of transplanting wolves to the Yellowstone ecosystem.

The plan calls for a zone management system to synchronize wolf management with other land uses. According to this system, three wolf management zones would be established in the ecosystem. Zone 1 would comprise critical wolf habitat, with management emphasis given to the recovery of the wolf. Zone 2 would be managed for a balance between wolves and other land uses. Wolves would be allowed in this area but not always assigned the highest priority. A Zone 3 designation would be assigned to areas where wolf damage would not be tolerated.[17]

The plan has generated bitter controversy. On one side of the issue are many environmental groups that value having wolves in the Greater Yellowstone area. On the other side are ranchers in Montana, Idaho, and Wyoming with interests in livestock and other agricultural commodities.

Elk and Wolves on Private Land

It may appear that, with the relatively small amount of private land near Yellowstone, the reintroduction of the wolf in the park would not have significant implications for landowners. Although precise measurements are not available, only about 5 percent of land in the Yellowstone ecosystem is privately owned.[18] But raw percentages are

17. Reported in Eric Wiltse's "Dillon Rancher Predicts Worst If Wolves Are Returned to Park," *Bozeman Daily Chronicle,* April 3, 1986, as the plan appears in the "Northern Rocky Mountain Wolf Recovery Plan," U.S. Fish and Wildlife Service.

18. The Greater Yellowstone Coalition estimates that 2 percent is privately owned, the Political Economy Research Center estimates 5 percent, and Defenders of Wildlife estimates 7 percent.

deceiving. Five percent is approximately 350,000 acres of land—land generally located on lower valley floors that is prime wildlife habitat. This brings private landowners directly into the conflict.

Three major rivers drain Yellowstone National Park to the north, the Yellowstone, the Gallatin, and the Madison. Of the three valley floors created by these rivers, two—the Madison and Paradise valleys of the Yellowstone River—are nearly all privately owned. This land provides range and riparian zones that are critical wildlife habitat. State and federal lands are often at higher elevations. In general, deer and elk summer at higher elevations and winter at lower elevations. Because the animals' nutritional needs are extremely high during late gestation and early lactation, the spring grasses on low-elevation sites are particularly important to their survival.

Edwin Nelson, a Paradise Valley rancher, estimates that he loses $6,000 worth of spring grasses to elk each year. Mr. Nelson's strategy is to set aside 640 acres of grazing land in case of a dry season between June and October. "We have the 640 acres as a backup to rotate the livestock onto in case we need to ease the pressure on our regular grazing land," Nelson says. "Last year [1985] was a dry one, but we couldn't rest our pasture because the elk had grazed the 640 acres down so far it was literally useless." [19]

State funds are usually inadequate to compensate ranchers for crop damage by wild game. Joe Egan, a wildlife biologist with Montana's Department of Fish, Wildlife, and Parks, points to one of the larger ranches in Montana's Big Hole valley and admits: "If we tried to pay wildlife damage costs on some of those ranches, we'd be washed right down the drain financially." [20]

In addition to causing damage to grasses and crop stores, elk attract hunters and predators. Duane Neal, an outfitter from Paradise Valley, explains why hunters are attracted to private land.

As game herds multiply, more animals are forced from federal to private land, attracting hunters to ranches for hunting opportunities. In addition, private land is more desirable for hunting because hunters can usually

---

19. Edwin Nelson, telephone interview with the author, Paradise Valley, Montana, July 16, 1986.

20. John Baden and Tom Blood, "Man and Beast Living in Harmony," *Denver Post*, May 19, 1984.

drive through private land, as opposed to the necessity to hike or pack into public land for good hunting.[21]

Similarly, when sportsmen hunt on private land and are not actively controlled, an owner's property is almost inevitably damaged. Even the most careful hunter might accidentally leave a gate open or drive across a wet field. In some instances, inexperienced hunters mistake livestock for game. Thoughtless hunters litter the land.

Ranchers will also be pressured if wolves are attracted to private land by game and livestock. It is not surprising, therefore, that headlines such as "Dillon Rancher Predicts Worst If Wolves Are Returned to Park" appear in local newspapers.[22] Ranchers are concerned about controlling their property, and the roaming and sometimes marauding wolf has come to symbolize their loss of control. This is why opposition from stockmen is one of the biggest hurdles wolf partisans must clear before the reintroduction of the wolf to Yellowstone National Park becomes politically feasible.[23]

Environmental groups are aware of the stockmen's concerns. To counter rancher opposition, some environmental groups are recommending a federally funded compensation program to pay for animals killed by wolves. Their model is a state-funded program in Minnesota that pays ranchers whose livestock is killed by any of the 1,200 or so timber wolves in the state. Under the aegis of the U.S. Department of Agriculture, the program has a $20-million budget and provides market value (up to $400 per head) of livestock lost to wolves.[24] Local Department of Natural Resource Conservation officers must verify that wolves are responsible for the death and determine the market value of the livestock killed.

Environmental groups have proposed a similar compensation program for the Yellowstone ecosystem as a way to reduce stockmen's concerns about the reintroduction of wolves to the area.

21. Duane Neal, telephone interview with the author, Paradise Valley, Montana, July 18, 1986.

22. *Bozeman Daily Chronicle,* April 3, 1986.

23. Craig Johnson, "Politics Delay Return of Wolf to Park, Panelists Say," *Bozeman Daily Chronicle,* June 3, 1986.

24. Steven H. Fritts, "Wolf Depredation on Livestock in Minnesota," Resource Publication 145 (Washington, D.C.: U.S. Department of the Interior, U.S. Fish and Wildlife Service, 1982), p. 4.

Problems in administering such governmental programs abound. Once such programs are established, they often remain inflexible in the face of change. For instance, if livestock depredation from wolves outgrows the wolf depredation compensation fund, how long would stockmen have to wait to receive compensation? The bureaucrats who administer the program would have to lobby Congress for additional funds, a time-consuming and uncertain process.

In contrast, private conservation groups thrive on fundraising efficiency. In the summer of 1987, seven wolves raided livestock herds on three northern Montana ranches, several hundred miles from Yellowstone. The value of livestock killed by the wolves, which were not part of a reintroduction program, was $3,149. However, the Defenders of Wildlife was able to raise private money to pay these ranchers in a fundraising effort that took only two days.[25] On the other hand, if the wolf population falls and cases of livestock deaths drop, the bureaucrats will have incentives to spend the money on other components of the program, even if the other components do not need it. When funding comes from the general treasury, the compensation program that does not spend its budgeted funds loses what it fails to spend.

In light of these incentives, a more efficient alternative is for environmental groups to post bond to compensate ranchers for wolf depredation on livestock in Greater Yellowstone. Environmental and sportsmen's groups can raise the money from their membership or from outside interests willing to assume some financial responsibility for the risk of releasing wolves in Greater Yellowstone. The Defenders of Wildlife has already raised $30,000 from private business for their compensation fund, should reintroduction occur. According to Hank Fischer, the group's Northern Rocky Mountain representative, Defenders' target is $100,000. Fischer is encouraged by the group's success and says fundraising projects that are underway include commissioning a Yellowstone wolf print and using the proceeds from sales to finance the fund.[26]

The "adjustor" role—determining if wolves were responsible for the kill—should be left to state fish and game personnel. This is often

25. Tom Blood, "Saving Wolves by Soothing Ranchers," *Wall Street Journal,* October 20, 1987.

26. Hank Fischer, telephone interview with the author, Missoula, Montana, March 28, 1989.

a difficult task. Was the animal killed by a wolf or by a coyote, bear, or bobcat? Has the carcass decomposed too much to determine the cause of death? If wolf sign is evident near the decomposed carcass, is the wolf responsible for killing the animal, or was the wolf scavenging an animal that died of another cause?

With private funding of compensation, state fish and game personnel will have different incentives than under the Minnesota program. Under the use it or lose it principle, if the administrators of a program do not spend funds appropriated to them, their budget may be reduced by the unspent amount the succeeding year. This encourages waste and inefficiency. With the government program in Minnesota, "about 73% of the calves for which compensation was paid in 1979 were calves that could not be accounted for; no remains were found, and no wolf involvement was verified."[27] In fact, many of the calves reported as being killed by wolves may never have been born. Some ranchers, uncertain about whether or not a cow is pregnant, may blame wolves for depredating a calf that was never conceived, and government personnel may not have the incentive to spend much time looking for remains. During one summer, a Minnesota rancher claimed that sixty of his calves were lost to wolves. Precautionary fertility tests conducted the following year revealed that 27 percent of his herd was not carrying calves.[28] Is it possible that the rancher's breeding program had been as inefficient the previous year?

How can private organizations raise enough funds so that the bonds do not run out in the middle of the year? One answer is for an umbrella organization like the Greater Yellowstone Coalition (GYC) to back the organizations that post insurance bond. The GYC embraces the concept of ecosystem management around the oldest and most famous national park in the United States. Many newspapers and periodicals would devote space for commentaries and articles released by the Greater Yellowstone Coalition about reintroducing wolves. These articles could mention the groups that raised contributions, giving these organizations positive regional and national exposure and enhancing their fundraising efforts.

This insurance system is also more equitable than the current government program. The cost of wolf depredation on livestock would

---

27. Fritts, "Wolf Depredation," p. 5.
28. Ibid.

be shifted away from ranchers and the general taxpayers and onto the shoulders of the environmental groups that are lobbying for the wolf's reintroduction. The Minnesota program, on the other hand, is funded by all U.S. taxpayers, including environmentalists, hunters, farmers, and those who do not care whether or not the wolf exists in northern Minnesota.

The private system is beneficial in another way. Stockmen in the Yellowstone ecosystem are concerned that the wolf will become more of a problem to livestock than the grizzly bear is; they want wolf populations controlled. Their anxiety is biologically well founded. Grizzlies generally do not begin producing offspring until the age of five and average only one cub per year. Wolves begin breeding at three and can have up to six pups per year.[29] Under the private bond proposal, environmentalists would have to monitor wolf populations to ensure that they do not reach excessive levels. If wolf predation on livestock increases, the interest earnings from the bonds posted will decrease as liability payments increase. In addition, ranchers will put pressure on conservation groups to increase the compensation fund or to lobby for smaller numbers of wolves. These incentives will encourage wolf supporters to advocate a wolf population that is consistent both with their love for the animal and their pocketbooks.

Most confrontations between wolves and stockmen would probably occur on land designated Zone 3, land where harmful wolves will not be tolerated because priority will be given for livestock raising and other resource uses. The antithesis of Zone 3 management is Zone 1 management—areas where wolf recovery would have the highest priority in land and resource management.

Conservation Organizations and Critical Wolf Habitat

What problems, if any, face the wolf in Zone 1 areas? Most of the Zone 1 habitat in the Greater Yellowstone ecosystem would be in the park itself or in surrounding national forests.[30]

According to Wayne Brewster, wolf coordinator for Glacier National Park, there are two major components of wolf management:

---

29. Ruth Rudner, "Call of the Wild: Of Wolves and Woman," *Wall Street Journal*, August 5, 1986, p. 26.

30. Wayne Brewster, telephone interview with the author, Helena, Montana, July 25, 1986.

providing populations of large ungulates for prey and preventing wolf depredation on livestock. Some wolves travel nearly 50 miles a day in search of food, and require large tracts of wild land with few people and minimum accessibility.[31] They need a habitat with rugged or wooded terrain that will provide cover sufficient for denning. Wolves also need small game to supplement their diet. Mr. Brewster observes that, if such an environment is available, a key to providing wolf habitat is to foster big-game populations, which means ensuring that there is enough winter browse for large ungulates.[32]

The difference between managing for elk winter habitat and allowing this winter habitat to deteriorate from overpopulation could be significant. On national forest land in Zone 1, if sufficient winter habitat was maintained for big game by natural and artificial means and elk populations were kept under control by hunting, small game might return. The Gallatin National Forest currently has winter range to support 5,600 elk, but the Forest Service appears to be more interested in harvesting timber than in preserving winter range.[33] The 1986 *Audubon Wildlife Report* states: "Timber management continues to receive a far greater proportion of the Forest Service budget than does any other activity. Foresters and engineers, who primarily design the roads required for logging, dominate the USFS both in numbers and in their position in the power structure.[34] The draft environmental impact statement for the 1985 Gallatin National Forest plan adds, "[M]ost of the effort to maintain and improve wildlife habitat is associated with timber harvest, grazing, burning, road management."[35]

From the USFS's viewpoint, this strategy makes sense. Timber harvesting is extremely expensive. Logging roads cost at least $56,620 per mile to construct; this item is budgeted at a minimum of $276,000 per year for the Gallatin National Forest. Wildlife habitat improve-

---

31. William F. Jensen, Todd K. Fuller, and William L. Robinson, "Wolf Distribution on the Ontario–Michigan Border near Sault Ste. Marie," Minnesota Department of Natural Resources, Forest Wildlife Populations and Research Group, Grand Rapids, Minnesota, August 1986 (Unpublished), p. 5.

32. Brewster interview.

33. U.S. Department of Agriculture, U.S. Forest Service, *Draft Environmental Impact Statement, Gallatin National Forest, Forest Plan* (Bozeman, Mont.: U.S. Forest Service, 1985), p. II-10.

34. *Audubon Wildlife Report, 1986* (New York: National Audubon Society, 1986), p. 2.

35. U.S. Department of Agriculture, U.S. Forest Service, *Draft Environmental Impact Statement, Gallatin National Forest*, p. IV-15.

ment is allocated only $13 to $30 per acre and is budgeted at from $13,000 to $30,000 per year.[36] As a result, the Forest Service has an incentive to harvest timber and build roads—financially intensive activities—to justify a larger budget for the next year. Such a system creates incentives to predict high future timber prices in order to justify timber harvesting levels.

The 1985 projected price trends that Gallatin National Forest planners used were labeled "questionable" by the Cascade Holistic Economic Consultants (CHEC), an organization that reviews forest plans for private interests. CHEC notes that the USFS instructed their consultants to project timber price rises in the Gallatin National Forest plan based on the assumption that demand for housing would remain strong, despite high interest rates. Even Forest Service economists have raised their eyebrows at the projected price trends. In a November 23, 1983, memorandum, they pointed out that although recreation and wildlife values were increasing, by using price-trend analysis *only* for timber "a strong and unjustifiable bias" for timber harvesting over other uses has developed.[37]

Resource management and use decisions driven by timber sales and road construction will probably lead to a decline in competing resources, such as wildlife habitat. Management Area 10 in the Gallatin National Forest, for example, has about 30 percent forest cover and was described by wildlife biologist Matt Reid as "prime elk winter range." Adjacent is Management Area 11, which contains 90 percent forest cover and was declared by Reid as "mainly summer range if it [is] useful to wildlife at all."[38] The Gallatin National Forest Plan designates that Management Area 10 be primarily used for harvesting timber and calls for clear-cutting of parcels of up to 40 acres. Management Area 11 will be managed "to attain a proper balance of cover and forage for big game through regulated timber harvest."[39]

36. Ibid., p. B-45. The USFS calculates that it builds approximately one mile of road per square mile of forest for harvesting timber. The USFS claims in the *Gallatin National Forest, Forest Plan,* p. II-11 that the current direction alternative would require 3,120 acres (4.8 square miles) of timber to be harvested annually for the first decade of the plan. The plan calls for 1,000 acres of habitat improvement every year under the current direction alternative (p. II-10).

37. Cascade Holistic Economic Consultants, "Review of the Gallatin Forest Plan and the EIS—Summary," Eugene, Oregon, 1985, p. 7. Timber is the only resource for which the USFS funds price-trend research.

38. Ibid.

39. Ibid. Clear-cuts will not exceed 25 acres for areas designated as summer range on Management Area 11 and will not exceed 20 acres for areas designated as winter range.

Gallatin National Forest wildlife staff officer Rich Inman acknowledges that the USFS is financially incapable of managing wildlife habitat on a site-specific basis in the Gallatin. Shortages of money and staff are the primary reasons the USFS must create a single management plan for critical elk winter habitat across the 1.7-million-acre Gallatin National Forest.[40] Gallatin's wildlife staff consists of two biologists, while twenty-seven people manage Gallatin timber harvests.[41]

It is uncertain how wolves, elk, and the Forest Service will interact if wolves are reintroduced to the Yellowstone ecosystem. How will the Forest Service weigh the need to preserve critical wolf habitat against timber harvesting? How will the agency adjust to the challenges of a new and major predator in its elk management areas?

One promising alternative to the Forest Service is to turn the management of critical wolf habitat areas over to one or more of the 500 private land trusts in the United States, such as the Audubon Society or the Nature Conservancy. These organizations are responsible for the protection of nearly 3 million acres of fragile and valuable ecosystems in the country.[42]

The Nature Conservancy has protected more than 2 million acres, from the 114-acre Rodman's Hollow in Rhode Island, an important bald eagle and peregrine falcon habitat, to the 12,445-acre Pine Butte Preserve in Montana, critical grizzly bear habitat.[43]

The Nature Conservancy's approach to managing critical bear habitat on the Pine Butte Preserve shows the commitment and management flexibility this land trust is willing to make on behalf of an important species. Grizzlies, like wolves, frequent wetland areas because of their rich plant and small-game communities. To preserve this sensitive habitat, the Nature Conservancy has taken steps such as replanting chokecherry shrubs that were overgrazed and fencing off wetland areas from deer, elk, and cattle.[44] Putting ecology above politics has enabled the threatened grizzly to thrive.

Such site-specific management is very difficult for public agencies

40. Rich Inman, telephone interview with author, Bozeman, Montana, July 28, 1986.

41. Gale Everett, Personnel Office, USFS, telephone interview with author, Bozeman, Montana, July 29, 1986.

42. John Baden and Tom Blood, "Troubled Wetlands and the Land Trust Movement," *Orvis News,* June 1985.

43. *The Nature Conservancy News,* 35 (September/October 1985).

44. Blood, "Wolf Reintroductions."

to achieve because their decisions must be governed by politics, not ecology or economics.

Government land use principles, detailed in the Federal Land Policy and Management Act of 1976 (FLPMA) and the Multiple Use–Sustained Yield Act of 1960 (MUSYA) may appear to differ from the Nature Conservancy's agenda. FLPMA and MUSYA mandate multiple use and sustained yield on federal lands; that is, "management of the public lands and their various resource values so that they are utilized in the combination that will best meet the present and future needs of the American people."[45] In contrast, the Nature Conservancy has a single goal: "identifying, protecting and managing ecologically significant land and the endangered plant and animal life that land supports." The Conservancy's philosophy of managing land means "providing or maintaining the conditions that will either perpetuate or improve the viability, quality and defensibility of the elements for which the area was protected."[46]

But there are similarities between some federal mandates and the practices of the Nature Conservancy. The U.S. Forest Service, for instance, sometimes recognizes areas of crucial environmental concern where special attention is required to protect rare plant and animal species.[47] Unfortunately, the Forest Service's multiple-use directive often creates conflicts between commercial and environmental concerns. In the Gallatin National Forest the budget favors commercialism.

The Forest Service seems reluctant to commit money and manpower to the preservation of key wildlife habitat management. It is logical that the USFS sell conservation easements or full property rights to a private land trust like the Conservancy. Private land trusts have strong incentives to preserve ecosystems. Their funds come from individuals concerned about environmental protection, so the support that a land trust receives is directly related to the effectiveness with which it carries out its mission. If a private land trust manages an area in a manner that supporters find unsatisfactory, the organization loses contributions and invites charges of breach of trust. Simply put,

---

45. Gary Hammond, "The Nature Conservancy: Protecting the Rare and the Beautiful," p. 28; Federal Land Policy and Management Act of 1976. This law, passed by the 94th Congress, was one of the major legislations coming out of the environmental movement.
46. Hammond, "Nature Conservancy," p. 29.
47. Ibid.

if a private land trust does not satisfy its customers, it will go out of business.

The work of the Natural Lands Trust on the Fortescue glades in New Jersey demonstrates the effectiveness of a private land trust. The Fortescue glades are comprised of tidal creeks, ponds, oak-pine wetlands, and estuarine marshes, which are crucial winter habitat for hundreds of waterfowl species. After acquiring 956 acres and working with dozens of landowners to preserve 2,500 additional acres, the trust hired a full-time resident supervisor and staff to prepare a master inventory of the refuge, to improve wildlife habitat, and to curtail illegal hunting. The staff is also developing an integrated network of nature trails with observation blinds so that naturalists can observe wildlife in this unusually beautiful setting.[48]

It is unlikely that private land trusts could manage all critical wildlife habitat in the Yellowstone ecosystem in the same way that the Natural Lands Trust is managing the Fortescue glades. But private land trusts can manage crucial habitat according to the needs and peculiarities of the specific area. Game-animal herd size can be regulated by controlling the number of hunters. Trust managers can balance permission to hunt with the ungulate prey base necessary to sustain elk and wolf populations and maintain the habitat's carrying capacity. Human access to sensitive areas such as denning sites can be controlled. Critical habitat would not be endangered by budgetary incentives that encourage Forest Service bureaucrats to give priority to wasteful timber sales.

Timber Subsidies and Balanced Use

Although many Forest Service holdings are not considered critical for wildlife survival, they may still be important habitat. A valley floor with dense cover, for example, may be favored elk calving ground; a tributary to the Yellowstone River may provide riparian cover for trout; a meadow supporting choice bunch grasses may provide summer forage for antelope. Forest Service timber management practices on these lands must be reformed before more wildlife is harmed. Some wildlife already suffers from the side effects of clear-cutting and extensive road building.

48. Baden and Blood, "Troubled Wetlands."

Fisheries can also be hurt by the oversedimentation associated with constructing logging roads. Robert Herbst, executive director of Trout Unlimited, describes what happens:

> In most instances, timber-cutting requires a considerable expansion of the network of roads within a forest, exposing soils to erosion. Timber harvest on areas of steep slopes of unstable soils further exposes more land to the eroding forces of rain and gravity. The result is often a heavy influx of sediment into the area's streams and lakes, severely affecting fish spawning and water quality.[49]

Erosion from road building and other timber harvesting activities has damaging effects on other wildlife habitat as well. Randal O'Toole of Cascade Holistic Economic Consultants sums up his observations on the effects of timber management on wildlife:

> Forest Service officials claim that timber management benefits other resources such as recreation, wildlife, and water. . . . CHEC has examined these claims in many forest plans and found that the contrary is more likely to be true: timber management is detrimental to most nonmarket resources [such as wildlife] and greatly increases management costs.[50]

The Knutson–Vandenberg (KV) Act of 1930 is responsible for much of the destruction of wildlife habitat in the national forests in the Yellowstone ecosystem. Established to ensure that the Forest Service would reforest timbered land to obtain a sustained yield, the act allows the USFS to retain a percentage of its timber sales revenues to fund reforestation activities. While the receipts from timber sales are sent to Washington, KV money remains with the USFS. Mr. O'Toole estimates that between 25 and 35 percent of the KV funds "may include salaries, rents, and travel, that are highly discretionary and receive virtually no oversight from Congress or Office of Management and Budget."[51]

In effect, KV provides incentives to the USFS to maximize the volume, not the value, of timber sold. The result is that a lot of low-grade timber, such as subalpine fir and lodgepole pine is cut and sold.[52] The most efficient means for the USFS to harvest this timber is clear-

49. Robert L. Herbst, "Living Brightwater," *Trout,* Autumn 1985, p. 54.

50. Randal O'Toole, "Maximum Forest Budget Means Maximum Timber Sale Losses," pp. 11–12, Available from CHEC, P.O. Box 3479, Eugene, Oregon, 97403.

51. Ibid., pp. 2, 7.

52. Ibid., p. 2.

cutting. Sales of high-quality timber such as mature ponderosa and western larch are blended with timber of negative value to produce a positive sum for the buyer and more KV funds for the Forest Service.

This system affects wildlife habitat in a less obvious way. Terrain at lower elevations is characterized by deeper soil and less slope than are found at higher elevations. The lower valued timber species, like white fir and lodgepole pine, grow at higher elevations, on thin, less stable topsoil and on steeper slopes, making topsoil in these areas easy to dislodge once trees are removed. Therefore, damage to habitat and wildlife species can be intensified from road building, clearcutting, and subsequent erosion when these low-value timber species are harvested.

The incentives generated by the KV Act can create a vicious cycle. The cost of reforestation is likely to be higher on fragile slopes at higher elevations where low-quality timber is harvested. This requires additional KV funds. Because more KV collections will be needed to reforest high elevations, even more low-quality timber will have to be harvested to fund the reforestation budget.

CHEC'S Randal O'Toole has suggested that the Forest Service's budget be based on net revenues from timber sales instead of on volume of timber sold.[53] Under this proposal, selling timber of marginal quality would not benefit the Forest Service. Rather, selling easily accessible, higher quality timber would be encouraged—an environmentally and economically rational outcome. High capital expenditures for activities like road construction would eat into Forest Service revenue levels and would have to be justified economically.

Such a check on road construction would directly benefit wildlife, including wolves. A study conducted on wolf habitat in Wisconsin correlated the historical demise of wolves in the state to road densities that exceeded 1 mile per square mile of forest. Researchers found that higher mortality rates are not just an indication of loss of habitat from road construction. The disappearance of the wolf was more directly linked to human use of roads running through the wolf's range. Most often, wolves were killed by vehicles or were trapped or shot illegally by hunters.[54]

53. Ibid., pp. 16–17.
54. Richard P. Thiel, "Relationship Between Road Densities and Wolf Habitat Suitability in Wisconsin," Wisconsin Department of Natural Resources, Bureau of Endangered Resources, Madison, Wisconsin, 1984.

A study conducted on the Ontario–Michigan border near Sault Ste. Marie concludes:

> Both this study and the work of Thiel indicate that where road densities exceed about 0.6 km/square km [approximately 1 mile/square mile], wolf populations cannot sustain themselves. Though official definitions of roads may vary between areas, the available data suggest that by evaluating road density one might obtain a preliminary estimate of the impact of development on already established wolf populations, or of the likelihood of re-establishing wolves in areas otherwise appropriate.[55]

Using the Michigan–Ontario study as a benchmark, we can see that current logging practices in parts of the Greater Yellowstone ecosystem result in road densities that would not lead to stable wolf populations. Bob Dennee, public relations director for the Gallatin National Forest, says that Gallatin timber harvesters generally plan "one mile of permanently maintained road per square mile of forest."[56]

Effective reform can reduce the number of roads; nevertheless, some roads will inevitably be built. In some instances, these roads might be closed after the area has been harvested. A road could be gated off to prevent traffic, or it could be reseeded after the logging operation is finished.

YELLOWSTONE WILDLIFE MANAGEMENT

Wildlife management in Yellowstone National Park has been a medley of changing politics and goals during this century. In the early 1900s, ranchers and public wildlife managers saw Yellowstone as hot pots, geysers, fertile streams, and splendid mountain ranges inside the park boundaries. They weren't aware that the ecosystem was a biological island whose significance reached into southwestern Montana, central Idaho, and northern Wyoming. Nor did they realize the importance of "bad predators" for maintaining healthy populations of "good animals." Ranchers and Yellowstone Park personnel envisioned an environment where livestock and desirable species of wildlife such as deer, elk, and bison could flourish, and they manipulated the Greater Yellowstone ecosystem to achieve that effect.

55. Jensen, Fuller, and Robinson, "Wolf Distribution," p. 6.
56. Bob Dennee, telephone interview with author, Bozeman, Montana, August 7, 1986.

With the proposal to reintroduce the wolf, the ideal of wildlife management in Yellowstone National Park has done a complete reversal since 1915 when wolf extermination measures were undertaken by rangers in the park. Those who believe that man and beast can live in harmony must realize that man has impacted the ecosystem too strongly to revert to a policy that is completely "natural." Many environmentalists favor reintroducing the wolf, but are opposed to wildlife management practices in Yellowstone National Park—practices they perceive as artificial. But how natural is anesthetizing a small pack of gray wolves in Minnesota or Canada, flying them to Yellowstone National Park and then releasing them with radio collars attached? At the same time, would environmentalists oppose replanting beaver habitat in northern Yellowstone Park on the grounds that doing so was "unnatural"?

The wolf recovery plan was approved by the U.S. Fish and Wildlife Service in August of 1987. The only hurdle left for the plan's implementation is that the National Park Service must write an environmental impact statement (EIS) before wolves can be reintroduced. However, soon after the recovery plan was approved, the Park Service stated that it would not write the EIS until the pro-livestock Wyoming congressional delegation backed the reintroduction plan.

Many environmental groups believe National Park Service chief William Penn Mott, Jr., was backpedaling because of the wolf pack (mentioned earlier in this chapter) that caused over $3,000 worth of damage to livestock in northern Montana during the spring and summer of 1987.

Wolf advocates are currently feeling the wear of a long battle that is two steps forward and one step back. But those favoring reintroduction would be wise to ask if wolves could survive in Greater Yellowstone. Currently, many government land use policies do not favor the wolf's presence. Environmental groups and concerned policy makers might use the delays to explore alternate wildlife management and resource policies or risk the possibility that wolves may not be able to survive in Greater Yellowstone.

6

OIL AND GAS DEVELOPMENT

Donald Leal
Geoffrey Black
John A. Baden

There is increasing evidence that oil and gas exploration and production can coexist with ecological integrity and high quality wildlife habitat.[1] The goal of this chapter is to explain how oil and gas production *and* environmental preservation can be fostered in Greater Yellowstone.

For years energy developers and environmentalists have battled over the development of energy resources in the Greater Yellowstone ecosystem. While natural resource conflicts among logging, road construction, resort development, livestock grazing, and oil and gas exploration affect the management of Greater Yellowstone, oil and gas exploration is probably the least understood and most bitterly contested of those disputes.

Since 1981, environmentalists have fought vigorously against energy development in the national forests surrounding Yellowstone National Park, contending that oil and gas exploration is "necessarily" harmful to the environment. They believe that oil and gas exploration and production are major threats to the Greater Yellowstone ecosystem and should at least be severely curtailed and preferably should

---

1. See, for example, John Baden, "Oil and Ecology Do Mix," *Wall Street Journal* lead op. ed., February 11, 1987 and also John Baden and Richard Stroup, "Saving the Wilderness: A Radical Proposal," *Reason*, 13 (July 1982).

117

be banned. Oil and gas developers contend that new energy development will be managed so as to produce little more than temporary and minor disturbances to the environment. They consider the large park areas that have been withdrawn from production to be exorbitant and see some of the operating restrictions they must work under as unreasonably severe. As oil imports rise toward 50 percent of total U.S. oil consumption, oil developers worry about the reserves left fallow because of public lands' being placed off limits to exploration and development (although at the prices prevailing during the latter part of 1988, few of these wells were economically viable).

Few would disagree that there are critical areas surrounding Yellowstone Park in which the risks of permanent environmental damage are too high to warrant commercial disturbance by oil and gas developers. In areas such as grizzly bear population centers, or the Island Park geothermal area, development should be prohibited. However, in Greater Yellowstone we believe protection efforts have been carried too far. In addition to the 2.5 million acres of Yellowstone and Grand Teton national parks, at least 45 percent of the national forest land surrounding Yellowstone National Park is, for all practical purposes, closed to energy development. This situation disregards the possibility that these resources can be sensitively developed. Restricting *all* development on these lands falsely implies that even minor and temporary environmental disturbances have infinite costs.

Restrictions on oil and gas exploration and production in Greater Yellowstone involve more than closing off land to development. Lengthy delays in processing lease applications and in activating current leases also arbitrarily inhibit activity. For example, a 1985 Montana district court decision indefinitely set aside all oil and gas leases on the Gallatin National Forest pending completion of a detailed environmental impact statement. Judging from past experience in the Rocky Mountain region, this delay could last for several years.

Environmentalists have also been influential in delaying oil and gas exploration efforts. Marathon Oil Company worked more than two years to overcome legal blockades before being allowed to drill an exploratory well in Shoshone National Forest. Under existing institutional arrangements, oil developers and environmentalists have been relying heavily on the courts and the legislature to protect their particular interests. Money spent by warring interests on lobbying legislatures and conducting legal battles could have been used to develop new, safer methods of energy extraction and to purchase endangered wildlife habitat.

Energy developers believe that large areas of the Greater Yellowstone ecosystem are highly likely to have large reserves of oil and gas. The southern part of the ecosystem lies on the Western Overthrust Belt of western Wyoming, southeastern Idaho, and northeastern Utah. The overthrust belt is part of a much larger geologic province, exhibiting large-scale folded and faulted rocks containing large traps in which oil and gas may have accumulated. The Western Overthrust Belt is thought to contain up to 7.5 billion barrels of oil and 30 trillion cubic feet of gas in Wyoming, Utah, and Idaho alone. The Wyoming portion of the overthrust belt, just south of the Greater Yellowstone, has been the site of large discoveries of oil and gas. Exploration activity has occurred in the northern part of the ecosystem near Bozeman, Montana, and commercial production has taken place in the eastern portion of the ecosystem near Cody, Wyoming. Farther north, the Canadian portion of the overthrust belt produced more oil and gas than any other part of Canada.

AN OVERVIEW OF OIL AND GAS LEASING IN NATIONAL FORESTS

The largest landholder in Greater Yellowstone is the federal government, which owns 95 percent of the land, held by the U.S. Forest Service (USFS), the National Park Service (NPS), the Bureau of Land Management (BLM), and the U.S. Fish and Wildlife Service. Typically, the National Park Service—custodian of Yellowstone and Grand Teton national parks—is the best-known landlord, but most of Greater Yellowstone is under the jurisdiction of the U.S. Forest Service. There are six regional forests in the region: Gallatin, Targhee, Shoshone, Bridger-Teton, Beaverhead, and Custer.

The principal agencies governing oil and gas leasing on the national forests are the BLM, which manages subsurface resources, and the USFS, which manages the surface resources. Under the Mineral Leasing Act of 1920 and the Mineral Leasing Act Amendments of 1947, the BLM has the authority to issue and cancel leases for oil and gas exploration and development. Lease applications on national forests are forwarded to the USFS for review and for recommendations to protect surface resources. Although the law does not require it, the BLM generally accepts Forest Service recommendations.

The passage of numerous environmental laws during the 1960s and 1970s, including the Wilderness Act of 1964, the Wild and Scenic Rivers Act of 1968, the National Environmental Policy Act of 1969, and the Endangered Species Act of 1973, meant that extensive environmental reviews and assessments became a routine part of oil and gas leasing on federal lands. Additionally, the governing federal land agents were now authorized to impose whatever restrictions thought necessary to ensure areas were protected from potential damage from oil and gas operations. By agreement with the BLM, the USFS was now responsible for ensuring private compliance with environmental legislation in the national forests.

Typically, after receiving lease applications on national forests, the Forest Service conducts an environmental review to determine areas of potential concern. These reviews, which generally include preparing an environmental assessment, are conducted either for an entire Forest Service region or, more typically, for an individual national forest. The environmental assessment identifies sensitive areas, either where no leases should be issued or where restrictions should be attached to leases to ensure that any exploratory activity complies with environmental laws.

In Greater Yellowstone, the Forest Service's operating stipulations for leases often include seasonal restrictions to protect recreational use or big-game breeding or calving. The most restrictive stipulation is "no surface occupancy," which prohibits any surface activity on the leased land, including drilling. The Forest Service forwards its recommendations to the BLM for review. If the BLM has no objections to the Forest Service's designated leasing areas or recommended lease stipulations, the lease is sold.

Another round of environmental review is begun when a leaseholder files for a permit to drill on national forest land. Before the well is permitted, the Forest Service performs another, site-specific, environmental assessment. If significant impacts from drilling activities are identified, the assessment is upgraded to a full-scale environmental impact statement (EIS). The Forest Service will then stipulate surface activity restrictions, such as limitations on access, drilling, and reclamation procedures, to ensure that the National Environmental Policy Act, the Endangered Species Act, and other applicable laws are not violated. If drilling is expected to occur in habitat that is occupied by threatened or endangered species—in Greater

Yellowstone, grizzly bear, bald eagle, or peregrine falcon—all proposed drilling activity must be approved by the U.S. Fish and Wildlife Service.

Public lands can be closed to leasing by a number of mechanisms, of which the two most important are "formal" and "administrative" withdrawals. In formal withdrawals, public lands are closed to oil leasing primarily through an act of Congress or a decision by a federal agency. The fastest growing type of formal legislative withdrawals is set-asides for wild and natural areas, such as those lands affected by the Wilderness Act of 1964. Administrative withdrawals generally result from land management decisions by public land use agencies, such as the USFS or BLM. Almost all such decisions are made at the local agency level, with no requirement that they be publicly announced. The amount of public land affected by these decisions is difficult to estimate, as numbers must be gleaned from Forest Service forest plans and BLM resource area plans. Thus, the acreage we report as closed by administrative withdrawals is probably understated.

Under the present federal onshore leasing program, tracts (which average 2,000 acres) are leased competitively or noncompetitively. To date, only noncompetitive leases have been issued in Greater Yellowstone.[2] The federal government's standard practice is to issue noncompetitive leases in areas, such as Yellowstone, where no commercial quantities of oil and gas have yet been discovered.

OIL AND GAS CONSTRAINTS IN GREATER YELLOWSTONE

By mid-1986, the land unavailable to oil and gas leasing on national forests surrounding Yellowstone National Park totaled nearly 4.4 million acres (see Table 6–1). The restricted land included designated wilderness areas, wilderness study areas, wild and scenic rivers, and other special situations (see Table 6–2 for land withdrawals in Shoshone National Forest).

Land withdrawals in Greater Yellowstone reflect a nationwide trend. When the Wilderness Act was passed in 1964, it immediately set aside 9.1 million acres of national forest land; since that time, the wilderness preservation system has increased almost tenfold and now con-

2. D. L. Leedy, L. W. Adams, and L. E. Dove, *Environmental Conservations and the Petroleum Industry* (Columbia, Maryland: National Institute for Urban Wildlife, 1985), p. 36.

Table 6–1.   Land Withdrawn from Leasing in Greater Yellowstone.

National Forest	Total Acreage	Acreage Unavailable for Leasing
Gallatin	1,735,412	821,374
Shoshone	2,433,125	1,498,135
Targhee	1,854,240	642,845
Bridger-Teton	2,740,765	946,852
Custer (Beartooth district only)	587,487	351,641
Beaverhead (Madison district only)	426,779	105,000
Totals	9,777,808	4,365,847

Table 6–2.   Acreage Not Available for Leasing in Shoshone National Forest.

Category	Acreage Unavailable for Oil and Gas Leasing	Percent of Total
Designated Wilderness*	1,379,048	92.0
Wilderness Study Areas**	14,700	1.0
Dunoir Special Area**	28,987	1.9
Grizzly Bear Situation I**	66,650	4.5
Wild and Scenic River**	6,660	.5
Research natural areas*	1,680	.1
Beartooth Highway withdrawal*	410	.02
Total	1,498,135	

* Legislatively withdrawn
**Miscellaneous areas totaling 117,000 acres

Source: U.S. Department of Agriculture, U.S. Forest Service, *Shoshone National Forest Land and Resource Management Plan* (Cody, Wyoming: USDA Forest Service, Rocky Mountain Region, January 1986).

sists of nearly 90 million acres. The USFS and BLM have another 35 million acres under study for wilderness designation. When national parks, national wildlife refuges, Alaska set-asides, and miscellaneous federal lands are included in the total of protected lands, a whopping 319 million acres, 45 percent of all federally owned land, have been removed from energy development.[3]

Energy exploration and development on federal lands have been

3. Chevron USA (Paper for the Bureau of Land Management and the Wyoming Game and Fish Department, Rock Springs, Wyoming, July 26, 1982).

constrained in other ways. For example, in addition to officially with-drawing federal lands from leasing, the Forest Service can impose a no surface occupancy restriction on an area. Under this restriction, developers can still reach a target beneath a sensitive area through directional drilling from a nonrestricted area. When the geology is as complex, however, as in the Western Overthrust Belt, slant drilling becomes prohibitively expensive. The 1982 paper by Chevron USA estimates that slant drilling would cost almost 40 percent more than the average for a wildcat well.[4] Thus the no surface occupancy re-striction can amount to a *de facto* withdrawal of federal lands.

A further constraint involves significant delays in permitting on federal lands. Even after firms secure valid leases, they cannot begin operations until an application for permit to drill (APD) is approved. The American Petroleum Institute, the General Accounting Office, and Everett and Associates each cite substantial and increasing reg-ulatory delays in handling APDs.[5] Even under "normal" circum-stances, an APD on federal lands in the Rocky Mountains required an average of sixty-seven days to process compared to an average of fourteen days on private land in the same region.[6] (By law, the pro-cess is supposed to be completed in thirty days.)

A recent U.S. district court decision threatens to further restrict the federal leasing system. In 1982 the Montana Wilderness Association filed suit over leasing practices on two national forests, and in 1985 Judge Paul Hatfield suspended all leases in Montana's Gallatin and Flathead national forests pending completion of "adequate" prelease environmental impact statements (EISs). The Montana court found in *Conner v. Burford* that:

> In this case, the leasing stage is the first stage of a number of successive steps which clearly meet the "significant effect" criterion to trigger an EIS. . . . Subsequent site-specific analysis, prompted by a proposal from a lessee of one tract, may result in a finding of no significant impact.

4. Ibid.

5. American Petroleum Institute, *Should Federal Onshore Oil and Gas Be Put Off Limits?* (Washington, D.C.: American Petroleum Institute, August 1985), p. 7.

6. American Petroleum Institute, *Analysis of the Processing of Permits to Drill on Federal Lands,* Research Study 029 (Washington, D.C.: American Petroleum Institute, 1982); GOA, "Actions Needed to Increase Federal Onshore Oil and Gas Exploration and Development," EMD-81-40, 1981; Everett and Associates, *Analysis of Delays in the Processing of Appli-cations for Permit to Drill and Prestaking Clearance Applications* (Washington, D.C.: Everett and Associates, 1981).

Obviously, a comprehensive analysis of cumulative impacts of several oil and gas development activities must be done before any single activity can proceed. Otherwise, a piecemeal invasion of the forests would occur, followed by the realization of a significant and irreversible impact.[7]

Each EIS had to include an assessment of the environmental impact, including the number of wells to be drilled and their potential damage, before a lease would be issued.

There are at least three problems with this requirement. First, trying to estimate the potential locations of drill sites is next to impossible without preliminary exploration.[8] Second, figures based on historical national averages that approximate activities in the Rockies indicate that the chance of drilling an exploratory well that results in an oil or gas find that can be commercially produced is less than 2 percent (see Table 6–3). With such a low probability of finding energy, it is extremely wasteful to tie up resources to conduct an intensive EIS on activities that are likely to do no harm.

Third, requiring an EIS at this early stage is an unnecessary addition to the environmental review process. Following a lease issuance, every proposed activity of a developer generates a site-specific environmental review. Any surface-disturbing activity must meet National Environmental Policy Act standards, and on the vast majority of leases, the U.S. Fish and Wildlife Service can terminate any activities detrimental to threatened or endangered species. The 1985 ruling does not enhance environmental protection.

Table 6–3. Historical Probability Estimates of Oil and Gas Development.

Activity	Probability
Exploratory drilling	25%
Discovery of oil and gas	10%
Development	1–2%

SOURCE: U.S. Department of Agriculture, U.S. Forest Service, *Oil and Gas Activity in the Northern Region* (Washington, D.C.: U.S. Forest Service, 1984).

7. *Conner v. Burford*, 605F Supp. 107 (D. Mont. 1985) *Conner, et al. v. Burford*, and *Mountain States Legal Foundation, et al.*, Cir. No. 85-3935, U.S. Court of Appeals for the Ninth Circuit, March 1986.

8. American Petroleum Institute, *Processing of Permits*, p. 1, Preliminary Exploration.

Although the ruling in *Conner v. Burford* applies only to leasing on two forests in Montana, environmental groups had hoped that the case would set a precedent for leasing processes on all national forests. Because the USFS and the BLM have applied the decision only to the sites specified in the case, environmentalists have turned to Congress for relief. The Sierra Club has taken the lead in a congressional campaign designed to establish "more precise" statutory requirements for preleasing environmental review. Under the Sierra Club's plan, adequate public notice and participation would be required in sensitive leasing decisions, and areas unsuitable for leasing would be identified and removed from consideration. This differs significantly from current practice in which decisions to remove areas from the leasing process are not made at this stage. The rationale for this procedure is that the decision to remove an area requires information that is not available at this stage, such as the precise location of a proposed activity and the feasible options available for mitigating disturbances. In addition, the USFS would be given responsibility to lease its own land, rather than just to advise the BLM; the USFS would be required to consult with other resource agencies, including the National Park Service and state wildlife agencies.

In addition to contending with obstructions to leasing, energy developers have also been increasingly hampered by court delays over proposed oil and gas activities *after* valid leases have been secured. In 1983 Marathon Oil proposed an exploratory well on its lease on the North Fork of the Shoshone River near the eastern edge of Yellowstone National Park. The USFS and BLM prepared an environmental impact statement and found that, under certain restrictions, the well would create only a temporary disturbance. The agencies concluded that Marathon would have to observe seasonal restrictions on drilling activity to protect big game and recreational use. Marathon chose to transport all equipment and personnel to the site by helicopter rather than build access roads. Hence, the potential for disturbance was further minimized. If the test well proved successful, subsequent activities would have to meet strict environmental standards. Development of the lease could be halted, for example, if the U.S. Fish and Wildlife Service determined that further activity jeopardized threatened or endangered species or their habitat.

Nevertheless, some local residents and environmental and sportsman groups attempted to block the well, concerned about what they perceived as potentially adverse impacts on elk and bighorn sheep. At the end of a two-year court battle, the Wyoming district court reaffirmed Marathon's right to drill on their lease. The company finally began drilling in 1985 with no degradation to wildlife and habitat. After the exhaustive legal battles, the well was found to be dry.

AN OPPORTUNITY FOREGONE: DEVELOPMENT OF ENERGY RESOURCES IN GREATER YELLOWSTONE

Some environmentalists consider land denial and severe restrictions on public land use the only ways wildlife can be protected. But oil and gas activity can be controlled to ensure that disturbances to the environment are temporary and minor. A host of case studies support this claim.

Studies on the extent of wildlife disturbance from oil and gas operations have provided important information on the potential for cooperative arrangements between energy developers and wildlife managers. For example, one group of studies relates to elk and petroleum operations in Michigan and Wyoming. In Michigan, James Everett Knight found that exploration and development caused only "short-term localized impacts" to elk in the area. The animals tended to return to drilling areas two weeks to a month after drilling was completed, and tolerated production more than exploratory drilling. Lightly traveled roads did not appear to be a threat to the elk.[9] In another study of the same elk herd, Knight concluded that seismic investigation for energy caused more disturbance to elk than did exploratory drilling and that serious harm was likely *only* if the animals were disturbed during rutting and calving periods.[10] This suggests that by timing seismic activity to avoid the rutting and calving periods, harm to the elk can be reduced or avoided.

In a study of the Snyder River basin in Wyoming, state wildlife biologists Bruce K. Johnson and Dave Lockman found that denying essential habitat to elk would place serious stress on the animals and decrease their chances for winter survival. However, Johnson and Lockman also found that the disturbance from exploration was min-

9. James Everett Knight, "Effect of Hydrocarbon Development on Elk Movements and Distribution in Northern Michigan" (Ph.D. dissertation, University of Michigan, Ann Arbor, 1980).
    10. Ibid.

imized by cooperation between companies and the state of Wyoming. Careful selection of access roads and the drill pad helped minimize the disturbance.[11]

As knowledge in this area expands to include other species and situations, new methods for reducing the possibility of disturbance will evolve. Entrepreneurs will have incentives to develop new methods for environmentally sensitive exploration and development of oil and gas. But research and development of these new methods will best occur with the cooperation of industry and environmental concerns. A willingness to allow carefully controlled petroleum operations in environmentally sensitive areas would clearly foster such research.

There are approaches to oil and gas activities that allow developers to minimize environmental disturbances during all phases of the development process, from drilling to production and reclamation.

During the drilling of an oil or gas well, numerous procedures can maintain the environmental integrity of the drill site and surrounding area. On the surface, the drilling pad is small (from 1 to 5 acres) and is essentially self-contained. Noise and air emissions are strictly controlled, safety valves and seals are installed to stop the flow of unwanted fluids or gases to the surface, and dikes and protective liners control spills. The drilling fluid used to lubricate the drill bit and circulate rock cuttings to the surface also seals off and protects the penetrated rock layers from contamination. Protective pipe and casing prevent communication between rock strata, ensuring that fresh water zones will not be damaged by zones containing saline water.

If the well is found to be noncommercial, the hole is sealed and all equipment is removed. The site is reclaimed by restoring the original contours of the land, replacing topsoil, and reseeding with native vegetation. When these reclamation procedures are carried out, it is often difficult to find an abandoned well site.

Reclamation efforts have been particularly successful in the Rocky Mountains, an area known for its pristine environment. Several successful projects within or close to the Greater Yellowstone ecosystem show the success of reclamation.

---

11. Bruce K. Johnson and Dave Lockman, "Response of Elk During Calving to Oil/Gas Activity in Snyder Basin, Wyoming," report A-1012, Wyoming Game and Fish Department, Cheyenne, Wyoming, 1980.

In 1978, Getty Oil leased a site in the Palisades, located in the Bridger-Teton National Forest in southwestern Greater Yellowstone. The lease was approved just before the area was recommended for Wilderness Study Area designation. An exploratory well was completed on the site in 1979, but no commercial quantities of oil were discovered. After completing the drilling, Getty worked closely with Forest Service personnel to reclaim the site, including revegetating the access road that had been built in extremely rugged country with slopes exceeding 70 percent in places. In 1981, Shell Oil Company reexcavated the reclaimed road and drilled a well a quarter-mile from the original Getty well. That well was also dry, and the area was again reclaimed, the original contours reestablished, the topsoil replaced, and native vegetation reseeded. According to one Forest Service engineer, the site is a "showcase" reclamation project where "you have to know where the site is to find it."[12]

Other examples of successful reclamation can be found near Grand Teton National Park in Wyoming. In 1984, Congress designated nearly 2,300 acres just east of the park as the Gros Ventre Wilderness Area. Two exploratory well sites drilled in the 1950s are located within the wilderness area. Even without any reclamation efforts by the original operators, the two sites had returned to their natural condition and were found to be suitable for wilderness designation.[13] A few miles south of Grand Teton in Little Granite Creek Canyon, there is a 5,500-foot exploratory well that Sinclair Oil drilled in the 1940s. Like the wells in the Gros Ventre Wilderness Area, the area has reclaimed itself, leaving no vestige of the drilling activity. At least seven other wells have been drilled in the area as recently as the 1960s, including one near-commercial gas well that reached a depth of 16,000 feet. Unaided by any reclamation efforts, restoration is so complete that one would be hard pressed to find any trace of disturbance.

Development of oil and gas resources in pristine areas can be carried out in a careful manner. During the past ten years, petroleum exploration and/or production has been conducted in sixty-two wildlife refuges and waterfowl production areas across the country. On the

12. Ken Baskin, "The Tug of War for the Wilderness," *Sun Magazine,* Autumn, 1985, p. 7.

13. Department of the Interior, Bureau of Land Management memorandum 3100 (410): Trip Report–Wellsite Review, Gros Ventre Wilderness, Rock Springs, Wyoming, August 12, 1985.

Arkansas National Wildlife Refuge in Texas, for example, an oil field with thirty-five producing wells has been operating without detriment to the environment for more than fifty years. The area is home to ten endangered species, including the peregrine falcon, the southern bald eagle, and the whooping crane.[14]

On Alaska's Kenai National Moose Range, the Swanson River field has been operating since Atlantic Richfield Company struck oil there in 1957. Refuge officials enforce strict controls. For example, each operator must put up a $50,000 bond to ensure that an area will be properly reclaimed once operations cease. There are currently fifty production and injection wells, and over 1,500 miles of seismic survey have been conducted. The refuge's moose population has suffered no ill effects from the oil and gas production and has, in fact, been steadily growing. The Swanson field also illustrates an important characteristic of most oil and gas activity—that much of it is not land intensive. Only 22,000 acres of the Kenai's 1.74 million acres have been temporarily disturbed by oil and gas activity.[15]

On the largest private refuge in the United States, the Rob and Bessie Welder Wildlife Foundation Refuge near Stinton, Texas, an oil and gas field has been operating since the 1930s. Under cooperative management by Marathon and other companies with the Welder Foundation, no significant disturbance has been apparent among the 400 types of birds and 180 species of mammals, reptiles, and amphibians. As the foundation director states, "The type of operation Marathon has practiced has not harmed the area's ecology or habitat. The care with which they monitor each lease has allowed the native vegetation to prosper within a few feet of the wells."[16] Revenues from the wells have contributed to research on wildlife and to the operation of the foundation.

Like the Welder Foundation Refuge in Texas, the Paul J. Rainey

14. Mark Ethridge and Ursula Guerrieri, "Survey of Oil and Gas Activities on Federal Wildlife Refuges and Waterfowl Production Areas," American Petroleum Institute Research Paper 031, Washington, D.C., September 1983; Max Pitcher, Conoco Inc., Statement before the Senate Energy and Natural Resources Subcommittee on Public Lands and Reserved Water, Washington, D.C., September 23, 1982.

15. "Environmental Concern Brings New Knowledge of Alaska Back Country," *Alaska Construction and Oil*, May 1979.

16. Keith Hay, American Petroleum Institute, "Can Energy Development Be Made Compatible with Protection of Wildlife Refuges?" (Remarks before the National Audubon Society's Alaska Regional Conference, Anchorage, Alaska, May 9, 1981).

Sanctuary Preserve in Louisiana is operated by a private nonprofit environmental organization, the National Audubon Society. The Rainey Preserve is a sterling example of how the benefits of energy development can be harmonized with environmental goals. This 26,161-acre preserve is an important wintering area for birds on the Mississippi flyway and is a nesting ground for ducks, geese, and terns. The area is home to minks, otters, white-tailed deer, and other mammals, as well as alligators.

The oil industry has operated in the Rainey Preserve for over twenty-five years under guidelines developed by the Audubon Society to protect the wildlife and its habitat. An Audubon pamphlet describes the situation: "There are oil wells in Rainey which are a potential source of pollution, yet Audubon experience in the past few decades indicates that oil [gas] can be extracted without measurable damage to the marsh. Extra precautions to prevent pollution have proven effective."[17] Rainey's wildlife managers have even used some of the petroleum industry's activities to improve habitat. When exploratory wells are abandoned, for example, the sites are converted into freshwater ponds that provide new habitat for the recovery of alligator and catfish populations.

A key benefit of the arrangement is that the Audubon Society has a significant source of revenue. Audubon collects nearly $1 million each year in royalties from the gas wells. With these revenues, Audubon maintains the ecological integrity of the Rainey Preserve and purchases endangered wildlife habitat elsewhere.[18]

This cooperative spirit is not found on national forest lands. Instead, environmentalists and energy developers are frequently locked into uncompromising adversarial positions over land use with the Forest Service serving as referee. We next explore improvements to this situation.

FOREST SERVICE INCENTIVES AND INFORMATION: IMPLICATIONS FOR SENSITIVE DEVELOPMENT

When environmentally sensitive oil and gas development is possible, the country is worse off if areas are arbitrarily set aside. Americans

17. John Baden and Richard Stroup, "Saving the Wilderness: A Radical Proposal," *Reason,* 13 (July 1981).

18. Baden and Stroup, "Saving the Wilderness," pp. 28–36.

are denied the opportunity to obtain more sources of domestic oil and gas, while a relatively small number of wilderness advocates receive special benefits. Unfortunately, current government policies ensure that we are arbitrarily withdrawing land from energy development at great cost to the taxpayer.

The Forest Service's response to proposed oil and gas drilling is significantly different from its attitude toward timber production. The agency maintains that if more noncommodities such as wilderness, wildlife, and other outdoor recreational opportunities are to be supplied, oil and gas must be "sacrificed." The Forest Service claims that although thousands of acres are affected each year by logging and extensive roading, lumbering is *beneficial* to wildlife. Many wildlife biologists and natural scientists have demonstrated that this is not the case, particularly in the Rocky Mountain region.[19]

We are left with a puzzle. Why do governmental agencies perpetuate environmentally destructive and financially costly logging in the Rockies, while precluding environmentally safer and economically more beneficial oil and gas developments?

Logging is an important source of jobs in many communities in or near Greater Yellowstone. To maintain the level of activity and support jobs, the logging fraternity has become increasingly well organized and adept at exercising political muscle. In 1985, for example, when Forest Service plans proposed a reduction in timber cuts, the citizens of Livingston, Montana, a town of 7,000, produced nearly 500 people to protest the cuts. The protesters included not only loggers, mill workers, and equipment dealers, but also grocers, insurance agents, filling-station operators, and other business people.

In marked contrast, the oil companies are not major employers in the area. Citizens believe that the local filling-stations' tanks will remain full even if exploration and development are blocked in the nearby national forest.

To understand why this disparity occurs when the Forest Service manages resources on our public forests, consider the incentives which

19. For example, Montana fish and game biologists found problems with sedimentation in the streams of the Flathead National Forest due to roads and clear-cuts. The National Wildlife Federation conducted a study in Bitterroot National Forest and found that only 35 percent of harvested areas had been successfully reforested, spelling trouble for resident elk and bear populations. Also see Dieter Mahlein, "Will Forest Plans Enhance Deer and Elk Habitat?" *Forest Watch* (April 1986), pp. 17–21.

affect resource decisions. The Forest Service operates with incentives different from those in a free-market structure. There are no markets for recreational uses such as fishing and hunting on Forest Service lands. Recreational resources are "free." As a result, the USFS uses arbitrary estimates of value, producing numbers that are cranked into elaborate models used to allocate various resources in the forest in ten-year increments. Using these economically unjustified numbers for all resources and activities that compete with timber production, the USFS "justifies" their favored timber production projects.

This tendency of the Forest Service to favor logging, even on marginally productive areas, is due to the way the agency's budget is prepared. Currently, the Forest Service ensures itself a budget increase if it emphasizes timber production, including such ancillary items as reforestation and road building—items that ensure steady budget increases. In the plan for the Gallatin National Forest, for example, nearly half of the total budget is allocated to timber production and road building. The amount allocated to fish and wildlife is 4 percent; minerals (including oil and gas) receive 3 percent. The budget incentive has a very different effect on the production of timber than it does on the production of fish, wildlife, and oil and gas.

The incentive for the Forest Service to maximize its budget also works to severely restrict oil and gas activity. The Forest Service spends little on activities connected to oil and gas production. With timber production, the Forest Service carries out budget boosting activities like reforestation and road building, but the agency's role in oil and gas is negligible. Energy development provides little, if any, justification for budget growth.

Another factor is the agency's opportunity to enhance its political support and discretionary power. As economist Gary P. Libecap notes:

> The Forest Service makes land allocation decisions both to build and maintain favorable political support for budget requests from interest groups and Congress and to meet internal bureaucratic management goals. These allocations imply broad discretionary authority by the agency over its output. Accordingly, the resource uses selected will be those that maintain or enhance bureaucratic control, *ceteris paribus*.[20]

20. Gary P. Libecap, "Regulatory Constraints on Oil and Gas Production on Forest Service and BLM Lands," in R. Deacon and M. Bruce Johnson, eds., *Forestlands: Public and Private* (Cambridge, Mass.: Pacific Research Institute for Public Policy, Ballinger Publishing, 1985), p. 139.

Oil and gas development detracts from the Forest Service's power to grant favors. Leasing is initiated by firms and the Forest Service merely responds to corporate decisions, an arrangement that diminishes the agency's authority over land use. The Forest Service can exert control over energy resources only by withdrawing land from production, imposing severe restrictions, and creating processing delays. When the agency prevents drilling, it prevents the acquisition of knowledge about how much the Forest Service land is worth in the marketplace, thus allowing the agency to make allocations for less profitable—and sometimes more environmentally threatening uses, such as clear-cutting timber.

Wilderness designation and the Wilderness Study Area procedure fit the Forest Service agenda nicely. Although the Wilderness Act allowed for exploration till 1984, the Forest Service effectively blocked such activity by imposing severe restrictions on potential developers. Hence, information on wilderness oil and gas potential is unavailable. As a bonus, the Forest Service was able to strengthen its political support from influential environmental groups.

HARMONIZING OIL AND GAS WITH ENVIRONMENTAL GOALS

The problems described above can be rectified. Typically, under Forest Service management, authority is separated from responsibility in land use decisions. The Forest Service has a residual claim in timber production; it has no such claim in oil and gas production since the agency does not benefit from any income. The size of the Forest Service's budget is relatively unaffected by the degree to which oil and gas development takes place. That is, the most significant returns from oil and gas activities are the royalties from producing wells, but these royalties go directly to the general treasury and not to the Forest Service budget. The agency increases its budget by imposing costly constraints on oil and gas activity. When the Forest Service is not fiscally accountable, it can "sacrifice" wildlife and watershed to increased timber production. To foster accountability in land use decisions regarding oil and gas and to foster environmental values on our national forests, we advocate a move toward open, competitive leasing of multiple-use lands and toward privatization of existing wilderness with oil and gas potential.

There is a good example of how such a system could work, one that both protects the environment and allows oil and gas production. Long ago, National Audubon Society executives recognized that if a careful and ecologically sensitive plan was developed for producing oil and gas within their preserves, the subsequent revenues could be used to improve existing preserves and acquire rights to new ones. Likewise, oil and gas companies found innovative ways to operate on fragile lands at an extremely low cost for environmental protection.

When acting in the market, the Audubon Society is continually on the lookout for ways to protect wildlife through the purchase of land or easements. The organization faces strong incentives to minimize the impact of its requirements for environmental preservation and to allow profit-making activities, thereby minimizing the cost of what it obtains. In much the same way, the owner or developer of a forest faces strong incentives to find ways to sell easements of environmentally important portions of the land to conservation groups whenever the sale can be made at a low opportunity cost. Environmental groups such as the Nature Conservancy currently own title, easements, or covenants to several million acres of land. On its own land, Audubon cooperates with energy firms to raise revenue to help meet its goals of environmental preservation. This cooperation contrasts sharply with its behavior when the land in question is publicly owned. In the case of public lands, Audubon and other environmental groups take the position that no cost is too great to pay for habitat or wilderness values.

A simple way to resolve the disparity would be to transfer wilderness areas with oil and gas potential to the private sector. The Palisades Study Area of Targhee National Forest in Idaho, for example, is a wilderness highly likely to contain promising oil and gas resources in addition to its wilderness value. The area has been held in limbo as environmentalists and developers vie over its fate. The Palisades Study Area and similar lands could be turned into productive ones for both parties by placing them under the control of private, nonprofit organizations whose goal is to preserve the area's ecology and to acquire easements and land preserves around the public forests to protect the land. The new custodians of the land would have to consider potential income-producing opportunities. They would have to carefully weigh the benefits to be gained from oil and gas development. They would probably feel more secure about such development knowing that they could personally regulate the activity. The potential for acquiring additional income to purchase tracts in the eco-system would be a strong incentive to arrive at an agreement with oil and gas developers. Under such an arrangement, everybody wins.

For multiple-use forests, one way to mitigate conflicts is to open oil and gas leasing to competitive bids from all parties. In this way, environmentalists as participants in the bidding process are forced to select those areas they value the most. The leases should be structured so that the environmentalists could hold leases indefinitely without developing oil and gas reserves. They could also allow oil and gas development on their leases and implement their own stipulations for protection.

SUMMARY

The situation in Greater Yellowstone is one of continual conflict between oil developers and environmentalists, exacerbated by misinformation generated by the Forest Service. There is also a misperception of the degree to which oil and gas production actually disturbs the environ-ment. Many well-intentioned but uninformed environmentalists do not acknowledge that the industry has responded to the need for ecolog-ically safe development. The Santa Barbara oil spill of 1969 still haunts the industry.

Perceptions can and will change when environmentalists and the oil industry find opportunities for cooperative, mutually supporting agreements. But change is unlikely until incentives are in place to promote such arrangements. This leads us to the single most impor-tant cause of current restrictions on oil and gas activity on federal lands: the incentive structure of our public land agencies. We have focused on the dominant landowner in Greater Yellowstone, the U.S. Forest Service. We could apply the same analysis to the Bureau of Land Management and other public land agencies.

The Forest Service severely restricts the amount of oil and gas ac-tivity on the national forests, an action that is directly tied to the agency's primary goal of maximizing its budget by emphasizing tim-ber production. Under existing negative incentives, wildlife and watershed resources will be sacrificed in the pursuit of bigger budgets while oil and gas development will be curtailed with additional ar-bitrary land withdrawals and extensive processing delays.

Change in this situation requires fundamental shifts which would impose accountability in resource decision making. One modest way to initiate the change is to focus on areas with high environmental value that have the potential for energy development. If a private, nonprofit organization whose goal is to protect environmental integrity were to manage such an area, it would be able to collect economic rents from carefully selected and controlled commercial activities. Under this arrangement, there are incentives for protecting environmental values and for furthering environmental goals in the ecosystem by cooperating with developers in conducting safe development.

PART III

POLITICS AND ECOLOGICAL REFORM

7

WHAT WASHINGTON DOESN'T KNOW ABOUT THE NATIONAL PARK SYSTEM

Alston Chase

Shortly after the Second World War, as a teenager, I lived in Heidelberg, Germany, where my father, an army officer, was stationed with the forces of occupation. At that time a joke was making the rounds of the *Gästhauser* about two men fishing the Elbe River that divided East and West Germany.

Throughout the day the man on the west bank caught one fish after another, while the fisherman on the east bank didn't get a bite. As evening approached, the West German, having caught his limit, headed for home. As he was departing, the East German yelled to him in frustration,

"How can you catch your limit when I must go home skunked?"

"That's easy to understand," replied the West German. "The fish on your side of the river are afraid to open their mouths."

When we consider our national park system, we find other fish who are afraid to open their mouths. And the reasons for their silence may tell us something, not only about our national parks, but also, perhaps, about ourselves.

A good place to begin our story is the spring of 1973. At that time the National Park Service (NPS) was in political hot water, not unlike the position it is in today. Two years previously, it had terminated John and Frank Craighead's grizzly bear research because these noted biologists had opposed the closing of the open-pit garbage dumps where grizzlies had fed for nearly a century.

The government's reason for the firing, as Deputy Assistant Secretary of the Interior Curtis Bohlen explained to Republican senator Robert Griffin of Michigan at the time, was that the Craigheads had attempted "to extend their products of research into the realm of policy and management decision making," an action, according to Bohlen, that "goes beyond the normal prerogatives of a scientific endeavor." That is, while it was all right for the scientists to do research, it was *not* all right for them to draw conclusions from their research, nor to inform management of their conclusions. These are restrictions which engineers at Morton-Thiokol might have found familiar in the wake of the *Challenger* disaster.

Even more damaging to the reputation of the Craigheads in National Park Service circles was that their advice had turned out to be correct. Following closure of the dumps, bears wandered further in search of food, invading towns and campgrounds. To protect people from bears, the National Park Service began killing these animals in large numbers. Between 1969 and 1970 alone, at least 101 bears were (permanently) removed from the population.

The Craigheads, meanwhile, warned that these actions threatened to extirpate the entire grizzly population in the park. The biologists' criticisms inspired a national controversy. In 1973 a news release from the Fund for Animals announced, "The management program in Yellowstone is an extermination campaign designed, in part, to make the Park 'safe' for campers."

To quell criticism, Assistant Secretary of Interior Nathaniel Reed established an interagency grizzly bear research project, to be headed by a Fish and Wildlife Service biologist named Robert Finley.

However, Finley found one impediment after another blocking his research efforts. His study plans first had to be approved by the park superintendent, Jack Anderson. Anderson would not allow Finley to tag bears, a practice Finley believed essential if he was to discover any useful information. When Finley questioned this constraint, Anderson (not a scientist himself) replied, "There are other techniques for identifying individual bears without having unsightly streamers which were used in the past."

Anderson, mysteriously, was supported by A. Starker Leopold, the prominent biologist then advising the Park Service, and when Finley tried to complain directly to Assistant Secretary Reed, he received a letter of reprimand for not directing his complaint through "proper channels."

The interagency team was not allowed to have access to original data collected by past park researchers. When Finley complained, the team was prohibited from doing any research in the park at all, and Finley's assistant, Bob Phillips, was abruptly transferred to do coal-mining research. Finley's choice for a new assistant, biologist Jay Sumner, was disqualified by authorities because he once had worked for the Craigheads. When Finley complained again, he found himself looking for another job.

Yet three months after Finley had complained to Superintendent Anderson that restrictions placed on research rendered all grizzly studies meaningless, Assistant Secretary Reed wrote Democratic Senator Philip A. Hart of Michigan, "Monitored observations of grizzlies in the back country of Yellowstone National Park indicate a very healthy, viable population with an increase this year over last in the number of cubs produced."

There was, of course, no justification for this claim, and indeed, a 1974 investigation by the National Academy of Sciences revealed that the grizzly population, rather than increasing, was decreasing at an alarming rate.

This gap between what scientists find in the field and what reaches Washington was not merely a past phenomenon; it exists today and it is growing.

When I began research in Yellowstone in 1981, the Park Service, in its published literature, was claiming a grizzly population of 350 and a black bear population of 650. The actual number of grizzlies estimated by its own biologists, however, was at that time under 200, and the number of black bears biologists believed to inhabit the park was closer to 50 than 650. When I reported this misrepresentation in the *Atlantic Monthly,* park officials stopped using these numbers. Today, however, they claim a black bear population of 500. When I asked how they arrived at that number I was told, "Because it seems right."

The July/August 1986 issue of *National Parks,* an organ of the National Parks Conservation Association, reported that Yellowstone supports "2,000 mule deer, and hundreds of moose, (and) bighorn sheep." Yet these claims too rest on complete fabrications. Rather than 2,000 mule deer, researchers last winter found 76; rather than "hundreds" of bighorns, the recent census found 132. As no census of moose has ever been done, Yellowstone authorities have no idea of the size of that population, but no independent biologist in the country believes there is more than a handful left.

Assuming that Nathaniel Reed and the fact checkers of *National Parks* magazine are honorable people (and I think we must assume they are), how are we to explain these discrepancies? We can only infer that there is a persistent information gap between Washington and the field, a gap between what researchers are actually finding, and what is reported. That there is such a gap with respect to information about Yellowstone helps to explain the enormous public surprise at the revelations found in my book, *Playing God in Yellowstone*. But Yellowstone is not an isolated instance of this phenomenon. The numbers of elk in Mount Rainier and Rocky Mountain national parks are persistently underestimated. For years the impact of burros on bighorns in Death Valley and grasses in Grand Canyon was ignored. Park scientists' evaluations of the critical status of alligators and woodstorks in the Everglades were suppressed for years.

Within the national park system we find an explicit mechanism for preventing embarrassing information from escaping the parks. This mechanism consists of seven elements.

First, research in the national park system is, in agency jargon, "mission oriented." That means, in the words of Starker Leopold, who helped to frame current policies, the role of scientists "is that of service to the superintendents, and to park administration in general." This entails in practice that researchers report to the superintendent; they are graded by the superintendent; and may only publish findings with the approval of the superintendent.

Second, "raw" or uninterpreted data is decreed to be private property of the Park Service researcher, to which the public is deemed to have no right. Those journalists and university scholars who ask for this data are routinely denied it. I tried without success for six months, for instance, to obtain the original flight reports, with breakdown by counting units, of one winter's elk census.

Third, nearly all research done in national parks by university scientists is by contract between the National Park Service and the individual researcher or his institution. Awarding of contracts is "delegated to field level," that is, the park superintendent decides who shall get a contract.

Fourth, in every park the chief of resource management reports to the chief ranger.

Fifth, given the nearly total control of resource management and research by the chief ranger and superintendent, one would suppose these individuals would themselves be professionally qualified in appropriate scholarly fields. Unfortunately, that is not the case. The average ranger is no more scientifically trained than the average highway patrolman. According to a recent poll by the Association of Park Rangers, only 2.2 percent of superintendents' prior training and experience had been in resource management. Law enforcement, landscape architecture, and maintenance constitute the principal educational background of these people.

Sixth, little NPS research is published. When something is published, the Park Service pays a stipend to those who grade the work as part of the "peer review" process. This ensures the selection of reviewers in favor of agency authors. It also tempts editors of academic journals to publish Park Service-funded reviewers, biasing the peer review process against those critical of the NPS.

Seventh, the potentially excellent system called research grade evaluation, the process by which scientists are evaluated by academic peers rather than by their manager-supervisors, is seldom used. Today there are only 70 individuals on Research Grade Evaluation in the entire 337 units of the national park system.

In other words, the national park system is organized along feudal lines. It looks not unlike the map of France did before the reign of Louis XI. Just as fourteenth-century France was a country with independent duchies and a weak king, so the national park system today is one of independent regions and a weak director. Each region is autonomous; Washington has no "line authority" over them. Given the isolation of the major parks, superintendents of these areas are themselves largely independent with nearly total control over what information leaves the parks.

Paradoxically enough, the current system grew out of attempts to upgrade the national park science program in the sixties. In 1963 a committee of the National Academy of Science, known as the Robbins Committee, discovered that the Park Service science program was nearly nonexistent. Expenditures in 1962 for natural history research were only $28,000 out of a total NPS budget of $40 million—less, the Robbins Committee noted, than the Park Service spent building one outdoor comfort station. The agency was under strong public pressure to reform. Unfortunately, attempts to build up its research arm were thwarted by the ranger corps, who saw development of a highly professional cadre of scientists and resource managers as a threat to their control.

At that time the only way reformers could gain acceptance of any increase in the science budget was to put the research and resource management programs under the control of the rangers. That is what they did.

There are several consequences of this arrangement:

- Superintendents—that is, managers—can prohibit studies that might make their decisions look bad.
- They can influence the results of these studies.
- Bad news does not get to Washington and therefore is not subject to the scrutiny of top officials within the Interior Department and the administration, the national press corps, or the mainline environmental groups.

Without sound scientific information reaching Washington, the director of the Park Service cannot make intelligent decisions.

The absence of sound research that could serve as the basis for planning encourages the politicization of decision making, in which pressure groups, rather than data, determine the ultimate resolution of issues.

Researchers who challenge this system, or who have the misfortune to do research that embarrasses management, suffer as a consequence. Thanks to their differences with the Park Service, the Craigheads effectively found their careers ended; research monies and opportunities dried up. Robert Finley had to leave the government for a post at the University of Colorado. Bob Phillips, as we saw, was literally banished to the coal mines. Reilly McClellan, a resource manager at Glacier National Park, was fired from the Service because he objected to placement of a sewage treatment plant in a floodplain. A Park Service historian, Dr. T. Allan Comp, was recently forced to leave the

Service because he listed more buildings on the National Register of Historic Places than his superiors wished. Aubrey Haines, a historian in Yellowstone, was sent into premature retirement because his studies showed that the "national park idea" was not conceived in Yellowstone, as Park Service myth would have it, but was the product of a publicity campaign by the Northern Pacific Railroad.

Knowing the fact of such whistle-blowers has usually been sufficient to inhibit the research of other scientists who work in our national parks.

How can we improve this dreadful situation? I think the answer lies in understanding ecology.

The business of the Park Service is resource management. Resource management is the protection of ecosystems. An ecosystem is an organized network of land, water, mineral cycles, living organisms and their programmatic behavioral control mechanisms—comprising, but not limited to, living things. An ecosystem tends toward equilibrium and growth. It is not just forested regions, ponds, coral heads, or aquaria that are ecosystems. Human organizations are also ecosystems.

"In the broadest modern usage," writes the renowned ecologist Howard T. Odum, "systems that include humans, such as farms, industries, and cities, are also regarded as ecosystems." Each is characterized, he notes, by an "energy signature to which each ecosystem may develop organization to maximize power."

Ecosystems can also be considered closed-loop energy flows, where the energy quantity decreases as it passes through the system, but the energy quality increases. Indeed, Odum notes, "customarily people don't regard these flows as energy, but usually call them *information*. Flows of genes, books, television communications, computer programs, human culture, art, political interactions, and religious communications are examples of information.

Any human organization, therefore, can be considered an ecosystem. Organizations are systems of material and individuals, together with a program for ensuring stability of the organization and the enhancement of its power.

Our new, expanded definition of an ecosystem is also a good description of the Park Service. This agency does not just manage ecosystems, it *is* an ecosystem. And like any other ecosystem, it is a closed-loop flow of information, tending to stability and growth.

Now consider the behavior of any manager in such a human eco-system. As the actions of organizations have greater effect than the actions of single individuals, the decisions of the manager will affect many other people. The higher he is on the organizational ladder, the more people his decisions affect. Being human, the manager will have a desire to limit his accountability for his decisions: accountability to his superiors, to his subordinates, and to the public. How does he do that?

By limiting access to the information on which he bases his decisions.

As every manager at every level tries to limit access to the information upon which he acts, we can define a bureaucracy as an ecosystem tending to stability, growth, and control of the flow of information.

Now consider the role of science, or research, in such an organization. Science is the flow of information. In the long run, no organization survives unless this flow is constant, and of high quality. But in the short run, science is *destabilizing*. Results of scientific research are unpredictable, and therefore conflict with the requirements of stability of the system. It is natural for managers to try to control the results of research. If they succeed totally, then the flow of information stops altogether and the organization dies.

To put this another way, consider a graph, where "power" is plotted on the X axis and "truth" on the Y axis. What would a truth-power curve look like? It would have a negative slope, not unlike the demand curve: *ceteris paribus,* the more power, the less truth: an insight that applies to institutions as well as to individuals.

For institutions, the greater the power, the greater the control of information, and therefore the greater is the organization's capacity for self-deception. An extreme example is the Soviet Union, where nearly the entire society is one bureaucracy, and where the control of information is nearly total.

For individuals, the higher on the organizational chart one reaches within an organization, the less reliable information one is likely to receive from subordinates. Of course, high-level managers *think* that they are receiving reliable information, but that is because they confuse what they are told with the truth. That is, their subordinates tell them things, and they mistakenly suppose that because they are told many things they are being *informed*. They confuse memos with information.

Why do the leaders of bureaucracies receive unreliable information? Because lower echelon managers are not only anxious to cover the reasons for their own decisions, they also realize their promotions depend on telling their superiors what their superiors wish to hear. A dramatic, and tragic, example of this phenomenon was what happened to the flow of information to Washington from Vietnam during our involvement there. Field commanders did not tell Washington the truth; they told Washington what they thought Washington wanted to hear. An identical syndrome was recently exposed within the National Aeronautics and Space Administration (NASA).

Similarly, with the park system: Those who work in Interior in Washington do not learn what is going on in the parks; they learn what the park superintendents think those in Washington want to hear. So while the grizzly population may be plummeting, Washington will be told it is on the rebound; while mule deer numbers may be under 100, officials will be told there are 2,000, and so on.

Hence, we arrive at a sobering principle: The more powerful the individual, the less well informed he is likely to be.

When the head is cut off from the body, the body dies. How can we counter this tendency toward self-decapitation by human organizations?

A private enterprise in which management decisions are not made on the best available information eventually goes bankrupt. Government agencies, however, do not go bankrupt; they simply go on, failing to do their job.

This is the case with the National Park Service today. While it remains responsible for a system of 337 national parks and monuments, it no longer *manages* these places, because it lacks the information to do so. It lacks the information because it does not have a viable system for obtaining and disseminating it.

How can we remedy this? In an ideal world, information gatherers—that is, researchers—would be turned loose in the freest conceivable environment, to pursue the truth where they find it. Then the products of their labors would be as widely disseminated as possible, so that managers simply could not ignore their findings when making decisions.

And while this is not the ideal world, there are, I believe, six steps the National Park Service could take to provide managers with better information.

First, give the Park Service more independence and scrutiny by establishing it as an independent agency, away from Interior. Consideration should be given to turning it into a semi-independent trust, along the model of the Smithsonian. Also, to reduce the power of the rangers in controlling the direction of the Park Service, we should consider making the position of director subject to Senate confirmation.

Second, make management more sensitive to the contributions of science by professionalizing the ranger corps. That is, create a cadre of resource managers required to have graduate training in academic disciplines in order to advance through the ranks, and make resource management the only career ladder that reaches all the way to the top. Qualifications for superintendents—all of whom should be resource managers—should not be dissimilar from those we expect of college presidents and museum directors.

Third, to ensure that information flows from the parks to Washington, establish, in Washington, an office of natural and historical studies to serve as a research facility for natural and historic preservation. This office should have line authority over science and cultural programs in the national parks. However, interdisciplinary research stations should also be established in or near each major national park.

Fourth, to insulate research (the information flow) from managers, the chief of research in each national park should report, not to his superintendent, but to the district chief scientist, who in turn should report to Washington. Likewise, the chief of resource management in each national park should report to a regional chief of resource management, rather than to the park chief ranger.

Fifth, to ensure a continuous, open flow of information to the public, publication of research should be made an absolute requirement for all government scientists. The number of scientists on research grade evaluation should be multiplied at least fivefold. At least 25 percent of all researchers should be recruited from university ranks, and the Park Service should establish clear guidelines for public access to the fruits of government research. It should be emphasized that "mission-oriented research" does not mean "service to the superintendent," but rather "research directed to the problems of the park."

Sixth, to minimize the possibilities of co-option of university scholars, funding for independent research should come, not from contracts awarded by each park, as now, but by a grants program administered by peer review panels composed of nongovernmental scholars, just as the National Endowment for the Humanities, the National Endowment for the Arts, and the National Science Foundation do today.

Are these things likely to happen?

I'd like to refer back to the earlier analogy. The Park Service is an ecosystem, and like other ecosystems, it is not entirely self-contained. All terrestrial ecosystems derive their energy, ultimately, from the sun, and the source of renewal for each must come from the same source. When ecosystems age, they go through a series of stages known as seral succession, ultimately reaching what is called climax. In Yellowstone, that is the progression from grasslands, to shrub, to deciduous trees, to pine, and eventually to spruce and fir. At each stage the system contains less diversity than the earlier stage, and is less capable of sustaining life. It is a process of aging that can only be reversed by lightning or by man-caused fires. Fire reverses seral succession, returning forests to savannahs and recreating a more diverse, robust, and younger ecosystem.

Similarly, renewal of the National Park Service can only occur through outside intervention. If this agency is to do its job, we must hope lightning will strike it—and soon.

8

PLAYING GAMES AT *NEWSWEEK*

Gene Lyons

"I told him I was guilty only of oversimplifying his file almost beyond recognition," [Murray said.] "The real trouble came when Smithers, who had only skimmed O'Hearn's file, oversimplified my oversimplification, and then Woody, who hadn't read it at all, oversimplified Smithers' oversimplification."

"I tried to explain to O'Hearn that there are certain natural laws," Sayler said. "Control over the story increases in inverse ratio to knowledge of what actually went on. If he wanted to have some power over what was in the magazine, he should have had the sense to stay away from the scene of the event."

Calvin Trillin, Floater

In retrospect, my own experience with what one is tempted to call the Yellowstone Triangle—as in Bermuda Triangle—is not at all surprising. Now any halfway successful journalist has to have a bit of Swift's Lemuel Gulliver about him: a perpetual innocence, a bottomless capacity to be amazed. Yet even Gulliver had his moments of cynicism. Almost ten years before setting out to write a *Newsweek* cover story dealing with Alston Chase's *Playing God in Yellowstone*, I had decided as the result of an investigative foray into the Texas Education Agency that all public (and many private) organizations obey "three iron laws of bureaucratic inertia: to grow, to protect themselves from competition, and to ward off outside scrutiny." So I shouldn't have been caught off guard.

Nevertheless, my first encounter with the Yellowstone Triangle left me baffled, confounded, bewildered, and finally infuriated. Here was the National Park Service, of all things, doing a passable imitation of the Nixon White House under siege. The NPS hedged. They fudged. The floundered. They changed the subject. They invented oxymoronic jargon. "Natural regulation," indeed. Why not "spontaneous regimentation"? They called Alston Chase some very bad names. Why, they even went so far, as Gulliver himself would put it, "to say the thing which was not." Or as very literal-minded persons would have it, the National Park Service lied—not once, but many times.

Most distressing of all, however, was that my editors bought it. Enough of it anyway, to transform a pointed exposé of a classic bureaucratic screwup and cover-up into a typical newsmagazine pseudo-crisis piece, chock full of vague pieties about rescuing innocent nature from wicked man. "Can We Save Our Parks?" *Newsweek* wondered in a July 28, 1986, cover story illustrated by a full-face photograph of a grizzly bear. The subhead was a bit mysterious: "The Struggle Between Man and Beast." (What was afoot? Terrorist elk? A Grizzly Liberation Front?) But the message was familiar. "Not for the first time in our history, but perhaps for the last, we are at a turning point in our relationship to the wilderness," the magazine told its readers. Tough choices lay ahead; hard thinking had to be done. The question was whether or not Americans wanted to preserve their national parks, as *Newsweek* cleverly put it, "from the normal succession of wilderness from range to farm to its climax cover of asphalt." In short, Chicken Little goes backpacking.

If solemn, the dilemma as the magazine posed it was anything but serious—as readers of this volume no doubt recognize. After all, can anybody be found who's *against* saving our national parks? Indeed, the *Newsweek* cover represented a triumph for an aspect of its "mission" at which the National Park Service unquestionably excels: managing the press. What began as an inquiry into the disastrous impact of specific policy decisions *inside* Yellowstone turned into a consideration of broader threats to the park's integrity from *outside* its boundaries. The effect was not only to shift most of the blame, but actually to strengthen the Park Service's hand.

Save Yellowstone? Why, of course. And the agency of that salvation? Why the very government agency, if readers will forgive the pun, that created the mess to begin with: the National Park Service.

Who else? And what did the National Park Service need to accomplish this miracle? Lots and lots of money. "The price tag is rising," *Newsweek* concluded. "The assaults on a magnificent wilderness keep growing—and the nub of the controversy is whether America is willing to pay the price to save it." Or, as I put it in my subsequent letter of resignation from the magazine, "With the house on fire and the mortgage overdue, *Newsweek* recommends running out to borrow from your brother-in-law."

But I am getting ahead of myself. The point is that not for nothing do the stalwarts in the Ranger Rick outfits enjoy what a recent poll determined to be a 95 percent approval rating from the American people—the highest in the federal government. The NPS needn't perform brilliantly to earn this benign image. Almost literally, it came with the territory. After all, what Boy Scout hasn't dreamed of becoming a park ranger? And certainly the NPS is far from being the only government bureaucracy able to parlay its own failures into increased power and larger budgets. (I would argue that the entire educational establishment subsists in rather the same way—also the Pentagon.) Indeed, the same appearance of selflessness that leads nineteen out of twenty adults to think well of the National Park Service when they think of it at all, also gives the agency substantial leverage—amounting almost to immunity—in the national press.

To understand how that process works, it's necessary to know something about the bureaucratic imperatives and the cultural ecology of the media itself. "They're afraid of it," a sympathetic colleague assured me when I called New York to ask how my story on the Yellowstone Triangle had become the focus of a fierce intramural struggle within the *Newsweek* building at 444 Madison Avenue. "Afraid of the National Park Service?" I asked. The story hardly touched the normal obsessions of the editorial power brokers known collectively as the Wallendas—high-flyers, you see—by their inferiors on the lower floors. "Let's put it this way," my colleague said. "The Washington bureau is full of people who, when they say 'we,' don't mean *Newsweek,* but the government." Not the government in any political sense, but the permanent government—the bureaucracy. And also, my colleague might just as easily have added, the shadow government of lobbyists, "think tanks," and "public interest" groups like the Sierra Club, the National Audubon Society, *et cetera, et al.*

To understand how and why such parties can come to exercise a powerful (though indirect) influence over a nominally independent press, it helps to know a little bit about how a *Newsweek* cover story is put together—by committee. Though the details differ from one organization to another, similar procedures apply in most of what we think of as the national media.

Like many such efforts, *Newsweek*'s "national parks" cover story began four months before it appeared through the efforts of a publicist—specifically, the fellow handling Alston Chase's book for Atlantic Monthly Press. What the publicist had to say about his client's forthcoming book caught the attention of a couple of *Newsweek* senior editors with roots or family ties in the Rocky Mountain West. For several reasons, *Playing God in Yellowstone* had particular appeal to the senior editor in charge of—among several others—my own department, Books. It goes without saying that successful cover stories boost the careers of the persons who originate, write, and edit them— also the prestige and the operating budgets of their departments. It should be noted, however, that all of the "back-of-the-book" departments (for instance, the Arts, Theater, Education) at a magazine like *Newsweek,* with its persistent bias toward "hard" national and international news, feel themselves both hard pressed and honor bound to produce cover stories at decent intervals. And even among back-of-the-book departments, Books was ranked almost at the bottom in terms of competitive prestige. Depending upon who you listened to, that was either because the Wallendas were anti-intellectual philistines, or because the Books staff were boring drudges who would have been more suitably employed handing out homework assignments to undergraduates. Frankly, I thought there was a little bit of truth on both sides.

Playing God in Yellowstone ended up in my hands for two reasons. One was that my editor knew I'd been growing increasingly restless in the Books ghetto. Having come to *Newsweek* from a career as a freelance writer for mostly monthly magazines, I missed reporting. Secondly, I live by choice in Arkansas, raise hunting dogs, and spend a good deal of my free time outdoors—hunting, fishing, canoeing, and hiking. Before coming to *Newsweek* I had reported and written several articles on biological/ecological themes—including a *Harper's Magazine* cover story dealing with wildlife management controversies in national parks in California and New Jersey and a widely reprinted account of the follies surrounding Arkansas' ill-fated "creation-science" law.[1] I do know something about wildlife management, a seeming advantage that turned into a handicap.

The first step was to secure an advance copy of Chase's book, which I read with mounting enthusiasm and dismay—enthusiasm for the brilliant job Chase had done and dismay over the mess *Playing God in Yellowstone* described. As his agent had predicted, I thought a story about Chase and his book would make an absolutely perfect *Newsweek* cover. What's more, we had to get moving. According to the agent, CBS's "60 Minutes" was interested and NBC News was sniffing around. One of us was going to want to secure, if not an "exclusive" with the author, at least his agreement to let *Newsweek* go first.

"If Chase is right," I argued in a memo formally proposing a cover story,

> we've got a (pardon me) Wilderness Watergate on our hands, and one that could not be better suited for a Memorial Day cover. . . . I see a shot of a grizzly bear, with the cover line "Where Have All the Grizzlies Gone? The Battle Over Yellowstone Park." Millions of Americans, I'm convinced, even those who have never visited Yellowstone, will be fascinated. As I see it, the running piece—which I'd like to write and report as much as possible—would deal with Yellowstone: Chase's argument, the NPS's defense of its policies, and how passionately people in the area feel about these issues. Sidebars might include summaries of wildlife management and related controversies at other national parks around the country (there are plenty), and perhaps a sketch of the author himself. He's a Princeton Ph.D. who sold the ranch/hideaway he and his wife owned in Montana in order to partly finance the writing of the book. So if he's right—and his book squares with everything I know about wildlife biology—he's a genuine American hero of the classical sort[2]

At least in part because the magazine always likes to have a cover story available for slow-news holiday weekends—especially one with no urgent time value that can be pushed ahead or held back as circumstances dictate—the Wallendas went for it. Just possibly the Books department would get its cover. Everybody knew that National would come barging in at the last moment with some breaking story about

---

1. Both *Harper's Magazine* essays, as well as the original version of the ill-fated *Newsweek* story under discussion, have been reprinted in my book *The Higher Illiteracy,* University of Arkansas Press, 1988.

2. Nothing I have learned in the interim has changed my mind about that.

the president's hangnail or his wife's wardrobe, and there was no telling what natural disasters, terrorist attacks, wars, or cataclysms would push what became known within 444 Madison as "Grizzlies" off the cover. But the flexible time frame was a big advantage, and politically speaking, the first step was the most important.

So off to Yellowstone I went. But not before knocking off "queries" for the Denver, San Francisco, and Washington bureaus. In retrospect, that was when the trouble started. Normally, you see, the writers of cover stories and other feature articles in magazines like *Newsweek* and *Time* do little, if any, of their own reporting. Once the subject of a story is agreed upon, queries are sent to the relevant bureaus, and correspondents in these bureaus are sent out to do the actual questioning and observing. The correspondents then wire long "files" to the writers in New York who piece them together into one coherent, polished account. The advantages of this system are obvious: the generation of massive amounts of raw data very quickly. Typically, correspondents have areas of expertise—even if that expertise consists mainly of knowing lots of phone numbers—that roughly correspond to the "beats" worked by reporters on daily newspapers. That is to say, there is a police reporter, a city hall person, somebody who covers the baseball team, and so on.

The bureau system also has several disadvantages. One is that the New York-based writer's distant, often entirely theoretical acquaintance with the people, places, and events he or she must sound very knowing about often results in prose with a certain slick, airless quality. In the absence of experience, it's easy to rely upon formulas. That was one of the reasons I wanted to go to Yellowstone myself.

Another weakness of the *Newsweek* bureau system is almost axiomatic in daily newspaper journalism. In time, beat reporters take on the coloration of their environment. The police reporter becomes more of a cop than a journalist. If he didn't, he couldn't do his job, because getting consistently reliable information day after day depends upon being trusted by one's sources. Hence, one of the first things a newspaper does when it catches wind of a major scandal involving the police department is to pull the beat reporter off the story.

From the point of view of the three bureaus queried, there were two big things wrong with "Grizzlies." The first was that "New York," and the Books department no less, were intruding upon their turf. But more than simple jealousy was involved. As in any hierarchical bureaucracy, *Newsweek* correspondents in the field are often convinced that their superiors in corporate headquarters know very little about what's actually going on anywhere outside Manhattan and must be set straight by whatever combination of persuasion, tactical maneuver, and obstruction seems appropriate. Often, of course, their suspicions are correct. But the idea—particularly for anybody with ambitions to rise within the organization—is to display one's own knowledge, expertise, and hard work without permanently alienating anybody important.[3]

Idealism, however, runs quite high among journalists. Most upsetting to the bureaus in my query was less their own territorial interest in National Park Service and environmental issues, than my summary of *Playing God in Yellowstone*. For if Alston Chase's exposé of NPS incompetence and malfeasance were correct, they and everybody else had been missing the biggest national parks story in decades. Hence Chase had to be wrong. And not just wrong, but dead wrong and a liar to boot. Which, of course, was precisely what their trusted sources in the NPS—and at several presumably selfless organizations like the National Audubon Society—wanted to tell them.

"Specious journalism and intellectual dishonesty," fumed Yellowstone superintendent Robert Barbee. "Full of blatant misrepresentations of fact. The premise is ludicrous," claimed the Audubon Society's Amos Eno (who, as a Nixon administration Interior Department official, was partly responsible for natural regulation). NPS director William Penn Mott, Jr., accused Chase of sensationalism, misquotation, and exaggeration. Numerous other mandarins of the environmental movement were equally unkind.

My own reporting, however, turned up very different results. In the first place, I actually read the book—which, to my knowledge, none of my eventual antagonists condescended to do. Certainly *Playing God in Yellowstone* squared with the facts of biology as I knew them. Indeed, my *Harper's Magazine* article of 1978 had examined in detail the very same National Park Service's controversial decisions to allow deer hunting in New Jersey's Great Swamp National Wildlife Refuge and "management kills" of deer by park rangers in Califor-

---

3. Actually, despite the withering tone, my personal experience is that the flow of information in journalistic bureaucracies tends to be a good deal more open than in most other kinds. Compared to the NPS, *Newsweek* resembles a New England town meeting. Scarcely an issue of the magazine appears without fierce and often angry intramural debate.

nia's Point Reyes National Seashore. In both instances the NPS's rationale had been the same: in the absence of predation, deer reproduced at a rate damaging to the environment, injurious to other species, and dangerous to the long-range well-being of the deer herd itself. How on earth, I wondered, could the same agency now deny the massive scientific evidence supporting those earlier decisions in the interest of "natural regulation"?

But like *Newsweek*'s bureau correspondents—and like most literate Americans, I suspect—I did have difficulty imagining that the National Park Service could be as inept and almost malign as Chase had portrayed it. The rangers I'd interviewed for the *Harper's Magazine* story had given quite the opposite impression. Hence I went to some pains to verify not only Chase's reputation for integrity but also the cogency and the accuracy of the book itself. On the ground in Yellowstone, the author proved a most impressive interview subject. More than simply telling me about his book, Chase guided me and a *Newsweek* photographer (somewhat inexplicably sent over from Johannesburg, South Africa) to specific sites that illustrated the overgrazing and other environmental damage he had written about. He also took us to areas at corresponding altitudes in the surrounding national forests (where ungulate populations are kept in check by hunting) to show us what the Yellowstone ecosystem was *supposed* to look like, as well as to provide a vivid rebuke to the NPS argument that conditions inside Yellowstone were the result not of too many elk but of climate changes. The photographer, who was from Zimbabwe, turned out to have had considerable experience taking pictures of African wildlife and environmental damage. (Had *Newsweek* ever used any of the great number of dramatic "before and after" shots he took to demonstrate "highlining," soil erosion, and denuded aspen groves, they would have provided powerful illustrations.)

The subsequent arrival of a *Newsweek* bureau reporter rather changed the tone of things. Somewhat inexplicably, the photographer and I thought, the fellow went out of his way to avoid meeting Alston Chase and made little effort to conceal his lack of enthusiasm for the whole project. But that was no problem. Besides curiosity, skepticism is a reporter's most valuable tool. We got on fine, I thought, and we decided to interview some NPS officials together.

My first question to Yellowstone chief of research John Varley set the tone for an odd day's work. Why, I asked, did I see large herds of mule deer grazing at dawn and dusk all up and down the Yellow-stone valley between Gardiner and Livingston, Montana, but hardly any inside the park proper? Varley explained that Yellowstone Park was not and never had been mule deer habitat. I commented that I thought it an odd coincidence that Congress had in 1872 quite by accident drawn a line precisely demarcating the boundary between elk and mule deer range. It wasn't until I received my colleague's file a week or so later, that I found out that before I entered the room, Varley had told *him* that, contrary to *Playing God in Yellowstone,* the previous year's mule deer census had been the highest in park history. In fact, I subsequently proved, when Chase provided me the actual document, that it had been the lowest—76 to be exact. An accom-panying topographical map shows mule deer in thick clusters up and down the valley, but stopping abruptly at the park boundary.

When asked to account for the bad effects of overgrazing I had been looking at all over Yellowstone for several days, Varley assured my colleague and me that permanent damage was a theoretical and practical impossibility. Why? Simple biology, he assured us. Con-sider the grasshopper, he urged. Perhaps impertinently, I objected that grasshoppers are heavily predated by almost every bird that flies. He'd have to do better. As he was by trade a fisheries biologist, Varley went on to say, perhaps the trout would make a better analogy. Bad choice. I am a devout trout fisherman; my brother-in-law and an ac-ademic friend are ichthyologists, both of whom do research in the area of trout reproduction. I indicated to Varley that I knew perfectly well that trout aren't herbivores at all, but predators, that they lay many thousands of eggs, a tiny proportion of which reach maturity— in part because adult trout prey on their own fry. What's more, mass die-offs of fish populations occur all the time for all sorts of reasons. Unless man-induced, they rarely make news. Was there any chance we could stick to the same phylum, at least, as elk? And specifically, was there any research data anywhere that indicated that elk or any other North American ungulate would quit reproducing in the absence of predation? And could Varley lead me to *any* scientist outside the National Park Service who could tell me where to find this data?

He conceded that the data justifying natural regulation did not ex-ist. Natural regulation, Varley contended, was an experiment set up specifically to test the hypothesis that some as yet unknown mecha-nism would induce the herd to quit expanding. How, I wondered aloud, did one design such an experiment involving migratory animals on a game preserve with no fences? "The science of wildlife management," the research director replied, "is part art. You don't have controlled experiments."

Altogether, interviewing the fellow was an exercise rather like chasing a squirrel around a tree. Now you see him, now you don't. Later, I learned that the NPS had not conducted a statistically valid elk count in five years. It seemed a hell of a way to run an art school. The point, however, is that the bureau guy bought every bit of it, even the trout story. Not a hint of my impertinence surfaced in his file, which recorded Varley's answers and his attacks on Chase's credibility with deadpan fidelity. Of course if you don't have controlled experiments, you don't have science. But nothing in my colleague's files, nor in the many hours of telephone conversations we had in the weeks following our day together in Yellowstone, indicated that he understood that.

My purpose here is not to rewrite *Playing God in Yellowstone*. So suffice it to say that every one of the interviews my colleague and I conducted together went pretty much the same way. Evidently, the NPS has been sacrosanct for so long that it has grown unaccustomed to dealing with reporters who do any more than write down what they're told and compose what are known in the trade as "puff pieces." Yellowstone park naturalist George Robinson even went so far as to pin the blame on Alston Chase when asked by my colleague to account for the fact that Frank Craighead's book *The Track of the Grizzly* may not be sold in NPS bookstores. Why, the publications committee Chase chaired for the Yellowstone Association (a private foundation) had never recommended it. Reminded that I had personally attended a meeting several days earlier in which Chase's committee had pointedly asked Robinson himself when Park Superintendent Barbee would decide on the Craighead book—as three years had passed since they'd first put it on his desk—Robinson took refuge in what he called a "bureaucratic misunderstanding." Pressed for specific examples of the many factual and scientific blunders he had insisted characterized *Playing God in Yellowstone*, Robinson failed to supply even one.

Nor, to come to the point, did anybody else interviewed by any of the *Newsweek* bureaus. Rhetoric of the kind quoted above they found aplenty; credible and verifiable examples of rebuttals to Chase, however, turned out to be in short supply. As I understood the concept of objective reporting, I kept saying in phone conversations that grew more heated as my deadline approached, it had something to do with the truth. Certainly no scientist myself, I did, however, know how to put together a scientific controversy piece: "Scientist A hypothesizes one thing, Scientist B another; here's what's at stake."

Yet *without exception*, every last one of the two dozen or more scientists I interviewed agreed with the basic premise of Chase's book. Nor did they have to plunge very deeply into sophomore biology to do so: "By removing predation," said University of Montana plant ecologist James Habeck, "they've removed the top of the entire food chain—with unforeseeable consequences. Sure, Yellowstone will still exist, geologically speaking anyway. But the cast of characters, plant and animal, will be entirely different."

What's more, the longer "Grizzlies" was delayed—for reasons I'll explain presently—the deeper I dug, going far beyond Chase's sources to experts in universities and in state and federal agencies coast to coast. I went to considerable lengths to check every allegation of in-accuracy in a twenty-seven-page rebuttal the NPS had prepared after *Outside* magazine published a chapter from *Playing God in Yellowstone* detailing the devastating impact of natural regulation on the park's grizzly bear population. In every verifiable instance, Chase's story checked; the NPS's didn't. Many of their allegations against his book were downright silly. Commenting upon Chase's version of a now-famous incident, in which a pair of grizzly cubs were left on Frank Island in the middle of Yellowstone Lake to starve to death after ice-out, for example, the government document went so far as to say that there were "no grounds for suggesting that the Park Service was re-miss. . . . The presence of considerable amounts of fresh scat on the island indicates that the bears were in fact getting substantial amounts of food and were not in danger of perishing."

In fact, according to a study Chase provided when challenged, the NPS's own wildlife advisory committee came to the following con-clusion:

> a cub grizzly . . . eventually died of starvation. Managers knew of a sow and two cubs on the island and were aware of the developing of a deteriorating nutritional situation. First the NPS decided to let the situ-ation develop naturally. . . . This incident and resulting indecision re-flects poorly defined objectives by the NPS.

In short, the animal had plenty of food; yet it starved. End of story. Chase's criticism was "reckless" and "irresponsible"; yet it exactly paralleled the finding of the NPS's own scientific advisers—as one suspects the anonymous author of the NPS rebuttal knew.[4]

The document reeked of intellectual dishonesty from start to finish. If Chase spoke of grizzly "incidents" decreasing during the sixties, the NPS debunked him with figures lumping grizzly and black bears together. (The smaller and more sociable blacks did most of the mischief.) If he listed the number of grizzlies killed inside the park previous to natural regulation (very few), he was rebuked with figures including the surrounding national forests—including kills by hunters. If he gave numbers for the Greater Yellowstone ecosystem—and Chase was always careful to specify—the NPS countered with figures from the park proper. Without saying so. To a casual reader predisposed against the book, the NPS rebuttal was quite persuasive. To any reporter who took the trouble I took, it was a revelation.

The point here is that nobody else at *Newsweek* took that kind of trouble, nor was disposed to put the matter on the table and have it out. Time and again, I told both Denver and Washington that my mind was *not* closed. If they or any of the NPS sources who were lobbying them so hard came up with any scientists who would defend the theory and practice of natural regulation, I would be not only happy but *compelled* to make explicit use of that information in my story. Otherwise my own definition of journalistic objectivity would compel me to point out, as I did in a part of my final draft that the magazine refused to print, that "'Natural Regulation' is based upon principles neither practiced nor accepted by any agency charged with the well-being of wildlife and habitat anywhere in North America— or, for that matter, the world."

What actually transpired at 444 Madison Avenue between my visit to Yellowstone and the publication of an oddly pureed (and unsigned) version of my story I can only conjecture. I was in Arkansas and got only broad hints. The first sign of trouble came indirectly: a copy of a curt memo from the senior editor assigned to the story essentially informing the bureaus that their objections had been noted but the piece was still on. "It is worth keeping in mind one of Chase's key points," the editor wrote,

4. Just to show that *Newsweek* correspondents were not the only members of the press to fall for an NPS snow job: a very unfriendly notice of Chase's book in the *New York Times Book Review* by Washington bureau reporter Phil Shabecoff denied that the Frank Island incident ever happened.

Neither philosophy nor science has ever been able to agree on the meaning of the word "natural." In commonsense usage, which Chase himself says he accepts, it reflects the classic dualism of man versus nature. In that case, "natural management" in Yellowstone or any other park is a literal impossibility . . . [and] the merely problematic now appears to be nearly incompatible. We should explore this irrespective of Chase's views on the subject.

I felt in good hands, even when the same editor reported to me that Washington had inquired about information it had gotten from an NPS source to the effect that the *Newsweek* story was an inside job, that Chase and I were old friends and that I was staying at his home near Livingston, Montana, while doing my interviews. Categorically false on both counts, as the editor knew. Until his book had been placed in my hands, I'd never heard of the man, nor he of me.

Besides the territorial dispute over who ought to be setting the agenda at the magazine for a story about a national park in Wyoming, the objections of the bureaus had a philosophical and emotional cast. Let me put it very simply: *Newsweek* is for the most part written and edited in Manhattan by persons who find the prospect of living there not merely endurable, but desirable. The domestic bureaus are in turn staffed by persons whose professional ambition is to succeed in making it to the big show in New York. As such they also tend to be persons whose ideas about nature and what is "natural" in matters of life and death concerning wild animals partake of the very sentimentality Chase cited as the underpinning of NPS policy.

"Sierra Club pantheism," I once called the attitude myself in the *Harper's Magazine* article mentioned earlier.

Tranquilized wilderness—nicely purged of scorpions, ticks, poisonous reptiles, and lethal microorganisms, thank you—has become the biggest theme park of them all. . . . If nature is benign, then by contemplating and merging oneself with it one can rediscover one's own primal integrity. Rather than cathedrals and monuments, we should be about the building of campsites.

Possibly that's a rather fanciful and literary way of putting it. But I think not. In the years since I've been paying reasonably close attention, I cannot recall ever having seen sport hunting mentioned in *Newsweek*—or in very many other national media outlets intended for general circulation—without an almost reflexive sneer. Not that anybody proposed closing Yellowstone to all but persons wearing hunter orange for a month or so each autumn. (Though it's possible such a policy could be made to go a long way toward solving Yellowstone's elk problems and paying for it too.) The sticking point was that even if my antagonists in the bureaus were hazy about biology, they were not stupid. They correctly deduced what was to them the most emotionally unacceptable consequence of Chase's argument: that an active wildlife management policy for Yellowstone or any other national park would have as one of its main components the death of many thousands of animals by human hands. Indeed, the very "Leopold report" that the NPS (and their carefully briefed *Newsweek* supporters) cited as the philosophical justification for running Yellowstone as "a reasonable illusion of primitive America" spoke to the problem directly.[5] Estimating the carrying capacity of Yellowstone's northern range as 5,000 elk, it recommended that rangers shoot excess animals during the park's off-season and donate the meat to charity.

But then, you see, I was the only reporter or editor at the magazine who took the trouble to *read* the Leopold report. The rest—very much like the NPS itself—came up with their own illusions of Yellowstone as a Garden of Eden and fought with near-religious fervor to impose them on *Newsweek*'s story. One bureau reporter informed me in a tone I can only describe as sentimental condescension that managing the elk herd would be impossible, as the magnificent beasts are too wild to control. Passing over the fact that elk lie around on the ground at Yellowstone Park headquarters like guernseys, I pointed out that the job had been done successfully for generations previous to natural regulation. After all, sport hunters all over the West paid large fees for the privilege of killing elk.

That correspondent and I never had another conversation, which was fine with me. What I wanted was reporting—interviews with scientifically qualified individuals who would defend NPS policies. What I got was rhetoric. Arguing about the story on the phone was like pointing out to certain kinds of religious enthusiasts that nobody can claim literal belief in the Bible without countenancing the stoning to death of sassy children, as Deuteronomy recommends. They just didn't want to talk about it.

5. A. Starker Leopold, a biologist who acted as adviser to the National Park Service et al. Wildlife Management in the National Parks. Report of the Advisory Board on Wildlife Management to Secretary of Interior Udall, March 4, 1963.

Not to my face, anyway. The greatest weakness of *Newsweek*-style committee editing is that the persons with the most authority over any article's final form are those who know least about it. Like the NPS itself, *Newsweek* and many other media organizations operate on a hierarchical flow of information. The various departments and bureaus function like little fiefdoms whose princes are expected to defend the prerogatives of their loyal subjects before the royal council of Wallendas.

Both senior editors who had worked on "Grizzlies" with me had read Chase's book carefully, and provided invaluable assistance at every turn. Of my first draft, one had commented, "While excellent in touching all the bases and being full of top-rate reporting, [the piece] suffers from structural problems." After offering detailed suggestions for resolving those problems, the editor went on to say,

> Here we have a classic example of what happens with too little foresight and too little scientific research. My final problem is that I think your ending is too weak as it stands. To say that this mess is fixable is, I think, a gross overstatement. Beyond that, Chase's book points up the dilemma of science vs. sentimentality. He has done a great job getting to the philosophical issues behind daily management problems, and we need to point this out.

(My too optimistic conclusion had been to observe that: "As government crises go, the Park Service mess is a relatively easy one to fix. The issues involved are not profound scientific mysteries. Expertise exists to be tapped.")

Unfortunately, *Newsweek* has at least three levels of editorial authority above the senior editor level. Each in turn has less detailed knowledge of any individual story than the level below it, but broader authority over its final form. Nor has the humble writer/reporter any standing at all in the debate; his senior editor must represent his interests. Confronted with continuing fierce opposition to the story by rival princes representing their minions in the bureaus, the Wallendas made a Solomonic decision. Rather than having the issue out on its evident merits, a bureaucratic compromise based upon the balance of powers within 444 Madison Avenue was negotiated.

"Grizzlies" as I'd proposed, reported, and written it, got downgraded—rather like a tropical storm—from a cover story to a sidebar accompanying a hastily patched together cover dealing principally with the threats to national parks in general due to crowding and urban sprawl. Nobody ever did manage to find a scientist who would endorse natural regulation in so many words. But the distinction was nicely blurred through judicious use of the ever-popular "crisis" angle: citing a Stanford ecologist to the effect that "a laissez-faire approach to management is simply untenable," and quoting an NPS biologist brave enough to come right out and admit that "some parks will have to actively manage, or lose, species," *Newsweek* managed to make these sound like very advanced concepts on the frontier of contemporary biological thought.

Never mind that the first paragraph of my original proposal had quoted Alston Chase to the effect that the NPS's refusal to manage wildlife actively in the name of natural regulation had *already* resulted in the loss or near extinction within Yellowstone of such species as antelope, bighorn sheep, black bear, while-tailed deer, mountain lion, beaver, wolverine, lynx, bobcat, fisher, and—of course—grizzly bear. The notion of an *external* threat to wildlife was sustained by a very clever line speaking of "our diminishing heritage of wildlife" as "our guarantors against the day when the United States becomes a nation of children and dogs."

The demonstrable fact that wildlife populations in much of America are in far better shape than at any time in the last hundred years is simply unknown, and culturally unacceptable, to most people inside buildings like 444 Madison Avenue. In my own state alone, deer, bear, turkey, wood duck, river otter, grouse, bald eagle, elk, beaver, and even alligators have passed from scarcity or near extinction to healthy and growing populations, thanks to state and federal game and fish agencies financed by license fees and excise taxes on hunting and fishing gear. If migratory ducks are to be saved, it will be the hunters' organization Ducks Unlimited that saves them.

My editor fought heroically, I know, to preserve as much of the integrity of my own work as was possible under the circumstances. But NPS officials were nevertheless quoted calling Chase a liar without having to cite even a single untruth; Yellowstone research director Varley questioned the sincerity of his motives. All references to the NPS's own dishonesty, including pointed accusations from internationally known scientists and easily documented falsehoods told to *Newsweek* reporters, vanished from the text. Scientific unanimity dwindled into the bland "many scientists," and Chase got taken to task—again without specifics—for oversimplifying the issues in a 446-page scholarly book with 1,100 footnotes. From where I sat, *Newsweek* had essentially appropriated the theme of Chase's book for its own uses, then prevented its reviewer from describing it as "must reading for any literate American who cares for the outdoors." I decided I didn't want to work there anymore.

What my story tells readers about the best means of approaching the media on wildlife/environmental subjects is difficult to say. At present the urban-sentimental, wildlife-as-welfare-client view of natural resource issues is the prevailing belief of the national press. Even the minority of writers and reporters intellectually equipped and culturally disposed to go beyond the "Bambi-versus-the-rednecks" stereotypes that characterize most coverage know that nobody can make a career doing this. For now, the best means of influencing the non-sporting public to reasonable positions on the environment would seem to be the very route Chase took: publishing in special interest magazines like *Outside* and general interest journals like *Atlantic Monthly* and *Harper's Magazine*.

The last I heard of Yellowstone research director John Varley, meanwhile, he was telling the *National Geographic* that one's view of the 1988 Yellowstone fires depends upon "whether we want man as the primary manager of these wild lands or whether we want mother nature as the primary manager." Playing God, indeed.

9

RESCUING YELLOWSTONE FROM POLITICS: EXPANDING PARKS WHILE REDUCING CONFLICT

Richard L. Stroup

[T]he central vision of preservation and access . . . is the genius of the [Park] system.

Conservation Foundation

The quotation from the Conservation Foundation book *National Parks for a New Generation* states the dilemma of national park management.[1] The National Park Service (NPS) needs the political support of the serious lovers of nature, a small but highly educated, organized, and vocal group of people who want to preserve the parks in a more or less natural state. But the Park Service also needs the support of a much larger group, tourists and others, many from urban areas, who want access to the parks but whose interest in them is seldom expressed politically.

For decades, the National Park Service has very successfully fostered the illusion that it is above politics. Pictured in their Smokey-bear hats, officials have effectively promoted the idea that they are simply the protectors of Nature. But of course they are not and cannot be. So long as the parks are owned and operated by government, the managers must be politically responsive to the various interest groups

---

1. Conservation Foundation, *National Parks for a New Generation: Visions, Realities, Prospects* (Washington, D.C.: Conservation Foundation, 1985).

and constituent pressures within the stated mission of each park. Congress controls the Park Service and its parent, the Department of the Interior. The Park Service in turn influences (some would say orchestrates) much of the pressure brought to bear on members of Congress. Political pressures, in other words, flow in several directions.

For a critical group, typified by the Conservation Foundation, Yellowstone is a last bastion of the purity of the wild, unspoiled by the scourge of the planet, *Homo trashius,* humankind. These are the serious preservationists. They consider parks, like wilderness areas, as cathedrals, places of refuge from the sins of our fathers and our brethren. Because parks are natural and people (in the view of this group) are not, people are viewed as intruders, trespassers on Nature. Members of this group recognize the political need for the Park Service to keep some peace with other interest groups, but they insist that theirs are the morally superior demands. In recent years, this group has had the most influence.

In contrast, most Americans think of a national park such as Yellowstone as a place where the magnificent grizzly lives, where Bambi wanders among the evergreens, and where Old Faithful spouts on schedule—the romance of the wild at its best. This group is much less knowledgeable about nature and much less organized politically, but its members represent large numbers of votes. The shallowness of the knowledge of this group and, specifically, its lack of the in-depth information needed to evaluate policy, is a problem for the Park Service. If a change in management strategy is needed, for example, getting these citizens to understand the need for the change can be very difficult. On the other hand, the same people are easily influenced by the carefully nurtured, extremely positive, benign image and appeal of the Park Service. Unfortunately, when the elk herd needs reduction or prescribed burns are appropriate, the ecologically unsophisticated general public may make sound management decisions difficult. Most do not understand that shooting elk or burning areas of Yellowstone may be important parts of a responsible management strategy, given the history of the park, the reduction in elk range outside it, and so on.

Politically, the Park Service and Congress must deal with many diverse groups, including those with commercial interests, such as park concessionaires and the businesses near park boundaries. In essence, the Park Service is expected to manage for the "public good."

Yet the very existence of different interest groups with conflicting goals, each quite legitimate, without further guidance from Congress, means that achieving the public good is a difficult task—and the previous chapters in this book make clear how inadequately that objective has been met.

FROM THE POLITICAL TO THE PRIVATE MARKETPLACE?

The task could be greatly simplified and the competing claims more effectively and efficiently sorted out if the park were in private hands. With property rights established, mutually beneficial trades would move resources and resource uses into much more productive patterns. Life could be made simpler and more productive for managers, and all interest groups would quite likely be better off than they are now. Why? The public is generally better served by people (bakers, merchants, and so on) seeking their own interest in trade than by those consciously seeking the public interest. Adam Smith made this point in *The Wealth of Nations:*

> By pursuing his own interest [the individual] frequently promotes that of society more effectually than when he really intends to promote it. I have never known much good to be done by those who affected to trade for the public good.[2]

Profit seekers pay close attention to the expressed desires of their prospective customers, and the latter express their desires thoughtfully and candidly—after all, they are parting with their own resources.

The same is true when the good is environmental, and the provider is a nonprofit interest group. They, too, know their own beliefs and values far better than others and can best assess the net impact of any proposed change in light of these values. In addition, while seeking to further their own narrow values efficiently, they have every opportunity and incentive to weigh carefully the desires of others with whom they may wish to trade. While perhaps caring not at all for the goals of others, these groups will (and do, in practice) find it useful to be cognizant of the desires of others, if only to take advantage of mutually beneficial exchange. Groups such as the National Audubon

2. Adam Smith, *The Wealth of Nations,* Edwin Cannan, ed. (Chicago: University of Chicago Press, 1976), Book IV, Chapter 2, pp. 477–478.

Society, the Nature Conservancy, and Ducks Unlimited deal constantly with landowners and others who seek different values but offer goods and services on a *quid pro quo* basis.

Still, while private property rights and market trading clearly offer potential gains for those with environmental and other goals and could improve the lot of each group, it seems unlikely that the national parks will soon be sold or even deeded to environmental groups. Accordingly, we need an arrangement that allows many of the benefits of privatization but would not involve the transfer of publicly owned lands.

This chapter will examine alternative institutional structures that might be useful for making decisions about national parks, in this case Yellowstone National Park. It will first explain the characteristics and logic of the politically directed bureaucracy that is the Park Service and then contrast this with a private firm in a similar land management situation. The workings and the results of private resource ownership and the market mechanism will be compared with those of public ownership and political control, and an alternative that combines some benefits of private ownership with maintenance of public ownership will be suggested.

POLITICALLY CONTROLLED MANAGEMENT

Civics textbooks suggest that democracy simply transforms the will of the people into political decisions, which are carried out by bureaucrats in the executive branch of government. Centuries of experience, however, have taught us something different. Bureaucrats are real people, with kids and dogs, just like everybody else. They have strong beliefs, especially about what they have chosen as their life work, and they have ambitions like the rest of us. Decision makers in the Bureau of Reclamation are likely to have a "beaver complex"— they love to build dams, and they truly believe that a river with a dam is better than a river without a dam. A park ranger probably believes that parks are the highest calling for any attractive, natural piece of land. A bigger, better funded park is a better park. In both cases, the sincere professional wants an expanded budget. More of a good thing, after all, is better than less. An expanded budget will also increase the likelihood of promotion for a good professional.

For managers who believe in their professional calling, a bigger budget offers the chance to promote the most effective people and to hire those the most promising. Thus, the conscientious, enthusiastic, and ambitious bureaucrat desires expansion. William Niskanen, in his book *Bureaucracy and Representative Government,* translated this desire into the hypothesis that the best assumption one can make about bureaucratic decision making is that it will attempt to maximize the bureau's budget.[3] As any theory must, this one oversimplifies. Yet one can admire the bureaucrat's sincerity, belief in mission, intelligence, integrity, and ambition and still subscribe to Niskanen's theory. All of those admirable characteristics are consistent with the bureaucrat's desire for a bigger agency budget. Of course, dedicated people in a private organization strive for expansion, too, but the owner is likely to be in much better touch with what is happening than is the average taxpayer or voter in the case of the Park Service.

For Park Service officials, working to gain support for the largest possible park budget means trying to please many constituents. It involves paying close attention to the wishes of politically potent groups who closely monitor Park Service activities, while simply providing public relations services—lip service and image management—to the general public. Most of the latter routinely confuse the National Park Service with the U.S. Forest Service (who, after all, invented Smokey the Bear). One result of Park Service public relations is that although the general public knows precious little about the policies of either agency, parks and park rangers have a much higher status with those people than do mere forests and foresters.

When a park (or any other natural resource) is run by a politically directed bureaucracy, the interest groups that are the best funded and are organized to monitor and lobby, will have the most influence. Because the general public is not organized, it will not receive the same sustained attention to its desires as will organized interests.

Today, the serious environmentalists hold sway in the Park Service. The frequency with which the "revolving door" into and out of the hierarchy of the National Park Service is used is testimony to the influence of environmental leaders.[4] Commercial interests have some influence, but the competition among them limits the potential profits and thus their willingness to spend time and money gaining influence. When the large, rather formless emotional energy of tourists and other

3. William Niskanen, *Bureaucracy and Representative Government* (Chicago: Aldine Atherton, 1971).

4. Chase, Alston, *Playing God in Yellowstone: The Destruction of America's First National Park* (New York: Atlantic Monthly Press, 1986), p. 341.

"warm fuzzy" sympathizers can be mobilized (usually by the Park Service and civilian organizations who cooperate with them), this vaguely pro-Park Service crowd can stampede Congress. Such a phenomenon seldom lasts long, however, and the steady pressure of more specialized groups generally wins the day.

Even Congress cannot take away privately held property without due process and compensation. But an important characteristic of political management that is attractive to political professionals (especially lobbyists) but frustrating to nearly everyone else is the fact that political questions are never really settled. A political result can never be bought or even leased; it can only be rented. All "rights" or "ownership" of a resource, then, are up for grabs nearly all the time. Anything Congress bestows it can take away; the Supreme Court has upheld this flexibility. One Congress cannot bind the next. A national shrine established during one term can be made a national dump the next if the political winds blow that way. Indian tribes found this out the hard way: many treaties have been broken, but the courts have declared that there was no violation of due process. Unlike private property rights, a congressional deal holds only so long as Congress, moment by moment, feels the urge—that is, the political pressure, to keep it. Not surprisingly, the political arena attracts "gladiators" who prefer the fight and the potential victory over simple negotiation. (One thinks quickly of Jay D. Hair, president of the National Wildlife Federation, among professional environmentalists, and former interior secretary James Watt, among the development oriented, as contemporary individuals who at times seem to relish the conflict itself.)

An interest group or a bureaucracy working in the political process has little incentive to pay attention to the desires of other groups competing for the same resources. The group's own goals tend to be sacred. The defense establishment, for example, believes that its priorities are more important than all others, and its rhetoric reflects that stance. The patriotism of those who do not support an expanded defense budget is strongly suspect. Farmers feel just as strongly about farm subsidies and teachers' unions about education spending. Each group firmly believes that its own priorities transcend all others. This is as true of the interest groups monitoring the National Park Service as it is of others.

William K. Reilly, then president of the Conservation Foundation but subsequently George Bush's administrator of the Environmental Protection Agency, expressed this single-minded focus when he wrote that "the parks have needs that arise regardless of current national priorities" and warned that "[f]or want of adequate protection policies, the nation could lose the parks in all their splendor."[5] In other words, the importance of parks trumps any other national goal. For the political lobbyist speaking in public, the extreme statement is expected on each seriously represented side of a contested issue. For the nonprofessional who takes this talk seriously, however, the emotions brought on by the rhetoric can make the affected parties less willing to be reasonable.

In brief, governmental control of parks and other resources—that is, politically directed bureaucratic control—has built-in drawbacks. The political process is contentious, rancorous, and unstable over time. People who typically know very little about technical policy issues (which includes most voters) can have a substantial influence. Usually, however, special interests carry much more clout than the general public.

PRIVATE-SECTOR RESOURCE OWNERSHIP AND MANAGEMENT

Of course, private-sector management has its flaws, too. Markets do not instantaneously and perfectly reflect what people desire; ugly and socially unwanted results can be found in markets, just as in government. However, failures in the marketplace are far more limited than we tend to think. Perhaps the most important are the unintended effects or important costs not borne by the decision maker. Such externalities usually stem from poorly defined property rights. For example, the private market cannot deal easily with air pollution, because no one owns the air. Due to lack of ownership, individuals typically lack the effective legal right to force polluters to control their emissions.

Similarly, clear-cutting in a forest may impose a cost on nearby landowners whose scenic view is diminished by the clear-cut or whose use of public streams is impaired by soil from the resulting erosion.[6] Without clear and enforceable ownership, there is no way for those harmed to collect damages or prevent the clear-cut. Under such con-

5. Comments by William K. Reilly in Preface, *National Parks for a New Generation*.

6. In England, where fishing rights (though not the fish or the streams themselves) are owned privately, owners of rights can and do obtain injunctive relief and damages where appropriate, thus stopping pollution damage to most streams where fishing is important. See Jane S. Shaw and Richard L. Stroup, "Gone Fishin,'" *Reason*, August/September 1988.

ditions, a case can be made for governmental restrictions on resource managers.

When bad results are unintended or when important costs are not borne by those who choose and benefit, the market situation is imperfect and alternative arrangements should be examined to find something better. Some features in West Yellowstone undoubtedly fall into this category; for example, large neon signs may help one business but be inappropriate for the merchants as a group, because the signs clash with the charm that draws people to the area. (Not far from Yellowstone, the developers of Big Sky, Montana, solved a similar problem by buying up a mountain valley, then subdividing it and selling tracts with restrictive covenants that allow only aesthetically acceptable development. These imaginative entrepreneurs used a market mechanism to solve a "market failure" problem, increasing the value of the land.)

There is another reason some people claim that the market is a failure: the observer may simply have different tastes than those who choose the market result. The market supplies things that some people clearly do want but that others dislike. Markets provide comic books, for example, which some believe are unnecessary and unproductive. Stock car racing and ballet are both provided privately, although neither has many aficionados and some people would pay to avoid each. Some well-educated people with sophisticated tastes consider markets to be fundamentally flawed because they allow outcomes that offend them. They don't want to accept market results ("commercialism") that are the outcome of voluntary exchange carried on to satisfy diverse but legitimate wants.

Environmental activists seem especially prone to this form of elitism where national parks are concerned. William Reilly is clearly offended by the "tawdry" gateway towns around Yellowstone.

> The sensitive stewardship traditions applied inside the national parks have not prevented "business as usual" outside—even adjacent to—park boundaries. The Gatlinburgs and West Yellowstones, tawdry gateways to some of our greatest natural parks, symbolize the contrasting traditions. These communities exemplify a land-use tradition that is, in its way, every bit as American as the parks. Americans have accepted both traditions, using park boundaries to separate domains.[7]

7. Ibid, p. xxviii.

While he concedes that the tawdry commercial sector outside the park represents an American tradition, he goes on to say that that tradition must make way for a better one.

> In the future, it will no longer be possible to reconcile the two traditions simply by fortifying boundaries . . . the tradition of park stewardship must gradually be extended beyond park boundaries, to domains where mainstream attitudes about private property and freedom of action still prevail today.[8]

There is no talk here of "market failure" in the sense of unintended consequences or even of results not accepted by the majority. Rather, Reilly takes issue with the idea that the masses are allowed to find their bait and tackle, their beer, and perhaps even their bowling near the park in the private sector. In Reilly's view, that kind of activity near the park defiles the park itself; it must gradually be eradicated.

Many commentators appear to think that private property and voluntary exchange slant the activities of people toward "inferior" businesses and allow them to indulge their "base and venal" tastes. Yet this is simply incorrect. The market serves a minority view when a majoritarian democracy would not. Organizations such as the National Audubon Society, the Nature Conservancy, the Hawk Mountain Sanctuary, and other groups and individuals have used private property and the market mechanism to accomplish what public opinion and bureaucratic inertia would not otherwise allow: the preservation of species and land before conservation captured the public imagination or where popular sentiment opposes what knowledgeable environmentalists recognize as important policy changes.[9]

In some respects, the private sector is a demonstrably superior mechanism for the conservation programs needed in and near Yellowstone National Park. Yet most observers do not believe that private solutions will be politically feasible any time soon. What may work, however, is a "halfway house" with many of the advantages of the market but without park land divestiture. This scheme retains ultimate congressional oversight.

---

8. Ibid.

9. For several examples of farsighted private stewardship, especially by nonprofit groups, see President's Council on Environmental Quality, *1984 Annual Report of the President's Council on Environmental Quality* (Washington, D.C.: Government Printing Office, Chapter 9.

THE ENDOWMENT BOARD CONCEPT

Some years ago I suggested a mechanism by which governmentally owned wilderness could be more effectively administered. I proposed a politically selected board with great discretionary powers that, instead of a mandate for "balanced" management, would have a fiduciary duty to a narrow set of goals, such as the preservation of wilderness. The land would be the "endowment" managed by the appointed board, the wilderness endowment board (WEB). Whoever wanted to use the land would have to offer in exchange something of greater value to the WEB. Parks are not the same as wilderness, but they share many of the same attributes. So do other endowments that are often managed by nonprofit groups.[10]

Environmentalists could learn a good deal about park management from those who run museums.[11] A museum's board of directors faces many of the same quandaries faced by advisers to the parks. The museum typically needs more space and additional art objects, but it has a limited endowment and a limited income with which to carry out its mission. Trades are commonly made of one kind of painting for another. All or part of a museum building may be exchanged for more and better space, for additional art objects, or for benefits that enhance the museum's underlying mission.

The park endowment board (PEB) could preserve and even enhance the park values specified for them without ignoring intensive recreation possibilities, scientific research, or even the potential mineral values of park lands. This system of management would introduce some of the advantages of private, voluntary relationships while maintaining governmental ownership and oversight. This system is also a first step toward reducing the unproductive conflict so frequently seen among the various groups of environmentalists, developers, recreation groups, and so on.

Park endowment boards would manage existing park areas as trusts or endowments for the public. There would be two steps in setting up a PEB for a tract of park land. The first is to establish the priority use (or uses, if they are thoroughly compatible) to which the tract—

---

10. See Richard L. Stroup and John A. Baden, "Endowment Areas: A Clearing in the Policy Wilderness," *Cato Journal,* 2 (Winter 1982).

11. John Baden points this out in the Introduction of this volume.

perhaps a whole park, perhaps not, depending on the tract's charac-teristics and Congress's desires—is to be dedicated. The PEB's mem-bers would be appointed by the president and confirmed by Congress. Individuals would of course be suggested for the board by established environmental and other park advisory groups.

The narrow responsibility of the park endowment board would be to protect and enhance the stated values appropriate to the park area. The board would be free to maintain, add to, or subtract from existing landholdings within its endowment as long as it carried out the board's fiduciary responsibility to enhance the values chosen by Congress. Some parts of its endowment can be expected to have far greater value to the board's mission than other parts, and the board might exchange, rent, or lease rights to those parts in exchange for land, covenants, added budget, or other considerations it considers important. Con-gress, however, would have a specified period in which to veto any divestiture.

Each park endowment board would have control, with account-ability to a narrowly defined mission. PEBs would face fewer con-flicts than the current National Park Service arrangement, since Congress would already have specifically dedicated each park tract. Fewer arguments over what should be emphasized would occur, so that managers would face fewer conflicting goals and could be more easily (and fairly) judged on their successes and failures.

These boards would *not* be established to promote the public in-terest as such, but *only* the public's interest in maintaining and in-creasing the stated values for that park. A PEB would not be a "consensus" group representing all points of view on the political, aesthetic, or economic spectrum. Instead, the members would act as trustees with a legal responsibility to use the institution's endowment to the best possible advantage to protect and enhance a narrower mis-sion specified by law. Separate boards would be created in different parks and perhaps for different sections of a given park, if a single board is deemed unable to properly judge trade-offs for all parts of the park. Cooperation among boards would often be necessary, of course, requiring mutually beneficial trades.

How would PEBs be financed? A financial endowment could be set up with each PEB, but should not be necessary. The grant of land itself should be sufficient. If preservation in the wilderness mode is the chosen mission for a tract, little management would be required, and the cost would be minimal. Fees from visitors and research organizations using the land, for instance, could finance the minimal management needed. For those parks where ease of access and interpretative services are desired, visitors could pay larger fees. Is this equitable? The current Park Service does little to measure the ability of its clients to pay. However, a 1980 Interior Department study indicated that in the case of the NPS Bryce Canyon unit, visitor household income averaged more than $30,000, compared to less than $19,000 for the average American family. Subsidizing the relatively rich by undercharging visitors, as we do now, does not seem as fair as letting users pay at least the maintenance costs of the service they receive.

For park units of all types, selling access to minerals, grazing, and a host of other possible benefits would be considered by PEBs, but it would only be permitted under the terms of the endowment if, on balance, it would enhance their stated missions. Boards would have flexibility to do as they see fit, subject to meeting their trust obligation. For example, suppose that a small percentage of a specific park area with no unique values contained significant quantities of oil or minerals. As an undisturbed part of the land of the park, the land might be evaluated by the PEB at, say, $100 per acre undisturbed, but the subsurface oil or minerals might yield millions of dollars per acre.

A board might decide to sell rights to the oil or minerals to the highest bidder, as long as the buyer agreed to the appropriate environmental constraints. The revenues could then be used to purchase more acres of land to add to the park endowment. The PEB could purchase land outright or development rights only. The board might buy the value of future timber sales in areas surrounding the park to preserve the timber and the habitat associated with old-growth or climax forests. By buying development rights, the board could vastly expand the acreage of protected land without actually purchasing it. It is also easy to imagine the board's turning down even a large sum of money if the development would occur on prime parkland and could not be done while preserving the park's values. A proposed exchange simply might not be worthwhile. The ability and the willingness of the PEB to consider a trade would not require it to accept any offered trade.

THE DIFFERENCE IS ACCOUNTABILITY

What is different about an endowment board? Why wouldn't it act just like another government agency? The primary difference is that the board would have freedom to act and would carry a narrower, and thus more easily monitored, responsibility. For this reason it would be more accountable for its actions. Board members would be responsible for choosing how to carry out the board's congressionally mandated mission, and they would be legally accountable for carrying it out properly. This is not the case under the national park system.

Although public officials nominally attempt to carry out the public interest, we have seen that the incentive structure of government makes it difficult for them to do so. The Park Service has multiple constituencies and multiple and conflicting missions; the agency's bureaucrats are pulled and tugged by an array of often tempestuous forces. Even when they see a clear mission, they are hampered by numerous restraints, including day-to-day political pressures. Thus, they are not clearly accountable for the result. While political figures, especially the director of the Park Service and the secretary of the interior, are theoretically accountable for major decisions, they serve a president who is in office for only a few years. As a result, they don't have the ability or the incentive to act with future generations in mind. And, of course, there is the troublesome matter of the conflicting goals that are "the genius of the park system." Faulty incentives— stemming from a lack of monitoring by anyone but organized interest groups, from professional ambitions that are narrower than the Park Service mission, and from distorted political pressures—routinely bring about policies in resource management agencies that are inequitable, inefficient, and sometimes environmentally destructive.[12]

Consider how government ownership under current arrangements has caused managers to ignore opportunities. Suppose for a moment that oil reserves existed within park boundaries and that the oil could be extracted with little impact on important park values. Even under such conditions, the park managers and supporters have an incentive

12. See Richard L. Stroup and John A. Baden, *Natural Resources: Bureaucratic Myths and Environmental Management* (Cambridge, Mass.: Pacific Research Institute for Public Policy and Ballinger Publishing Co., 1983) for examples and further explanation of such problems.

to oppose drilling and extraction. Any revenues from drilling would go to the Treasury rather than to the park and could not help enhance park goals. Understandably, Park Service officials generally don't even want anyone to know of any mineral or petroleum deposits within or near the park. If no one knows, there is no danger of drilling.

Contrast this attitude with that of a museum official in a similar situation. Would that official be upset if the frame of a famous painting in the museum's collection were discovered to contain several pounds of gold? For this manager, the solution is a simple one. If the gold could not be extracted without destroying more of the painting's value than the extraction produces for the museum, on balance, then the museum board of directors would simply decline the opportunity to extract the gold. Under the current arrangement in the national parks however, managers have no incentive to give up the tiniest item of value to allow the extraction of the most enormously valuable mineral.

THE FUTURE OF THE PARKS

Despite the missed opportunities, environmental leaders who currently hold sway politically with the Park Service enjoy the current arrangement. They are winning most of the contemporary battles. The political balance of power, however, can and does change. Public opinion and political coalitions are notoriously unstable. As environmental groups increasingly flex their political muscle, and as some recreation groups react, smart money might bet that the balance of power in some settings will shift. The current balance of power, which is based in part on the public's misperceptions, may prove to be unstable if interest groups with differing goals find it advantageous to educate the public or to supply their own version of the truth. Should this occur, would park supporters prefer the lands to be managed by naturalists with no need to compromise (but lots of ability to do so, if doing so would further park goals) or by the National Park Service, which is subject to shifting political winds?

The park endowment board would not replace public ownership of parks with private ownership. But it *would* replace some of the damaging incentives found in governmental structures with incentives that lead to beneficial relationships. Moreover, it has some significant political attractions.

The PEB approach would reduce conflict and ill will in managing the national parks. Different parks could be given differing goals, and PEB members would be chosen to manage each park tract with added flexibility and to work constructively toward more narrow goals. Whoever wanted new or different activities within the park would have to devise a way to more than compensate for any harm done to the congressionally mandated park mission. Just as a museum board is willing and able to make trade-offs that enhance the museum, a PEB would make trade-offs that enhance the mission of the park.

Although we rarely read about it in the newspapers, environmental organizations that are farsighted or lucky enough to own their own land have long been willing to negotiate calmly and constructively to further their aims when approached about options that may pose some danger to the lands they protect. When they can advance the interests of their cause through cooperating with others, they generally do so. Organizations such as the National Audubon Society and the Nature Conservancy allow and benefit from oil and gas leasing and other development on property they own and preserve. Firms that do business with them are willing to meet the organizations' environmental standards; further, they must more than compensate for any loss they impose. Any deal made must be mutually beneficial, creating more value than it destroys. This is the only condition under which drilling is allowed. Both sides find that they can better serve their own missions by cooperating than by obstructing. Even if each set of leaders has no regard for the goals of the other set, each can further its own mission by standing ready to trade for its own advantage. In a system of voluntary relationships, harmony is advanced because decision makers further their own goals by acting as if they care about the preferences of others.

In sum, the reform suggested here promises substantial advantages in economic efficiency and environmental quality. The establishment of PEBs would help expand park boundaries without rancor or additional burden on the economy. It would also decrease the conflicts over resource development. To realize these goals, a coalition of fiscal conservatives and people concerned with park conservation must be built. The park endowment board proposal would move us in that direction.

Assigning effective ownership would be possible for most park values, including, for example, habitat for endangered species. Private organizations for decades have been willing and able to protect habitat through covenants and rental arrangements. Specific government entities, such as the Fish and Wildlife Service, also have budgets for such preservation measures.

We must also remember that in the areas where governmental involvement may be justified the difficulties of bureaucratic management are most severe. The same lack of information on harms done (and potentials bypassed) that reduces the effectiveness of ownership and hampers private resolution of conflicts over air pollution and clear-cutting will also hinder the achievement of efficiency in any system of political control. We still don't know who is hurt, how great is the damage, or who is at fault. Politicizing the issue often makes it even more difficult to rationally resolve complex and emotional issues such as mining in the backcountry, protecting private pastures from damage due to elk and deer foraging, and oil drilling in wildlife habitat. Further, unless and until private contracts are written, political solutions can be reversed at any time.

PART IV

POSTSCRIPT

10

MAN AS AN ECOLOGICAL FACTOR WITHIN NATURE

Vernon L. Smith

The debate over the management of the Yellowstone ecosystem centers on two fundamental issues: (1) what is the role of man in nature and (2) what is the best institutional arrangement for implementing this role? Both of these questions are crucial to our understanding of all natural resource management issues. They become all the more important in Yellowstone because of its high visibility and emotional character.

On the question of the role of man in the environment, there are basically two positions. One is that man is separate from nature. In this view, nature is considered perfect and man fallible. Mixing the two would only interfere with a perfect system. In this view, man should leave nature to take its own course and learn from it.

The alternative view is that man is an integral part of nature and cannot be separated from it. According to this view, man must read the signals from nature and take his actions accordingly. There is little man can do about the weather, earthquakes, or other natural events; he must simply leave nature to take her own course. For other natural phenomena, however, man can alter the environment in ways that are thought to make it "better."

The answer to the question of how man's role should be integrated

I am indebted to Terry Anderson and John Baden for many helpful comments.

into nature depends on which of the above two roles is appropriate. If man is separate from nature, then his role is to leave it alone. No management is appropriate. On the other hand, if man is an integral part of the environment, institutions must be devised that determine what values are important and how information about these values is to be generated.

Management in the Yellowstone ecosystem clearly must confront the questions of the role man should play and the institutions that should best promote that role. Some people subscribe to the notion that Yellowstone is a natural ecosystem that should be left to take its own course. Starving elk should not be fed in the winter, forest fires should be left to burn, and wolves should be replaced to undo man's damage. There are also those who think more hands-on management is necessary.

Obviously, given the political institutions, it is impossible to have no management. Moreover, few people think that the political sector should not be responsible for this management. Accepting these constraints, we must ask whether these institutions adequately reflect the values and adequately generate the information necessary to manage. The preceding chapters suggest that management of political lands is deficient on both counts. Before turning to some general implications of how institutions might be reformed, let's consider man as an ecological factor from a long-term historical view.

THE PREHISTORIC VIEW

At the close of the last great ice age, about 12,000 years ago, the first Americans are thought to have entered this continent, crossing the Bering land bridge into Alaska. These first invaders of North America were the indirect descendants of *Homo erectus,* a tool-using hominid, culturally as well as biologically distinguishable from other animals. *H. erectus* dates from approximately the beginning of the Pleistocene ice age, 1.7 million years ago, and his use of fire may have begun as early as 700,000 years ago. These first Americans were the direct descendants of *Homo sapiens,* who replaced *H. erectus* and who have spread throughout the world within the last 100,000 years.

The last Pleistocene is of particular ecological significance, especially to the concerns represented in this book. With the exception of Africa, most megafaunal (adult mammals weighing over 100 pounds) extinctions in the Pleistocene occurred in the last 100,000 years, and much of this loss—particularly in North America—has occurred in the last 15,000 years. These American extinctions include four species of ground sloth, two of bear, the dire wolf, a saber-toothed and a scimitar-toothed cat (tiger), a cheetah, the giant beaver (*Castoroides,* the size of a black bear and the largest North American rodent during the Pleistocene), *Equus,* tapir, two species of peccary, camel, two species of llama, two of deer, the stag moose, pronghorn, shrub ox, two species of musk ox, yak, two subspecies of bison, mastodon, mammoth, and other less familiar megafauna. Although the American bison managed to survive, two earlier subspecies (*B. antiquus* and *B. occidentalis*)—both hunted by Paleo-Indians—became extinct from 8,000 to 11,000 years ago. All the *proboscidia* (mammoth, mastodon) were lost in North America between 9,000 to 12,000 years ago. Projectile points used to kill mammoth and mastodon are widely distributed throughout the United States. Although the horse was widely hunted in Europe, direct association between man and horse is uncommon in North America, where, paradoxically, the horse originated.

The remarkable association between megafaunal extinctions and the worldwide migration of man, and the direct evidence of hunting by man, has given rise to the prehistoric overkill hypothesis. As noted by Paul Martin,

> [U]nlike changes in climate, the global spread of prehistoric *Homo sapiens* was confined to the late Pleistocene. Prehistoric man's role in changing the face of the earth can conceivably include major depletions of fauna, an anthropogenic "overkill." . . . Sudden extinction following initial colonization of a land mass inhabited by animals especially vulnerable to the new human predator represents, in effect, a prehistoric faunal "blitzkrieg."[1]

Two large oceanic islands, Madagascar and New Zealand, illustrate the sudden acceleration of extinction in recent times. These islands were not occupied by men until about the year 1,000 whereupon these islands suffered heavy faunal extinctions. Earlier extinctions in Africa and Australia (inhabited by man) left these nearby islands unaffected. It is hard to reconcile these facts with the hypothesis that climate change caused these extinctions.

1. Paul Martin, "Prehistoric Overkill: The Global Model" in P. S. Martin and R. G. Klein, eds., *Quaternary Extinctions: A Prehistorical Revolution* (Tucson, Ariz.: University of Arizona Press, 1984), p. 357.

THE EARLY HISTORICAL VIEW

By the time most Northern Europeans had arrived on the Great Plains, the Indians had domesticated the horse, reintroduced into North America by the Spanish in the sixteenth century. As I have discussed elsewhere, the reintroduction of *Equus* had a profound effect on the Plains Indians.[2] With the eclipse of the American big-game hunting period 8,000 to 12,000 years ago, the Paleo-Indian response to this change in opportunity cost was to turn more extensively to agriculture (domesticated maize appears to date from 5,000 to 6,000 years ago) supplemented by hunting and gathering. But the horse brought a major technological revolution leading many tribes (for example, the "fighting" Cheyenne to the North and the Pawnee to the South) to abandon or reduce dependence on their horticulture and pottery arts and to revert to the bison chase.

The great bison herds of the Plains consisted of the dwarfed remnants of the two larger subspecies hunted by the Paleo-Indians. The ecological niche into which these prolific animals fitted had been vacated by the mammoth, *Equus,* camel, earlier bison, and other herbivores. Two-thirds of the North American megafauna had become extinct, and much of the carrying capacity of the land was now expressed in the huge biomass of bison. These animals, destined ultimately, I believe, to be decimated by the Indian's bow and horse, were instead killed quickly by Buffalo Bill and the U.S. cavalry. Could it have been otherwise, given the impending westward migration and the conversion of sod to meat, grain, and fiber for the support of the expanding white population?

The first tool users had property. Although the archaeological record of property is clear for nearly two million years, the property *rights* record is more obscure. But it is likely that property rights are also of ancient prehistoric origin. All the extant hunter cultures studied over the last century had sophisticated property right and trading traditions. Furthermore, property rights were rights to act and were thus quintessentially human rights, not merely or only rules governing the ownership of tangible durable property. Thus, among the Indians

2. For a discussion of this and other aspects of Prehistoric hunter-gatherer cultures, see Vernon L. Smith, "The Primitive Hunter Culture, Pleistocene Extinction, and the Rise of Agriculture," *Journal of Political Economy,* 83 (August 1975): 727–756.

of the Pacific Northwest, one had sealing rights on a particular rock or fishing rights on a particular eddy in a particular river every second day. The latter rights were independent of who "owned" the land for agricultural or other uses along the river. All such rights could be bequeathed or sold. Similarly, kinship groups in the Pacific Northwest owned transferable rights to salmon streams. The *potlatch* of the Pacific Northwest as the *kula, moka,* and *abutu* in other parts of the world were the ceremonial means of recognizing the transfer of property rights, including public goods such as crests, trading routes, and peace—the latter often being "purchased" by the exchange of daughters so that stateless societies became bound by kinship ties.

As much our heritage as Yellowstone Park, this history is part of who and what we are today, this instant, and evermore. We exploit as much as love all that is nature, for we are as much a part of that nature as the fires that devastated over one million acres of Yellowstone Park. Devastated? Why not renewed? For renewed they will be! Never mind that the National Park Service (NPS) bureaucracy will emphasize that its politically inspired policy of "Smokey the Bear" protection, followed by an equally politically inspired, natural-burn policy, will now be followed by a "nature's way, come see the renewal" campaign. Yellowstone *will* be reborn. Possibly it can be destroyed by man, but not by fire—not by *this* stroke of nature's hand.

LEARNING FROM THE LONG VIEW

Several lessons are suggested by this discussion. First, *humanity,* beginning with *H. erectus, has always been an intense user of nature for self-interested ends.* Cro Magnon and modern humanity evolved from a physically superior predator into a predator without peer. The mass killing of *Equus* in Europe and of bison in the United States is well documented. Once the technology of mammoth hunting was developed with the perfection of the Clovis fluted point, this became humankind's specialty. When the mammoth became extinct man turned to bison hunting, concentrating his efforts on *B. antiquus* and *B. occidentalis.* When these subspecies were gone, humankind turned to agriculture and bison hunting became relatively rare.[3] (In 1541 Coronado reported that the Apache were subsisting on bison hunting.)

---

3. Ibid. Also see Douglas North and Robert Thomas, "The First Economic Revolution," *Economic History Review,* 30 (1977): 229–241.

Then, with the reintroduction of the horse by the Spanish, Americans returned to the bison hunt. This selectivity strongly suggests a second lesson: *The cultures of man were sensitive to opportunity cost.*[4] Humankind's failure to continue bison hunting as their primary livelihood after the two bison subspecies became extinct suggests that the latter were more vulnerable than surviving bison, given the technology of the time. But man did not hesitate to return to hunting when the horse made hunting more productive than growing maize. The opportunity-cost view of humankind's development was stated implicitly by a Kung bushman who when asked by an anthropologist why he had not turned to agriculture, replied, "Why should we plant, when there are so many mongongo nuts in the world?" In effect, human cultures chart new directions when the old have become too costly relative to the new. A third lesson: *man's impact upon his environment is not an event new to the modern industrial age.* Prehistoric man's transformation of his environment was not only due to his hunting prowess, but also to his gathering technology and the wide migration that introduced exotic plants wherever he went. Although the tools of destruction were meager by modern standards, the flora and fauna of that era were far more vulnerable to human predation and disruption. What survived into the modern period were the more stubbornly resistant, remote, and adaptable species of plants and animals.

Finally, at some point in history, prehistoric *hunter-gatherers developed property rights,* the major theme in the New Resource Economics and in this book. This laid the foundation for labor specialization and the exchange of goods beyond the family and the tribe, establishing unsuspectedly and unintentionally an organizational engine for the creation of vast wealth and greater well-being. For the first time, humankind was able to combine the information and incentives of independent decentralized action with the coordination provided by a market economy, without submission to authoritarian control.

The origin of the most sophisticated forms of property rights was probably in the late pre-agricultural period when hunter-gatherers became more sedentary. The evidence for this is the archaeological

---

4. See Vernon L. Smith, "Hunting and Gathering Economies," in *The New Palgrave* (London: Macmillan, 1987), pp. 695–699, for an opportunity-cost interpretation of the cultural development of *Homo sapiens.*

record of increased paraphernalia: pots for boiling and stones for grinding seeds too hard to eat on the run; animal sledges and boats for transporting personal property; the domesticated wolf, nature's other great predator that employed social organization in the hunt; spears and atlatls (a device for throwing a spear), bows and arrows—investment goods using leverage, energy storage, and ballistics principles; even houses and small villages. Thus humankind became less mobile, more practiced in the ways of property and larger scale communities, and the stage was set for applying humankind's knowledge of seeds and animals to agriculture and the husbanding of domesticated animals. These developments were the first steps towards the industrial and our own communication revolutions. But through the millennia humankind has continuously responded to change by substituting new kinds of labor, capital, and knowledge for old, and developed new products and institutions to replace the old when the environment altered the costs of labor.

Property rights, in turn, nurtured sophisticated land management. Extensive studies of aboriginals' use of fire for game and plant management demonstrate clearly that primitive men had a sophisticated understanding of the reproductive cycles of shrubs and herbaceous plants. He used fire to encourage the growth and flowering of the plants that he gathered and to discourage the growth of weeds. People had to know when, where, how, and how often to apply the tool of controlled burning for managing plant and animal resources. Primitive peoples knew that one can advance the growing season two or three weeks by spring burns that warm the earth; that in dry conditions fires must be set at the top of hills to avoid wildfires, but in humid air they must be set in depressions to avoid being extinguished; that the burning of forest underbrush stimulated the growth of oak whose acorns could be gathered, and attracted moose who don't like underbrush; and that deer and other animals congregate to graze the tender new plants that sprout after a fall burn.[5]

MAN AND NATURE TODAY:
THE YELLOWSTONE ECOSYSTEM

As I read the criticism of the National Park Service for their natural-burn policy, and the congressional call for hearings, investigations,

---

5. Henry T. Lewis, *Patterns of Indian Burning in California: Ecology and Ethnohistory,* Ballerina Press Anthropological Papers No. 1, 1973.

and inquiries into this "outrageous policy," I am reminded of the incompetence of public policy *processes* to respond to anything but *immediate* demands. Political processes must always respond to the "don't-just-stand-there-do-something" imperative. Natural burn was a compromise between protection and controlled burn management, the latter, of course, made necessary by over a half-century of excessive fire protection. The Park Service—at last—had the right idea, but it is naive to think that a controlled-burn policy was politically possible, and that the NPS had the technical competence to implement it. There are probably Indian groups that could do the job properly, but the NPS is neither well practiced nor motivated to contract out management functions. Natural burn has worked well in the mountains around Tucson, because no other policy is or ever has been viable, given the frequency and severity of our summer lightning storms, which keep fuel accumulation (deadwood) at a minimum.

What of the grizzly and the elk or the question of reintroducing lost species such as the wolf into Yellowstone? Can the NPS management properly deal with any of these issues? The answer is plainly no. Both economic theory and observation make it clear that there is no way to aggregate diverse preferences to sustain any particular "public interest" outcome. The idea that the public interest could be defined and served by central control was wrong when the NPS was founded, and it is wrong today. Diversity of preference can only be served by tailoring policies to the needs of each large ecosystem—Yosemite, Grand Canyon, Glacier National Park, and so on. There is no way that centralist NPS policies can accommodate the differing needs of each ecosystem.

Private ownership organizations can if they so choose. One group using its own funds and property can choose to preserve the grizzly, excluding tourism and other activities that are incompatible with these "problem" animals. Another can reintroduce the horse on its own property, although few seem to appreciate that this great animal was once a natural part of the American landscape. (Today, wild forms of *Equus* are perceived as man-made instruments of destruction, causing soil erosion and excessive competition for bighorn sheep and deer.) Similarly, the wolf can be reintroduced if some group is willing to pay liability claims when *Canis* ranges beyond the group's property boundaries. Oil and gas development can be undertaken by environmental groups that own their own wildlife preserves and choose to take responsibility for mixing these activities. In short, different groups or individuals can choose to satisfy their own tastes and to conduct their own ecosystem experiments on their own preserves. The NPS cannot, because it must ultimately satisfy the median voter. Consequently, its job is not defined or definable. Scientists will define it one way, tourists another, and Wild Horse Annie in still another way. Neither science nor ecosystem policy can satisfy every voter any more than can the product policies of General Motors or the programming policies of a symphony orchestra or museum.

I think it is likely that we will lose many more species. The grizzly and wolf—these wonderful animals—will go; this might occur sooner under public management and might even be avoided under private ownership, but ultimately they are probably as doomed as the great *proboscidia,* bison, and sloth to make room for man. I hope I am wrong. As I began writing this chapter, resources were being volunteered to save three whales trapped in the Arctic ice. Before I finished, one was lost and two were believed to have been set free. The willingness to pay revealed value of these great animals was over one million dollars each. Today, more of us care, and with the right institutions this could make the difference. Sadly, I expect that we will not make the needed changes and our caring will merely prolong, minutely on the scale of *homo*'s interval on earth, the time that the surviving great beasts of nature will coexist with humankind.

But there is hope, and that hope is expressed throughout the pages of this book. The New Resource Economics has focused attention on the role that individual and group initiative, fueled by the responsibility that results from property rights, can play in reversing the decline in our environmental capital. Such decline is not inevitable provided that we can depoliticize environmental management and adopt the time-tested and ancient property right institutions which the New Resource Economics reminds us are necessary if we are to bring the power of private incentives to bear upon resource management.

BIBLIOGRAPHY

Aderhold, Mike. "Yellowstone Water: There's Only so Much." Montana Outdoors 8:2 (1977):13–18.

Adler, Jerry, Mary Hagler and Jeff Copeland. "The Fall of the Wild." Newsweek, 28 July 1986.

American Petroleum Institute. "Analysis of the Processing of Permit to Drill on Federal Lands." Research Study 029. Washington, D.C.: American Petroleum Institute, 1982.

———. "Should Federal Onshore Oil and Gas Be Put Off Limits?" Washington, D.C.: American Petroleum Institute, 1985.

Anderson, Robert. "A Report on Allenpur Dam." Livingston Enterprise, October 1986.

Anderson, Terry. "The Public Trust vs. Traditional Property Rights: What are the Alternatives?" In Proceedings from Western Resources in Transition: The Public Trust Doctrine and Property Rights. Bozeman, Mont.: Political Economy Research Center, 1986.

———. Water Crisis: Ending the Policy Drought. Baltimore, Md.: Johns Hopkins University Press and the Cato Institute, 1983.

Anderson, Terry and P. J. Hill. "The Evolution of Property Rights: A Study of the American West." Journal of Law and Economics 18:1 (1975):163–79.

Audubon Wildlife Report, 1986. New York: National Audubon Society, 1986.

Baden, John. "Crimes Against Nature: Public Funding of Environmental Destruction." Policy Review 39 (Winter 1987).

————. Earth Day Reconsidered. Washington, D.C.: Heritage Foundation, 1980.

————. "Oil and Ecology Do Mix." Wall Street Journal, 24 February 1987.

————. "Take Politics Out of the National Parks: Let Nature Groups Bid For Control." Wall Street Journal, 23 November 1988.

Baden, John and Tom Blood. "How to Save Yellowstone." St. Louis Post Dispatch, 2 October 1985. Also published in The Salt Lake Tribune, 29 September 1985; The National Inholder, Winter 1985–1986; and Bozeman Daily Chronicle, 29 September 1985.

————. "Man and Beast Living in Harmony." Denver Post, 19 May 1984.

————. "Troubled Wetlands and the Land Trust Movement." Orvis News, June 1985.

Baden, John and Richard Stroup. Bureaucratic Myths and Environmental Management. San Francisco, Calif.: Pacific Research Institute for Public Policy, 1983.

————. "Saving the Wilderness: A Radical Proposal." Reason 13:2 (July 1982):28–36.

Baskin, Ken. "The Tug of War for the Wilderness." Sun Magazine, Autumn 1985.

Blood, Tom. "Wolf Introductions Producing Howls—Yellowstone Unsuitable for Wolves." Albuquerque Journal, 25 February 1989.

————. "Saving Wolves by Soothing Ranchers." Wall Street Journal, 20 October 1987.

Bloom, Marshall. "Montana Jungle Boat Ride." Montana Troutline 6:1 (1986).

Boris, Connie and John Krutilla. Water Rights and Energy Development in the Yellowstone River Basin: An Intergrated Analysis. Baltimore, Md.: Resources for the Future and Johns Hopkins University Press, 1980.

Bozeman Daily Chronicle, 7 May 1986, p. 12.

Buchanan, James M. The Demand and Supply of Public Goods. Chicago: Rand McNally, 1968.

Buchanan, James and Gordon Tullock. The Calculus of Consent: Logical Foundations of Constitutional Democracy. Ann Arbor, Mich.: University of Michigan Press, 1962.

Calabresi, Guido. "Transaction Costs, Resource Allocation and Liability Rules." Journal of Law and Economics 11 (1968).

Cappaert v. United States, 426 U.S. 128, 96 S. Ct. 2062 (1976).

Cascade Holistic Economic Consultants. "Review of the Gallatin Forest Plan and the EIS—Summary." Eugene, Ore., 1985.

Chase, Alston. Playing God in Yellowstone: The Destruction of America's First National Park. New York: Atlantic Monthly Press, 1986.

Cheung, Steven N. S. "The Structure of a Contract and the Theory of a Non-Exclusive Resource," Journal of Law and Economics 13 (April 1970).

Clark, William. "A Free-Flowing Yellowstone: The Reservations Challenge." Montana Outdoors 10:2 (1979):22–23.

Clarke, Jeannie Nienaber and Daniel McCool. Staking Out the Terrain, Albany, NY: State University of New York Press, 1985.

Coase, Ronald. "The Problem of Social Cost." Journal of Law and Economics 3 (October 1960).

Cole, Glen F. "An Ecological Rationale for the Natural or Artificial Regulation of Native Ungulates in Parks." Transactions of the Thirty-sixth North American Wildlife and Natural Resources Conference. Washington, D.C.: Wildlife Management Institute, 1971.

————. "Elk and the Yellowstone Ecosystem." The Yellowstone Library, 1969.

Congressional Research Service. Greater Yellowstone Ecosystem: An Analysis of Data Submitted by Federal and State Agencies. Congressional Research Office, Committee on Interior and Insular Affairs, Committee Print #6, 99th Congress, Second Session, p. 82, Washington, D.C.: U.S. Government Printing Office, 1987.

————. Water Resources of the Missouri River Basin. Environment and Natural Resources Policy Division, Washington, D.C.: U.S. Government Printing Office, 1976.

Conner v. Burford. 605F Supp. 107 (D. Mont. 1985).

Conner, et al. v. Burford and Mountain States Legal Foundation, et al. Civ. No 85-3935, U.S. Court of Appeals for the Ninth Circuit (March 1986).

Conservation Foundation. National Parks for a New Generation: Visions, Realities, Prospects. Washington, D.C.: Conservation Foundation, 1985.

Council on Environmental Quality. 1984 Annual Report of the President's Council on Environmental Quality. Washington, D.C.: U.S. Government Printing Office, 1984.

Culhane, Paul J. Public Lands Politics: Interest Group Influences on the Forest Service and the Bureau of Land Management. Resources for the Future, Inc. Baltimore, Md.: Johns Hopkins University Press, 1981.

Dahl, Robert. Pluralist Democracy in the United States: Conflict and Consent. Chicago: Rand McNally, 1967.

Demsetz, Harold. "Toward a Theory of Property Rights." American Economic Review 57 (May 1967).

Driver, Bruce. Western Water: Tuning the System. Denver, CO.: Western Governors Association, 1986.

Duffield, John. "The Worth of Fishing." Montana Outdoors 19 (1988).

Duffield, John, John Loomis, and Rob Brooks. The Net Economic Value of Fishing in Montana. Helena, Mont.: Montana Department of Fish, Wildlife, and Parks, 1987.

The Ecological Society of America. Conserving Biological Diversity in Our

National Forests. Washington, D. C.: Wilderness Society, 1986.

Egan, Timothy. "Land Sought as Buffer Around Parks." New York Times, 3 March 1989, p. 8.

Ekey, Robert. "Campsite Closure Will Be Expensive." Billings Gazette, 28 March 1986.

———. "Park Service Stands Pat On Fishing Bridge." Billings Gazette, 27 February 1987.

———. "Timber Program Lost $1 Million." Billings Gazette, 17 March 1989.

Ethridge, Mark and Ursula Guerrieri. "Survey of Oil and Gas Activities on Federal Wildlife Refuges and Waterfowl Production Areas." American Petroleum Institute Research Paper 31. Washington, D.C.: American Petroleum Institute, September 1983.

Everett and Associates. "Analysis of Delays in the Processing of Applications for Permit to Drill and Prestaking Clearance Applications." Washington, D.C.: Everett and Associates, 1981.

Fairfield, R.P., ed. The Federalist Papers: A Collection of Essays Written in Support of the Constitution of the United States, p. 16. Baltimore, Md.: Johns Hopkins University Press, 1981.

Fritts, Steven H. "Wolf Depredation on Livestock in Minnesota." Resource Publication 145, p. 4. Washington, D.C.: United States Department of the Interior, Fish and Wildlife Service, 1982.

Gallatin Canyon Study Team. "Impacts of Large Recreational Developments Upon Semi-Primitive Environments: The Gallatin Canyon Synthesis Report Executive Summary." Bozeman, Mont.: Institute of Applied Research and Montana State University, December 1976.

Government Accounting Office. "Actions Needed to Increase Federal Onshore Oil and Gas Exploration and Development." EMD-81-40, 1981.

Hammond, Gary. "The Nature Conservancy: Protecting the Rare and the Beautiful." Western Wildlands 10:1 (Spring 1984).

Hardin, Garrett and John Baden. Managing the Commons. San Francisco, Calif.: W.H. Freeman and Co., 1977.

Hayek, F.A. "The Use of Knowledge in Society." American Economic Review 70 (September 1945).

Henkel, Mark. The Hunter's Guide to Montana. Helena, Mont.: Falcon Publishing Company, 1985.

Herbst, Robert L. "Living Brightwater." Trout 26:4 (Autumn 1985).

Houston, Douglas B. The Northern Yellowstone Elk: Ecology and Management. New York: Macmillan, 1982.

———. The Northern Yellowstone Elk, Part I and II: History and Demography. Yellowstone National Park, Wyo., April 1974.

Huffman, James. "Instream Water Use: Public and Private Alternatives." In Water Rights: Scarce Resource Allocation, Bureaucracy, and the Environment. Edited by Terry L. Anderson. Cambridge, Mass.: Pacific Research Institute for Public Policy and Ballinger Publishing Co., 1983.

International Paper Company. "A Forester's Guide to Wildlife Management in Southern Industrial Pine Forests." Technical Bulletin 10 (January 1980).

Jensen, William F., Todd K. Fuller and William L. Robinson. "World Distribution on the Ontario-Michigan Border Near Sault Ste. Marie." Unpublished report of the Minnesota Department of Natural Resources, Wildlife Populations and Research Group, Grand Rapids, Minn., August 1986.

Johnson, Bruce K. and Dave Lockman. "Response of Elk During Calving to Oil/Gas Activity in Snyder Basin, Wyoming." Report A-1012. Wyoming Game and Fish Department, Cheyenne, Wyo., 1980.

Johnson, Craig. "Beautiful, Bountiful Gallatin River." Bozeman Daily Chronicle, 21 September 1986.

———. "Forester Calls Macroserve Unrealistic." Bozeman Daily Chronicle, 25 January 1987.

———. "Politics Delay Return of Wolf to Park, Panelists Say." Bozeman Daily Chronicle, 3 June 1986.

Johnson, Ralph. "Public Trust Protection for Stream Flows and Lake Levels." U.C. Davis Law Review 14:2 (1980):265–67.

Josephy, Alvin. "The Agony of the Northern Plains." Edited by Lon C. Ruedisili and Morris W. Firebaugh. In Perspectives on Energy: Issues, Ideas, and Environmental Dilemmas. 2nd ed., pp. 205–25. New York: University Press, 1978.

Kirk, Ruth. Exploring Yellowstone. Seattle, Wash.: University of Washington Press, 1972.

Knight, James E. "Effect of Hydrocarbon Development on Elk Movements and Distribution in Northern Michigan." Ph.D. dissertation, University of Northern Michigan, 1980.

Krutilla, John and Anthony Fisher. The Economics of Natural Environments. Baltimore, Md.: Johns Hopkins University Press, 1968.

Landers, D.H., J.M. Eilers, et al. Characteristics of Lakes in the Western United States. Volume I. Population, Descriptions and Physico-Chemical Relationships. EPA/600/3-86/054A. Washington, D.C.: U.S. Environmental Protection Agency, 1987.

Leal, Don and John Baden, "Put the Parks Above Politics." St. Louis Post-Dispatch, 6 May 1986.

Leedy, D.L., L.W. Adams and L.E. Dove. Environmental Conservation and the Petroleum Industry. Columbia, Md.: National Institute for Urban Wildlife, 1985.

Lewis, H.T. Patterns of Indian Burning in California: Ecology and Ethnohistory. Ballerina Press Anthropological Papers No. 1, 1973.

Libecap, Gary. "Regulatory Constraints on Oil and Gas Production on Forest Service and BLM Lands." In Forestlands: Public and Private. Edited by R. Deacon and M. Bruce Johnson. Cambridge, Mass.: Pacific Research Institute for Policy and Ballinger Publishing Co., 1985.

Lyon, L. Jack, Terry N. Lonner, et al. Coordinating Elk and Timber Management: Final Report of the Montana Cooperative Elk-Logging Study 1970–1985, pp. 37–48. Bozeman, Mont.: Montana Department of Fish, Wildlife, and Parks, 1985.

Mahlein, Dieter. "Will Forest Plans Enhance Deer and Elk Habitat?" Forest Watch: The Citizen's Forestry Magazine, April 1986, pp. 17–21.

Martin, P. "Prehistoric Overkill: The Global Model." Quaternary Extinctions A Prehistorical Revolution. Edited by P.S. Martin and R.G. Klein. Tuscon, Ariz.: University of Arizona Press, 1984.

Martin v. Waddel, 41 U.S. (16 Pet.) 367 (1842).

McNamee, Tom. "Yellowstone's Missing Element." Audubon 88:1 (January 1986):12.

Missouri River Basin Commission. Missouri River Basin Management Plan. Omaha, Neb.: Missouri River Basin Commission, 1980.

———. Report and Environmental Assessment, Yellowstone River Basin and Adjacent Coal Area Level B Study, Vol. 1–2. Omaha, Neb.: Missouri River Basin Commission, 1978.

Montana Coalition for Stream Access v. Curran, 683 P.2d. 163 (1984).

Montana Coalition for Stream Access v. Hildreth, 684 P.2d. 1089 (1984).

Montana Land Reliance. "Conservation Easements." Helena, Mont. (1983).

———. 1978–1984. Annual Report. Helena, Mont. (1984).

Muller, Robert and Theodore Oberlander. Physical Geography Today. New York: Random House, Inc., 1978.

National Park Service. "Information Paper—Northern Yellowstone Elk Herd." 17 September 1968.

National Park Service and U.S. Forest Service. "The Greater Yellowstone Area." September 1987.

The Nature Conservancy News 35:5 (September/October 1985).

Niskanen, W. Bureaucracy and Representative Government. Chicago: Aldine & Atherton, 1971.

North, D. and R. Thomas. "The First Economic Revolution." Economic History Review 30 (1977): 229–41.

Olson, Mancur, Jr. The Logic of Collective Action: Public Goods and the Theory of Groups. Cambridge, Mass.: Harvard University Press, 1965.

O'Toole, Randal. "Inefficiency in the National Forests—A Review of the Sales-Below-Cost Issue." Forest Watch: The Citizens Forestry Magazine. Eugene, Ore., 24 September 1985.

———. "Maximum Forest Budget Means Maximum Timber Sale Losses." Eugene, Ore., Cascade Holistic Economic Consultants.

————. Reforming the Forest Service. Washington, D.C., Island Press, 1988.

Pero, Thomas R. "Yellowstone Fisher Fund." Trout, Autumn 1986.

Political Economy Research Center. Proceedings from "Western Resources in Transition: The Public Trust Doctrine and Property Rights." Bozeman, Mont. 1986.

Pollard v. Hagen, 44 U.S. (3. How.) 212 (1845).

President's Council on Environmental Quality. 1984 Annual Report of the President's Council on Environmental Quality. Washington, D.C.: Government Printing Office, 1984.

Reese, Rick. "Greater Yellowstone: The National Park and Adjacent Wildlands." Montana Geographic Series, No. 6, Montana Magazine, Helena, Mont., April 1984.

Reid, T.R. "The Land Set Aside for Yellowstone Was a Great Mistake." Washington Post, 15 July 1985, p. 23.

Roos-Collins, R. and Friends of the River Foundation. "Intervention in the Federal Energy Regulatory Commissions's Review of Hudro-Power." Federation of Fly Fishers, West Yellowstone, Mont., 1982.

Rudner, Ruth. "Call of the Wild: Of Wolves and Woman." Wall Street Journal, 5 August 1986, p. 26.

Sax, Joseph and Robert Rieter. "Glacier National Park and Its Neighbors: A Study of Federal Interagency Relations." Ecology Law Quarterly 14:207, 1987.

Shabecoff, Phillip. "Science Group Ties Acid Rain to Earth Harm." New York Times, 14 March 1986, p. 8.

Shaw, J.S. and R.L. Stroup. "Gone Fishin'." Reason, August/September 1988.

Simmons, Randy and John Baden. "The Theory of the New Resource Economics." Journal of Contemporary Studies 7:2 (Spring 1984).

Smith, A. The Wealth of Nations. Edited by Edwin Cannan. Chicago: University of Chicago Press, 1976.

Smith, Vernon L. "The Primitive Hunter Culture, Pleistocene Extinction, and the Rise of Agriculture." Journal of Political Economy 83 (August 1975):727–56.

————. "Hunting and Gathering Economies." In The New Palgrave, London: Macmillan, 1987.

Sowell, Thomas. Knowledge and Decisions. Basic Books, Inc., New York (1980).

Stone, Albert. Montana Water Law for the 1980s. Missoula, Mont.: University of Montana School of Law, 1981.

Stroup, Richard and John Baden. "Endowment Areas: A Clearing in the Policy Wilderness?" Cato Journal 2:3 (Winter 1982).

————. "Externality, Property Rights and the Management of Our National

Forests." Journal of Law and Economics (April 1974). Reprinted in The Economics of Legal Issues. Edited by Henry Manne. West Publishing Co., 1975.

―――. Natural Resources: Bureaucratic Myths and Environmental Management. San Francisco, Calif.: Pacific Research Institute for Public Policy, 1983.

―――. "Property Rights and Natural Resource Management." Literature of Liberty, October/December 1979.

―――. "Property Rights: Out Best Environmental Tool." Enterprise Magazine, November 1984. Reprinted in CIS Policy Report 1:6 (December 1985): 6–7.

Stroup, Richard L., John Baden and Jane S. Shaw. "Wilderness Endowment Boards: Alternative to Wilderness Disputes." Forest Planning 6:3 (June 1985).

Thiel, Richard P. "Relationship Between Road Densities and Wolf Habitat Suitability in Wisconsin." Wisconsin Department of Natural Resources, Bureau of Endangered Resources, Madison, Wisc. (1984).

Trelease, Frank and George Gold. Cases and Materials of Water Law. 4th ed. American Case Book Series. St. Paul, Minn.: West Publishing Co., 1986.

Tullock, Gordon. The Politics of Bureaucracy. Washington, D.C.: Public Affairs Press, 1965.

U.S. Department of Agriculture, U.S. Forest Service. Gallatin National Forest Plan. U.S. Forest Service, Bozeman, Mont. (1985): 11–68.

U.S. Forest Service. "Targhee National Forest Plan." USFS and USDA, St. Anthony, Id. (1985).

U.S. Geological Survey. Water Resources Data for Idaho, Volume 1: Great Basin and Snake River Basin Above King Hill. Water Data Report ID-80-1, Washington, D.C.: Government Printing Office, 1980.

―――. Water Resources Data for Montana. Water Data Report MT-79-1. Washington, D.C.: Government Printing Office, 1979.

United States v. Appalachian Electric Power Company, 311 U.S. 377, 61 S. Ct. 291 (1940).

United States v. New Mexico, 238, U.S. 121 88 S. Ct. 265 (1967).

United States Water Resources Council. Section 13(a) Water Assessment Report: Synthetic Fuel Development for the Upper Missouri River Basin. Washington, D.C.: U.S. Water Resources Council, 1981.

Wilderness Society. "Management Directions for the National Forests of the Greater Yellowstone Ecosystem." Washington, D.C.: Wilderness Society, January 1987.

Wiltse, Eric. "Dillon Rancher Predicts Worst if Wolves are Returned to the Park." Bozeman Daily Chronicle, 3 April 1986.

Winters v. United States, 207 U.S. 564, 28 S. Ct. 207 (1908).

Wrenn, Douglas. "Barrier Islands." Environmental Comment (February 1981).

Wright Water Engineers and Frank Trelease. A Water Protection Strategy for Montana: Missouri River Basin. Montana Department of Natural Resources and Conservation, Water Resources Division, Helena, Mont. (1982).

INDEX

ABOUT THE EDITORS

John A. Baden is currently Chairman of the Foundation for Research on Economics and the Environment (FREE). He received his Ph.D. in Government in 1969 from Indiana University.

Baden is co-author of several books, among them *The Vanishing Farmland Crisis: Critical Views of the Movement to Preserve Agricultural Land, Natural Resources: Myths and Management,* and *Bureaucracy vs. Environment: The Environmental Costs of Bureaucratic Governance.*

His articles have appeared in the *Cato Journal, Economic Inquiry, Journal of Law and Economics, Policy Studies Journal, Public Choice, The Public Land Law Review,* among others.

Donald Leal is a Research Associate at the Political Economy Research Center. Prior to that he was Manager at the BDM Corporation in McLean, Virginia. He received his M.S. in statistics in 1972 from California State University at Hayward.

Leal has co-authored several published papers including *Marketing Instream Flows and Groundwater, Building Coalitions for Water Marketing, Inside Our Outdoor Policy, Going with the Flow: Expanding Water Markets,* and *Sale of Federal Lands.* He is co-author of a forthcoming book on free market environmentalism.

Leal's articles have appeared in *The Chicago Tribune, Economic Affairs, The Orange County Register, The Wall Street Journal,* and *Western Business.*

ABOUT THE AUTHORS

Geoffrey Black is currently pursuing a Ph.D. in economics at the University of Washington emphasizing natural resource economics. He received his M.S. degrees in geology and economics from Montana State University.

Professionally, Black has been involved with resource utilization for the past ten years. He worked as a geologist on geothermal exploration programs in Nevada and northern California, and on copper exploration programs in northern Maine. He spent four years as a petroleum geologist for Chevron USA, Inc., where he was responsible for oil and gas development projects in Montana. He recently taught economics at Montana State University, while performing studies as Research Associate at the Political Economy Research Center in Bozeman, Montana.

Tom Blood is currently working as a marine naturalist in Washington state. He worked as a Murdock Research Fellow at the Political Economy Research Center in Bozeman, Montana, where he researched issues in wildlife, water, and land-use policy. He received his M.A. from the University of Washington in Communications and Public Policy.

His articles on wildlife policy have appeared in publications such as *The Denver Post, The San Francisco Chronicle, The Wall Street Journal,* and *Western Wildlands.*

Alston Chase is a writer and independent scholar currently serving as Adjunct Professor of Philosophy at Montana State University. He received his Ph.D. in philosophy from Princeton University in 1967. He is an alumnus of Harvard University and Oxford University.

Chase has served as the Chairman of the Board of the Yellowstone Association (dedicated to promoting research and education in Yellowstone), Director of Chase Ranch (an environmental summer school), and Executive Director of the Northern Rockies Foundation (a nonprofit organization dedicated to fundraising for environmental, educational, and cultural organizations in Idaho, Montana, and Wyoming).

His writings have appeared in *The Atlantic, The Educational Record, Humanities, The New York Times, The Rockefeller Foundation Working Papers, The Wall Street Journal,* and *The Washington Monthly.* He has also contributed scholarly papers on multidisciplinary science and systems ecology to Sigma-Xi, the Scientific Research Society, and the National Science Foundation.

Chase's recent book, *Playing God in Yellowstone: The Destruction of America's First National Park,* has stirred a national debate about park management.

Michael D. Copeland is Associate Professor of Economics at Montana State University in Bozeman where he has been teaching since 1968. He received his Ph.D. in economics from the University of Colorado in 1971. Copeland became the Executive Director of the Political Economy Research Center in Bozeman, Montana, in 1987.

His main areas of research are tax forecasting and the demand for outdoor recreation. He has been involved in many PERC conferences designed to teach free-market principles to journalists and congressional staff aides, among others, and in conferences dealing with environmental and privatization issues.

Andrew C. Dana received his J.D. degree at Stanford University School of Law where he served as Editor-in-Chief of the *Stanford Environmental Law Journal* and of *The Endangered Species Act: A Guide to its Protections and Implementation.* He received his M.A. in Geography from the University of Washington in 1984.

The initial draft of Dana's chapter in this volume was written in 1986 while he was a Research Fellow at the Political Economy Research Center in Bozeman, Montana. Dana has co-authored several articles including "Conservation Easements and the Common Law," (with Michael Ramsey), and "Toward a Policy Syntheses: The New Resource Economics."

Dana's editorials have appeared in the *Bozeman Daily Chronicle, The Denver Post, The Orvis News,* and the *St. Louis Dispatch.*

Jo Kwong is Director of the Philanthropy and Environment Program at the Capital Research Center in Washington, D.C. Prior to that, she was a postdoctoral fellow in private sector non-profit management at the Institute for Humane Studies, and a postdoctoral fellow at the Political Economy Research Center. Kwong received her Ph.D. in Natural Resource Economics and Management from the University of Michigan at Ann Arbor in 1986.

Kwong has lectured on free market environmentalism, corporate philanthropy and the environmental movement, and the corporation, state, and society. Her writings have appeared in *American Land Forum Magazine, Detroit News, Harvard Journal of Law and Public Policy, The New York Times, The Orange County Register, Urban Land,* and *The Wall Street Journal.*

Gene Lyons is currently a free-lance writer working on a book manuscript and writing regular book reviews for *The New York Post.* Lyons received his Ph.D. in English from the University of Virginia, Charlottesville, in 1969. He has held various professorships at the University of Massachusetts at Amherst, University of Arkansas at Little Rock, and the University of Texas at Austin.

From 1980 to 1986 Lyons served as General Editor for *Newsweek.* He has published literally hundreds of feature articles, essays, and reviews for *Esquire, Harper's, Inside Sports, The Nation, New York Post, New York Review of Books, The New York Times Book Review, The New York Times Magazine, Texas Monthly,* and *Tri-Quarterly.*

Lyons has won the National Magazine Award, the Clarion Award, the National Endowment for the Arts Fellowship Grant, and was a Ford Foundation Fellow.

Vernon L. Smith is Regents' Professor of Economics at the University of Arizona and currently serves as President of the Public Choice Society. He received his Ph.D. in economics from Harvard University in 1955.

Among his many accomplishments, Smith was the founding president of the Economic Science Association, was twice awarded "Best *Economic Inquiry* Article," served on the Board of Editors of the *American Economic Review,* and was the Vice President of the Southern Economic Association.

He has co-authored *Economics: An Analytical Approach* and *Economics of Natural and Environmental Resources.* He has edited volumes 1, 2, and 3 of *Research in Experimental Economics,* and edited *Schools of Economic Thought: Experimental Economics.*

Smith's articles have appeared in *American Economic Review, Economic Inquiry, International Economic Review, Journal of Political Economy, Quarterly Journal of Economics, Scandinavian Journal of Economics,* and *Supreme Court Economic Review.*

Richard L. Stroup is a Professor of Economics at Montana State University and a Senior Associate of the Political Economy Research Center. He received his B.A., M.A., and Ph.D. from the University of Washington. From 1982 to 1984 he was Director of the Office of Policy Analysis at the Interior Department.

Stroup is a widely published author on natural resources and environmental issues and has also written on tax policy and labor economics. His work has been a major force in the development of the approach to resource problems known as the New Resource Economics. His recent research focuses on hazardous waste policies and ways of coping with environmental risk.

Stroup is the co-author of *Economics: Private and Public Choice* and *Natural Resources: Bureaucratic Myths and Environmental Management.* He is also co-editor of *Bureaucracy vs. the Environment: The Environmental Cost of Bureaucratic Governance.*

PACIFIC RESEARCH INSTITUTE
FOR PUBLIC POLICY

The Pacific Research Institute produces studies that explore long-term solutions to difficult issues of public policy. The Institute seeks to facilitate a more active and enlightened discourse on these issues and to broaden understanding of market processes, government policy, and the rule of law. Through the publication of scholarly books and the sponsorship of conferences, the Institute serves as an established resource for ideas in the continuing public policy debate.

Institute books have been adopted for courses at colleges, universities, and graduate schools nationwide. More than 175 distinguished scholars have worked with the Institute to analyze the premises and consequences of existing public policy and to formulate possible solutions to seemingly intractable problems. Prestigious journals and major media regularly review and comment upon Institute work. In addition, the Board of Advisors consists of internationally recognized scholars, including two Nobel laureates.

The Pacific Research Institute is an independent, tax exempt, 501(c)(3) organization and as such is supported solely by the sale of its books and by the contributions from a wide variety of foundations, corporations, and individuals. This diverse funding base and the Institute's refusal to accept government funds enable it to remain independent.

OTHER STUDIES IN PUBLIC POLICY BY
THE PACIFIC RESEARCH INSTITUTE

OFFSHORE LANDS
Oil and Gas Leasing and Conservation on the Outer Continental Shelf
By Walter J. Mead, et al.
Foreword by Stephen L. McDonald

ELECTRIC POWER
Deregulation and the Public Interest
Edited by John C. Moorhouse
Foreword by Harold Demsetz

TAXATION AND THE DEFICIT ECONOMY
Fiscal Policy and Capital Formation in the United States
Edited by Dwight R. Lee
Foreword by Michael J. Boskin

THE AMERICAN FAMILY AND STATE
Edited by Joseph R. Peden and Fred R. Glahe
Foreword by Robert Nisbet

DEALING WITH DRUGS
Consequences of Government Control
Edited by Ronald Hamowy
Foreword by Dr. Alfred Freedman

CRISIS AND LEVIATHAN
Critical Episodes in the Growth of American Government
By Robert Higgs
Foreword by Arthur A. Ekirch, Jr.

THE NEW CHINA
Comparative Economic Development in Mainland China, Taiwan, and Hong Kong
By Alvin Rabushka

ADVERTISING AND THE MARKET PROCESS
A Modern Economic View
By Robert B. Ekelund, Jr. and David S. Saurman
Foreword by Israel M. Kirzner

HEALTH CARE IN AMERICA
The Political Economy of Hospitals and Health Insurance
Edited by H.E. Frech III
Foreword by Richard Zeckhauser

POLITICAL BUSINESS CYCLES
The Political Economy of Money, Inflation, and Unemployment
Edited by Thomas D. Willett
Foreword by Axel Leijonhufvud

WHEN GOVERNMENT GOES PRIVATE
Successful Alternatives to Public Services
By Randall Fitzgerald

TO PROMOTE THE GENERAL WELFARE
Market Processes vs. Political Transfers
By Richard E. Wagner

For further information on the Pacific Research Institute's program and a catalog of publications, please contact:

PACIFIC RESEARCH INSTITUTE FOR PUBLIC POLICY
177 Post Street
San Francisco, CA 94108
(415) 989-0833